CHANGE THE WORLD

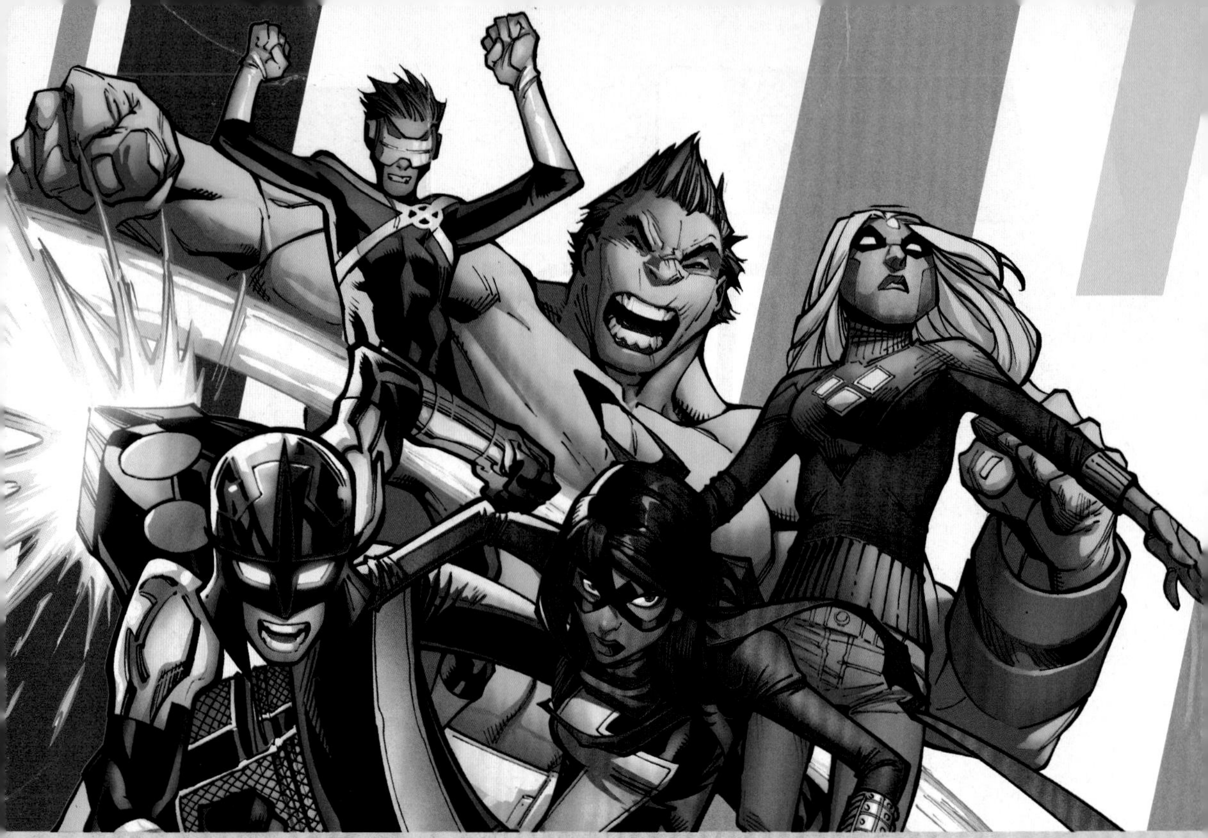

In the aftermath of the second superhuman civil war, the world has become disillusioned with its heroes. The next generation has to be better. They have to be...

CHAMPIONS

CHANGE THE WORLD

WRITER: **MARK WAID** PENCILER: **HUMBERTO RAMOS**

INKER: **VICTOR OLAZABA** COLORIST: **EDGAR DELGADO**

LETTERER: **VC'S CLAYTON COWLES**

COVER ART: **HUMBERTO RAMOS & EDGAR DELGADO**

ASSISTANT EDITOR: **ALANNA SMITH** EDITOR: **TOM BREVOORT**

SPECIAL THANKS TO DENNIS MALLONEE

COLLECTION EDITOR: **JENNIFER GRÜNWALD**
ASSISTANT EDITOR: **CAITLIN O'CONNELL**
ASSOCIATE MANAGING EDITOR: **KATERI WOODY**
EDITOR, SPECIAL PROJECTS: **MARK D. BEAZLEY**
VP PRODUCTION & SPECIAL PROJECTS: **JEFF YOUNGQUIST**
SVP PRINT, SALES & MARKETING: **DAVID GABRIEL**
BOOK DESIGNER: **JEFF POWELL**

EDITOR IN CHIEF: **AXEL ALONSO**
CHIEF CREATIVE OFFICER: **JOE QUESADA**
PRESIDENT: **DAN BUCKLEY**
EXECUTIVE PRODUCER: **ALAN FINE**

CHAMPIONS VOL. 1: CHANGE THE WORLD. Contains material originally published in magazine form as CHAMPIONS #1-5. First printing 2017. ISBN# 978-1-302-90618-4. Published by MARVEL WORLDWIDE, INC., a subsidiary of MARVEL ENTERTAINMENT, LLC. OFFICE OF PUBLICATION: 135 West 50th Street, New York, NY 10020. **Printed in Canada.** DAN BUCKLEY, President, Marvel Entertainment; JOE QUESADA, Chief Creative Officer; TOM BREVOORT, SVP of Publishing; DAVID BOGART, SVP of Business Affairs & Operations, Publishing & Partnership; C.B. CEBULSKI, VP of Brand Management & Development, Asia; DAVID GABRIEL, SVP of Sales & Marketing, Publishing; JEFF YOUNGQUIST, VP of Production & Special Projects; DAN CARR, Executive Director of Publishing Technology; ALEX MORALES, Director of Publishing Operations; SUSAN CRESPI, Production Manager; STAN LEE, Chairman Emeritus. For information regarding advertising in Marvel Comics or on Marvel.com, please contact Vit DeBellis, Integrated Sales Manager, at vdebellis@marvel.com. For Marvel subscription inquiries, please call 888-511-5480. **Manufactured between 3/10/2017 and 4/11/2017 by SOLISCO PRINTERS, SCOTT, QC, CANADA.**

10 9 8 7 6 5 4 3 2 1

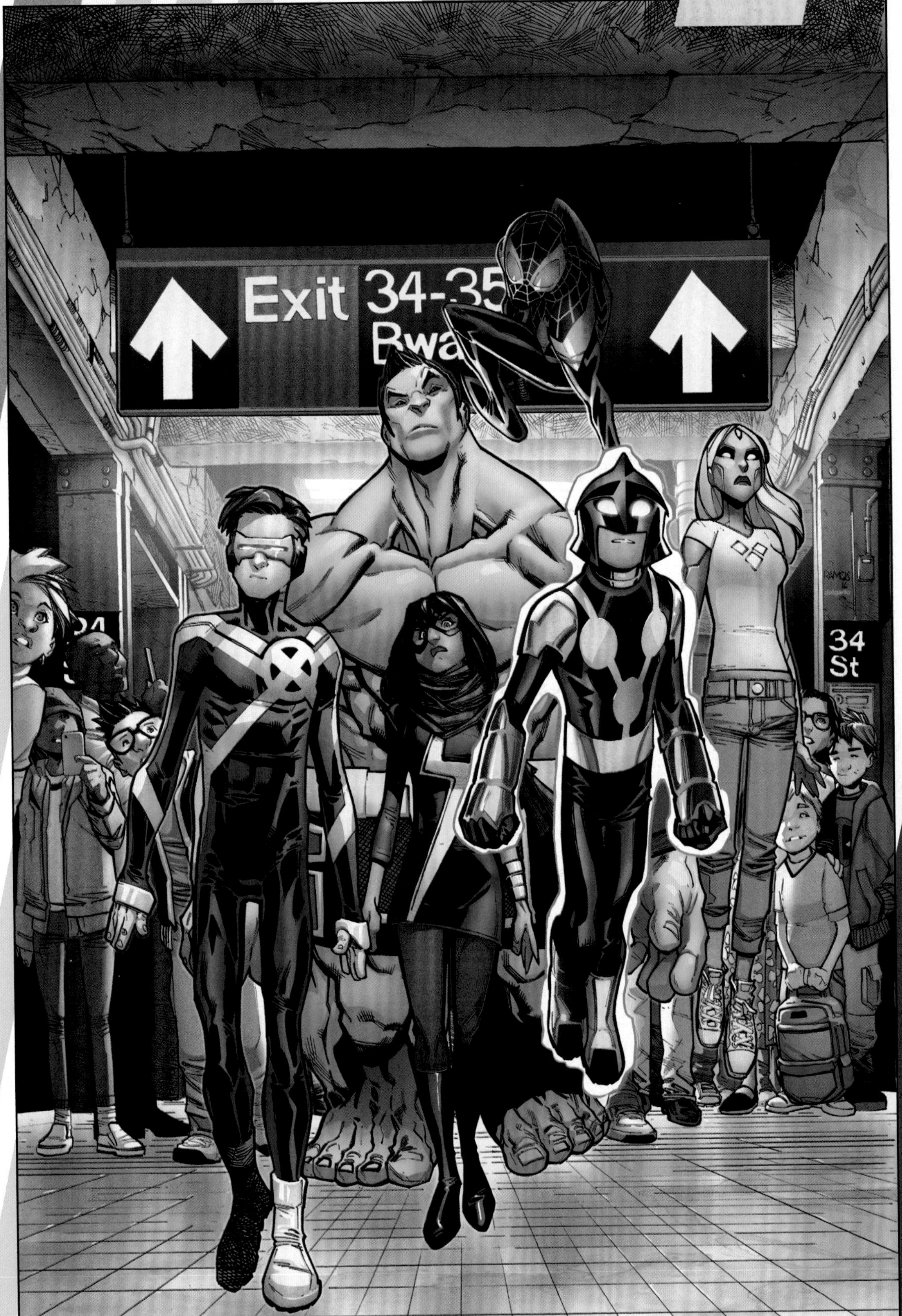
Exit 34-35
Bwa
34
St

1

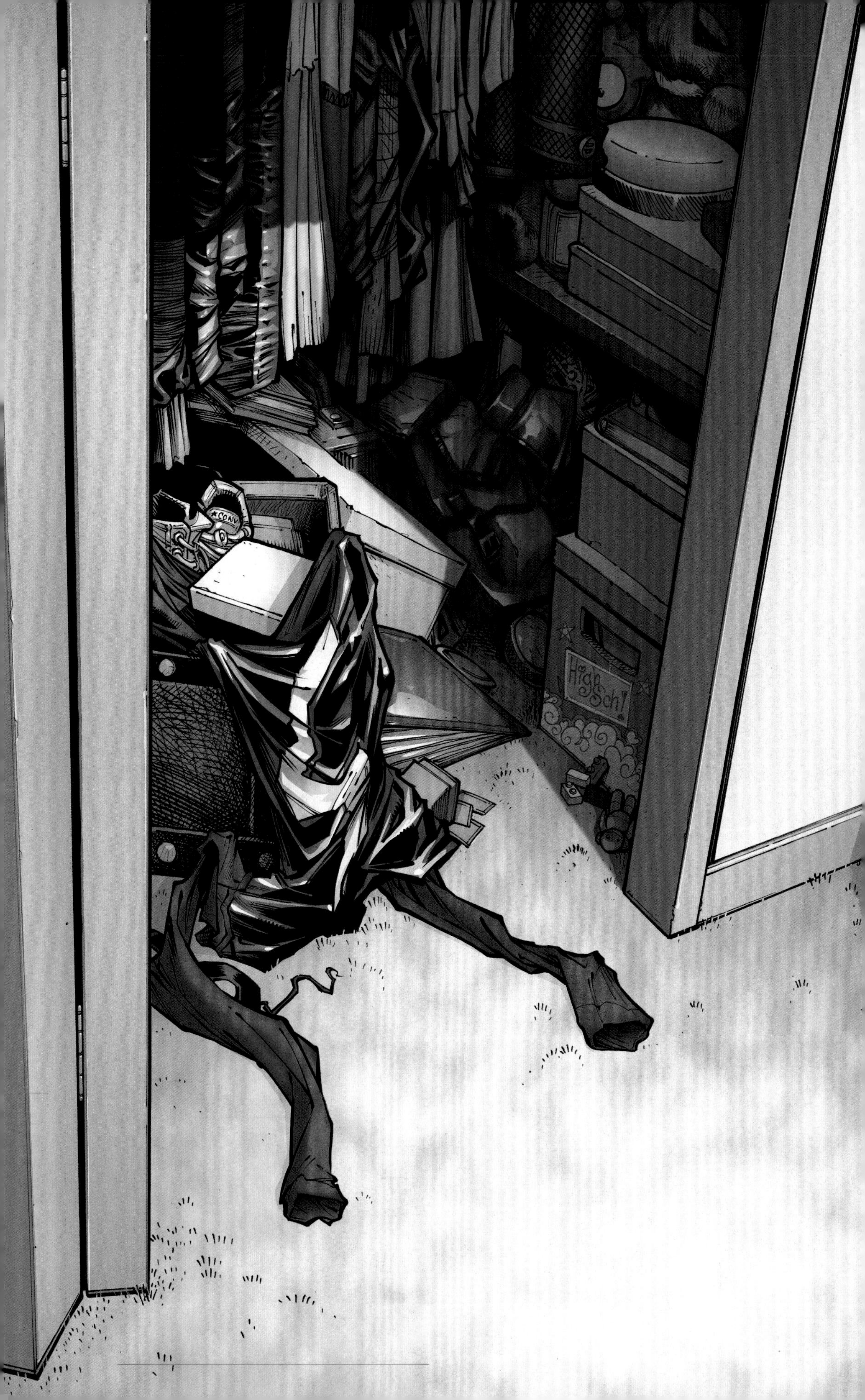
CONV
High Sch!

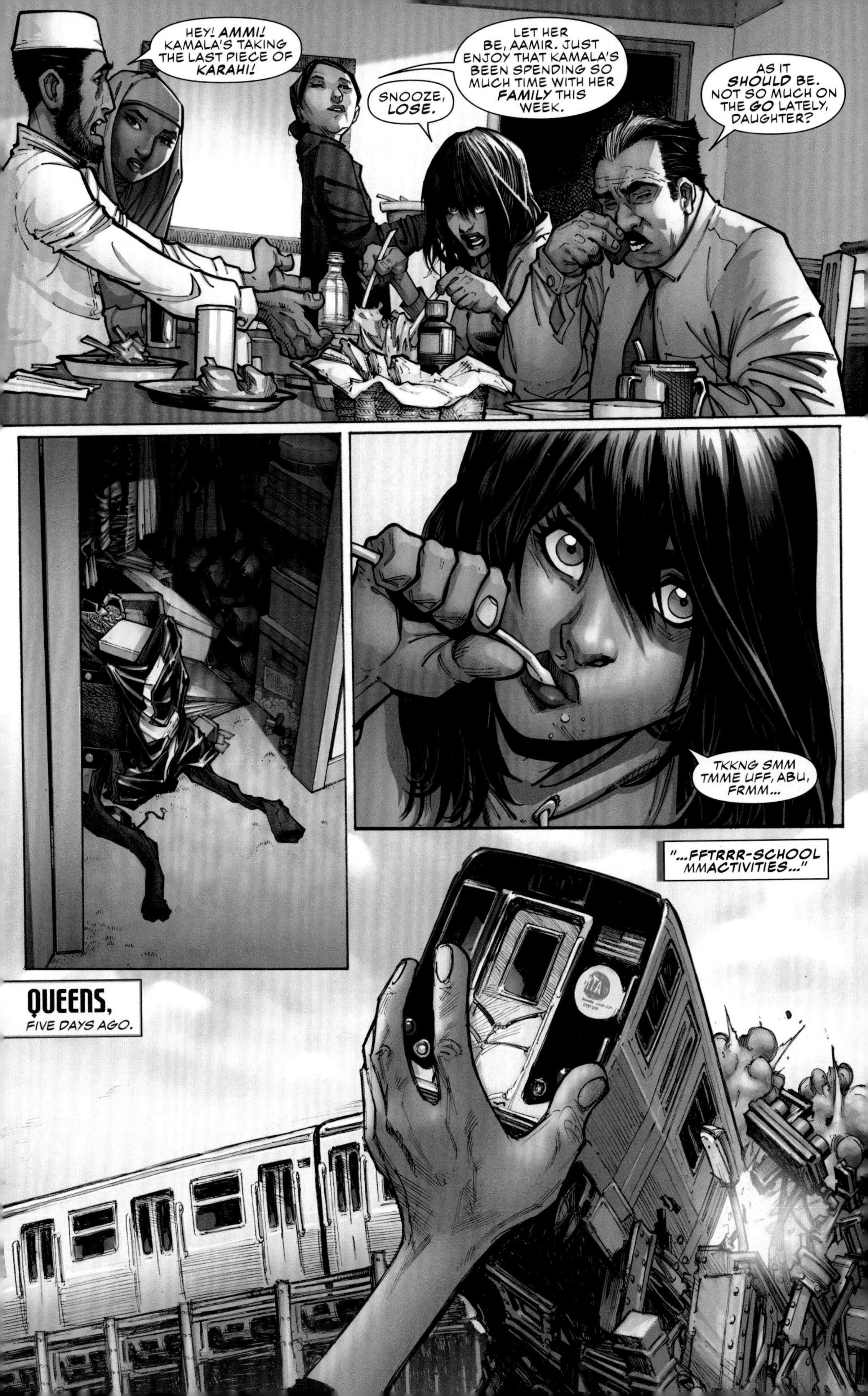
HEY! AMMI! KAMALA'S TAKING THE LAST PIECE OF KARAHI!
SNOOZE, LOSE.
LET HER BE, AAMIR. JUST ENJOY THAT KAMALA'S BEEN SPENDING SO MUCH TIME WITH HER FAMILY THIS WEEK.
AS IT SHOULD BE. NOT SO MUCH ON THE GO LATELY, DAUGHTER?
TKKNG SMM TMME UFF, ABU, FRMM...
"...FFTRRR-SCHOOL MMACTIVITIES..."
QUEENS, FIVE DAYS AGO.

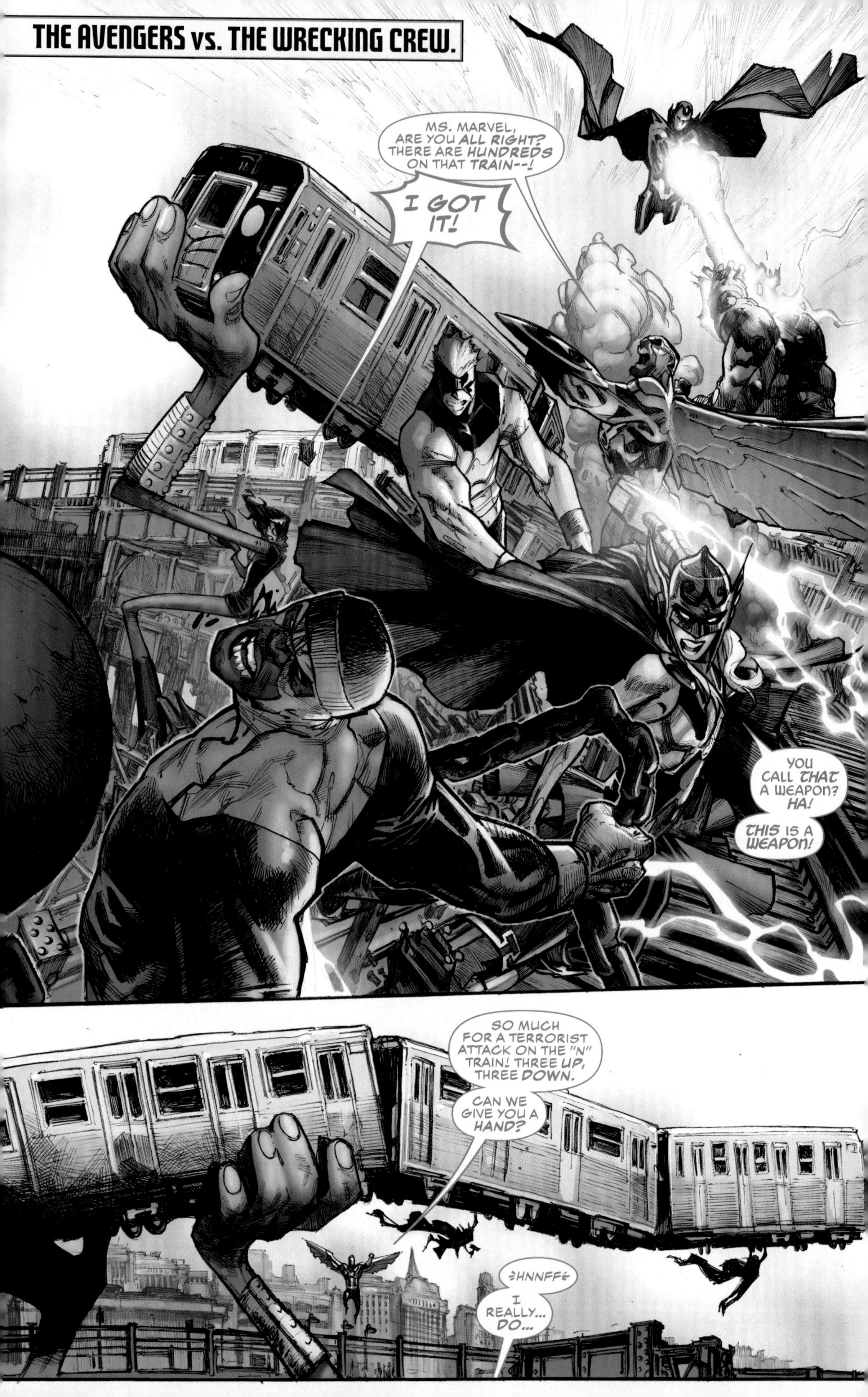
THE AVENGERS vs. THE WRECKING CREW.
MS. MARVEL, ARE YOU ALL RIGHT? THERE ARE HUNDREDS ON THAT TRAIN--!
I GOT IT!
YOU CALL THAT A WEAPON? HA!
THIS IS A WEAPON!
SO MUCH FOR A TERRORIST ATTACK ON THE "N" TRAIN! THREE UP, THREE DOWN.
CAN WE GIVE YOU A HAND?
HNNFF
I REALLY... DO...

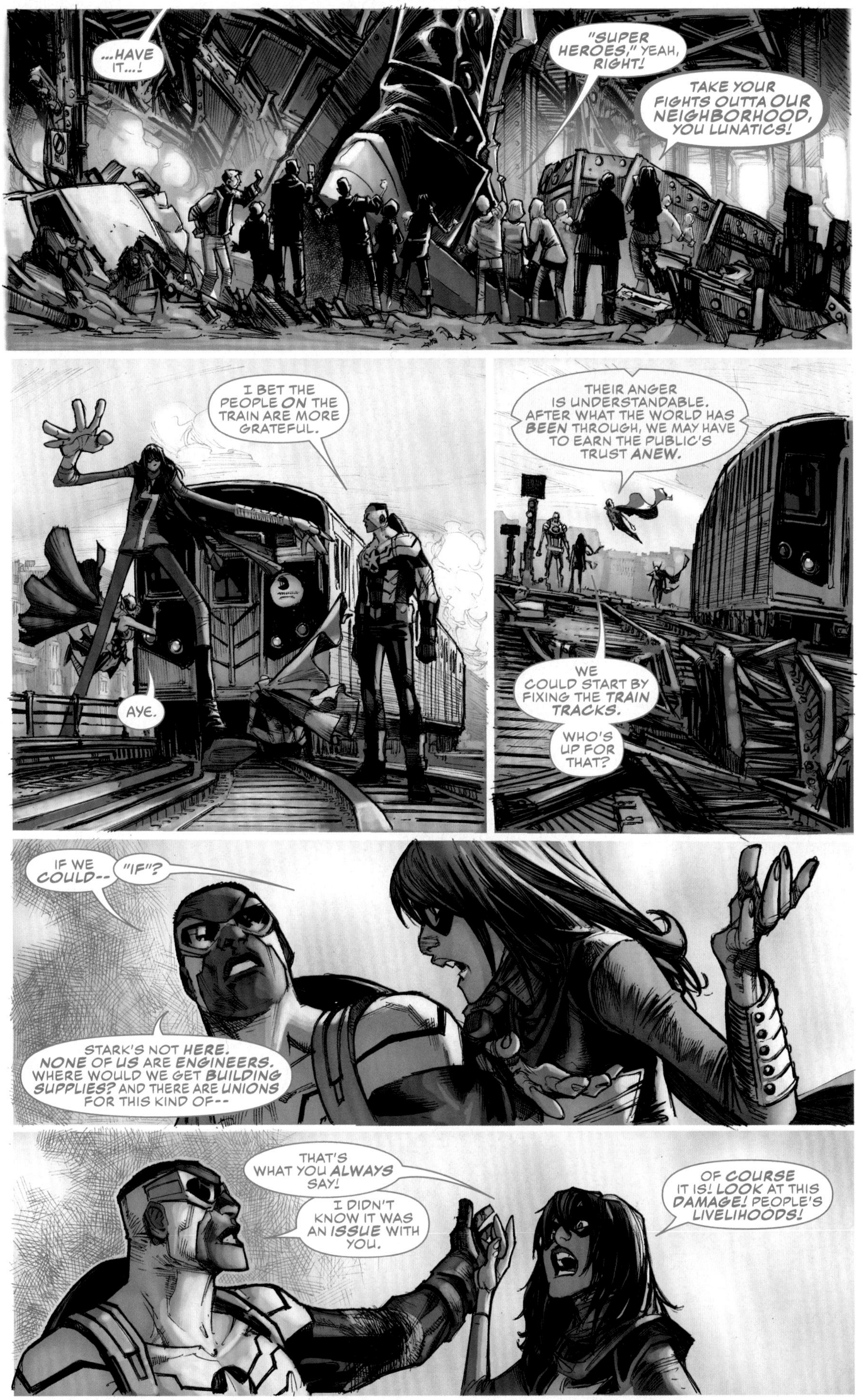

...HAVE IT...!
"SUPER HEROES," YEAH, RIGHT!
TAKE YOUR FIGHTS OUTTA OUR NEIGHBORHOOD, YOU LUNATICS!
I BET THE PEOPLE ON THE TRAIN ARE MORE GRATEFUL.
AYE.
THEIR ANGER IS UNDERSTANDABLE. AFTER WHAT THE WORLD HAS BEEN THROUGH, WE MAY HAVE TO EARN THE PUBLIC'S TRUST ANEW.
WE COULD START BY FIXING THE TRAIN TRACKS.
WHO'S UP FOR THAT?
IF WE COULD--
"IF"?
STARK'S NOT HERE. NONE OF US ARE ENGINEERS. WHERE WOULD WE GET BUILDING SUPPLIES? AND THERE ARE UNIONS FOR THIS KIND OF--
THAT'S WHAT YOU ALWAYS SAY!
I DIDN'T KNOW IT WAS AN ISSUE WITH YOU.
OF COURSE IT IS! LOOK AT THIS DAMAGE! PEOPLE'S LIVELIHOODS!

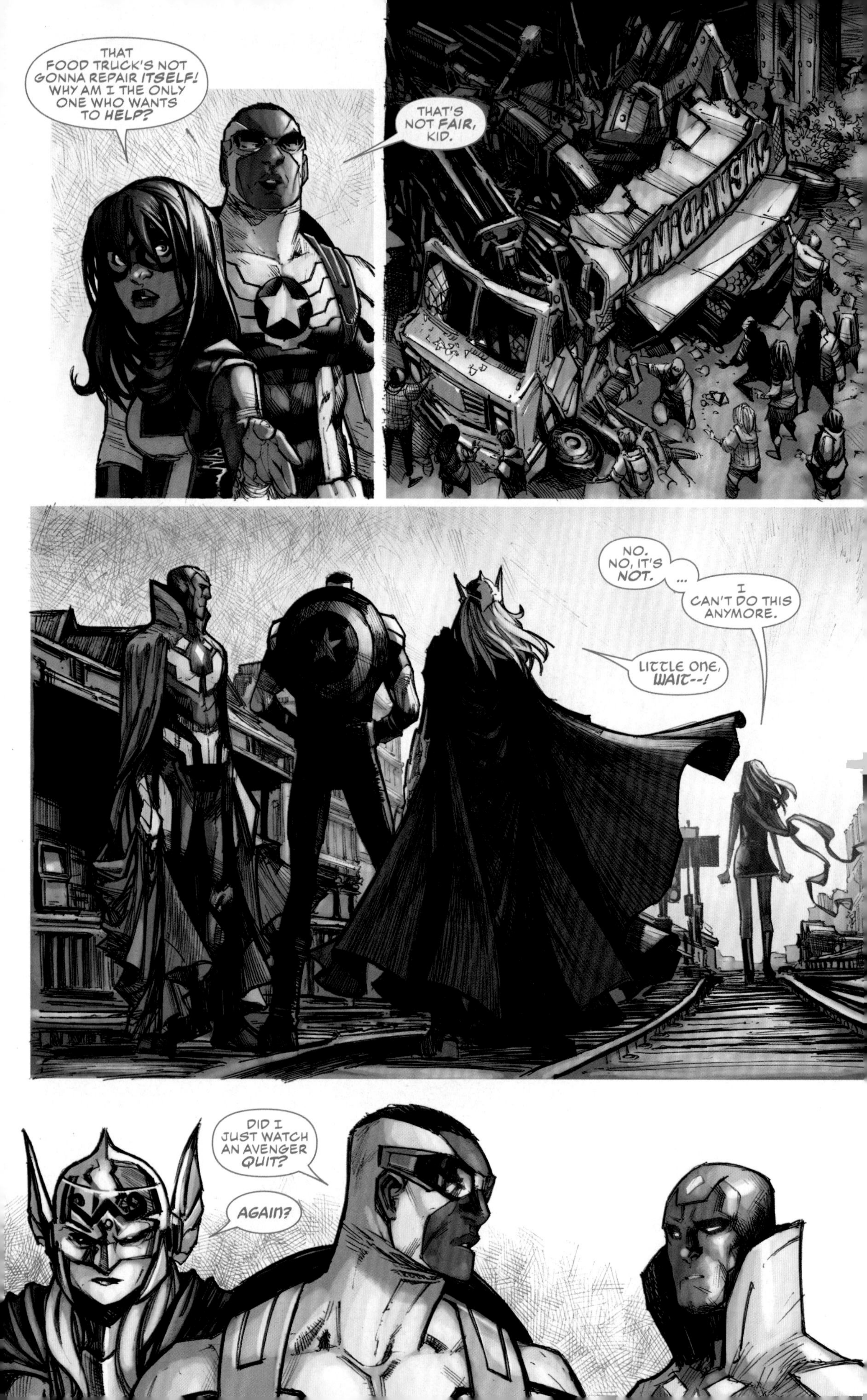

THAT FOOD TRUCK'S NOT GONNA REPAIR ITSELF! WHY AM I THE ONLY ONE WHO WANTS TO HELP?
THAT'S NOT FAIR, KID.
NO. NO, IT'S NOT.
...
I CAN'T DO THIS ANYMORE.
LITTLE ONE, WAIT--!
DID I JUST WATCH AN AVENGER QUIT?
AGAIN?

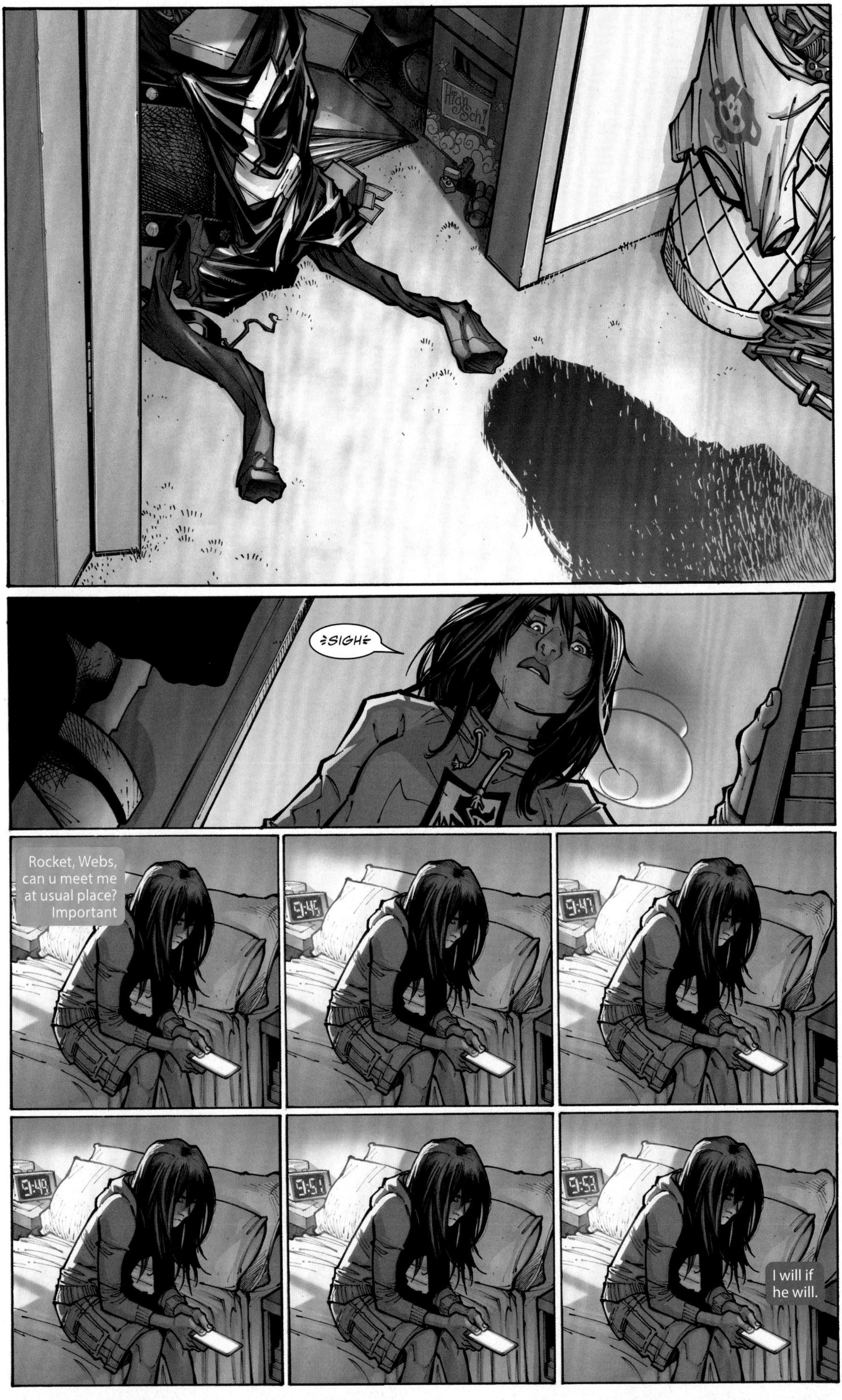
High Sch!
SIGH
Rocket, Webs, can u meet me at usual place? Important
I will if he will.

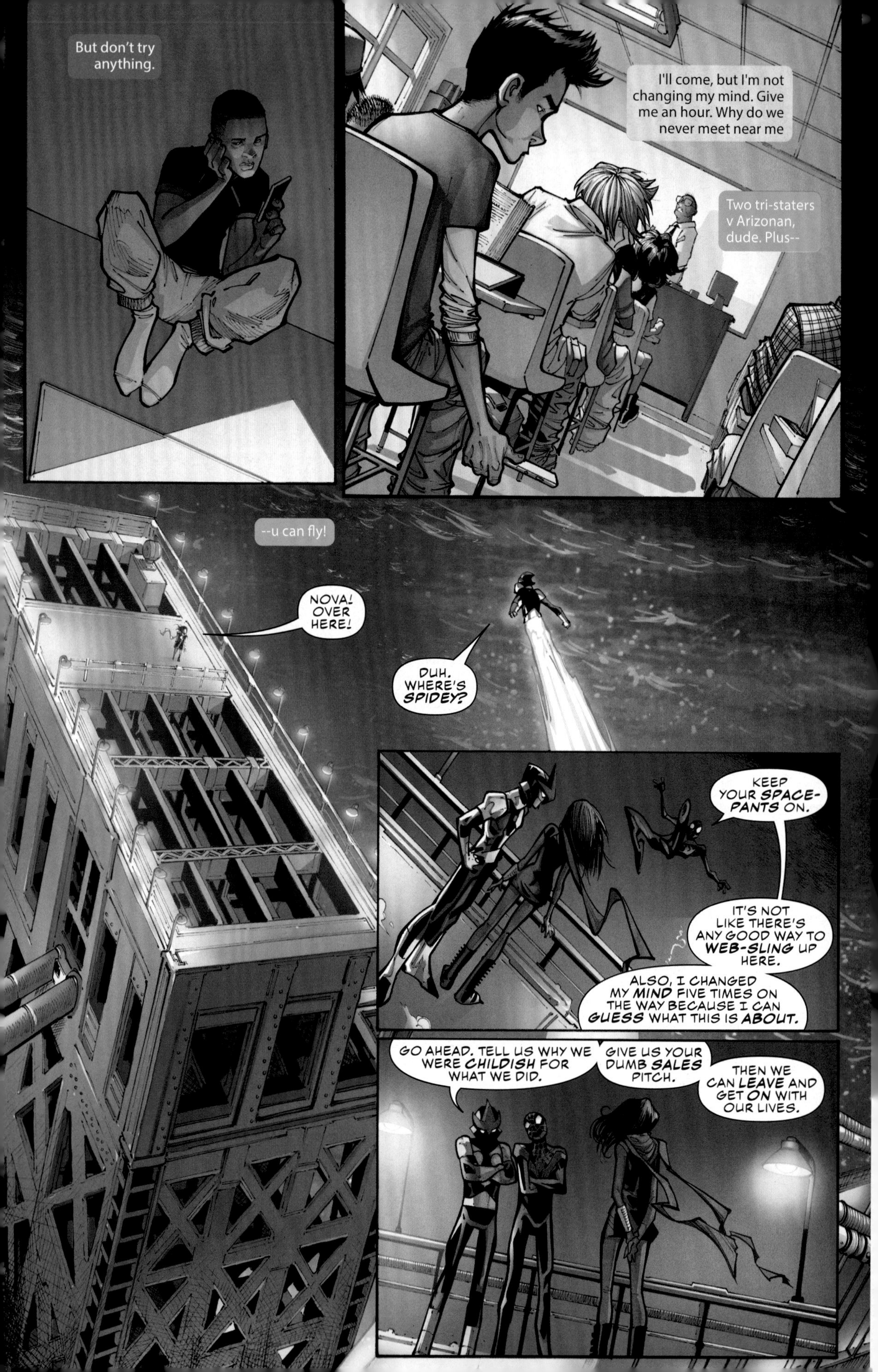

But don't try anything.
I'll come, but I'm not changing my mind. Give me an hour. Why do we never meet near me
Two tri-staters v Arizonan, dude. Plus--
--u can fly!
NOVA! OVER HERE!
DUH. WHERE'S SPIDEY?
KEEP YOUR SPACE-PANTS ON.
IT'S NOT LIKE THERE'S ANY GOOD WAY TO WEB-SLING UP HERE.
ALSO, I CHANGED MY MIND FIVE TIMES ON THE WAY BECAUSE I CAN GUESS WHAT THIS IS ABOUT.
GO AHEAD. TELL US WHY WE WERE CHILDISH FOR WHAT WE DID.
GIVE US YOUR DUMB SALES PITCH.
THEN WE CAN LEAVE AND GET ON WITH OUR LIVES.

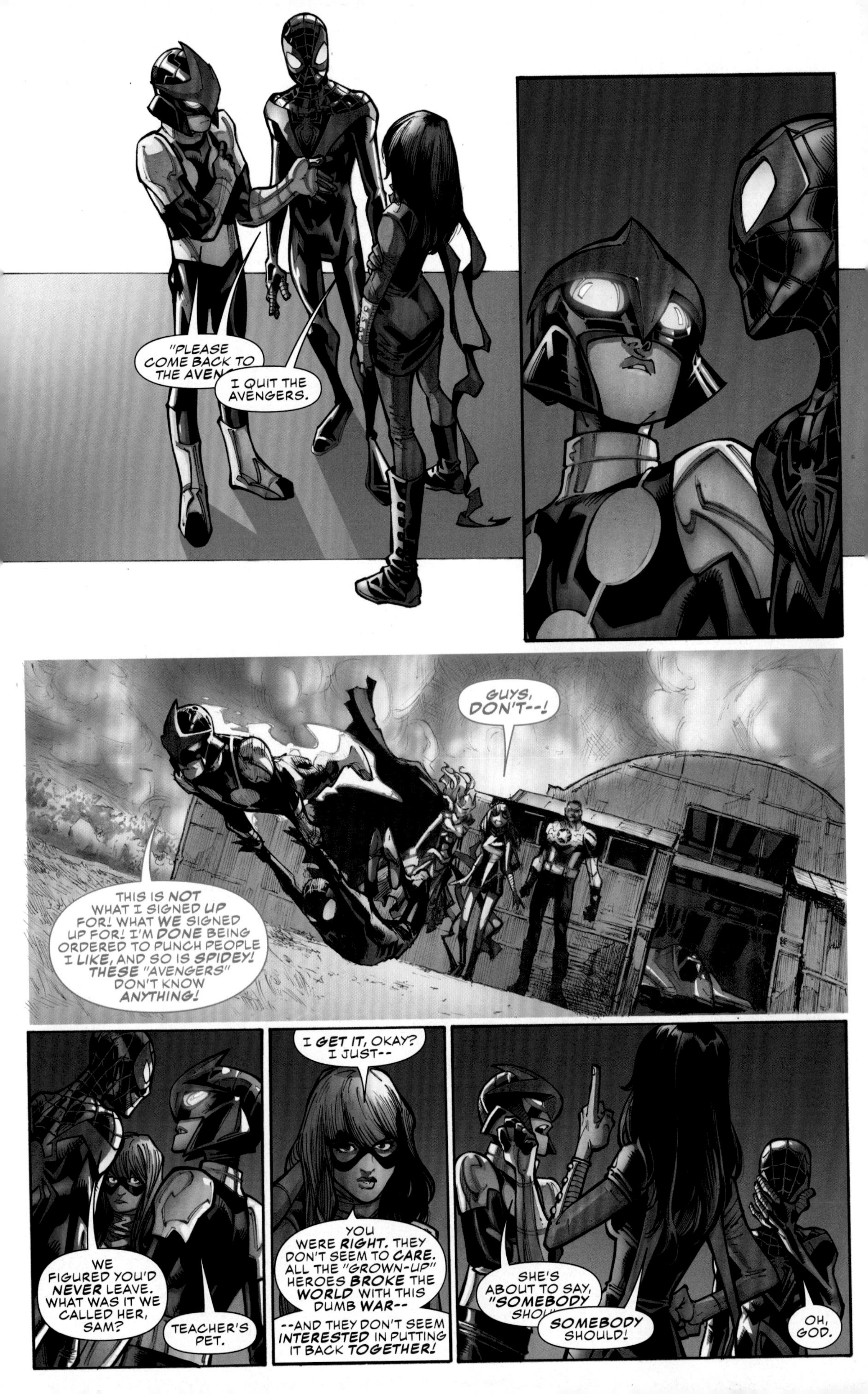
"PLEASE COME BACK TO THE AVEN--
I QUIT THE AVENGERS.
GUYS, DON'T--!
THIS IS NOT WHAT I SIGNED UP FOR! WHAT WE SIGNED UP FOR! I'M DONE BEING ORDERED TO PUNCH PEOPLE I LIKE, AND SO IS SPIDEY! THESE "AVENGERS" DON'T KNOW ANYTHING!
WE FIGURED YOU'D NEVER LEAVE. WHAT WAS IT WE CALLED HER, SAM?
TEACHER'S PET.
I GET IT, OKAY? I JUST--
YOU WERE RIGHT. THEY DON'T SEEM TO CARE. ALL THE "GROWN-UP" HEROES BROKE THE WORLD WITH THIS DUMB WAR--
--AND THEY DON'T SEEM INTERESTED IN PUTTING IT BACK TOGETHER!
SHE'S ABOUT TO SAY, "SOMEBODY SHOU--
SOMEBODY SHOULD!
OH, GOD.

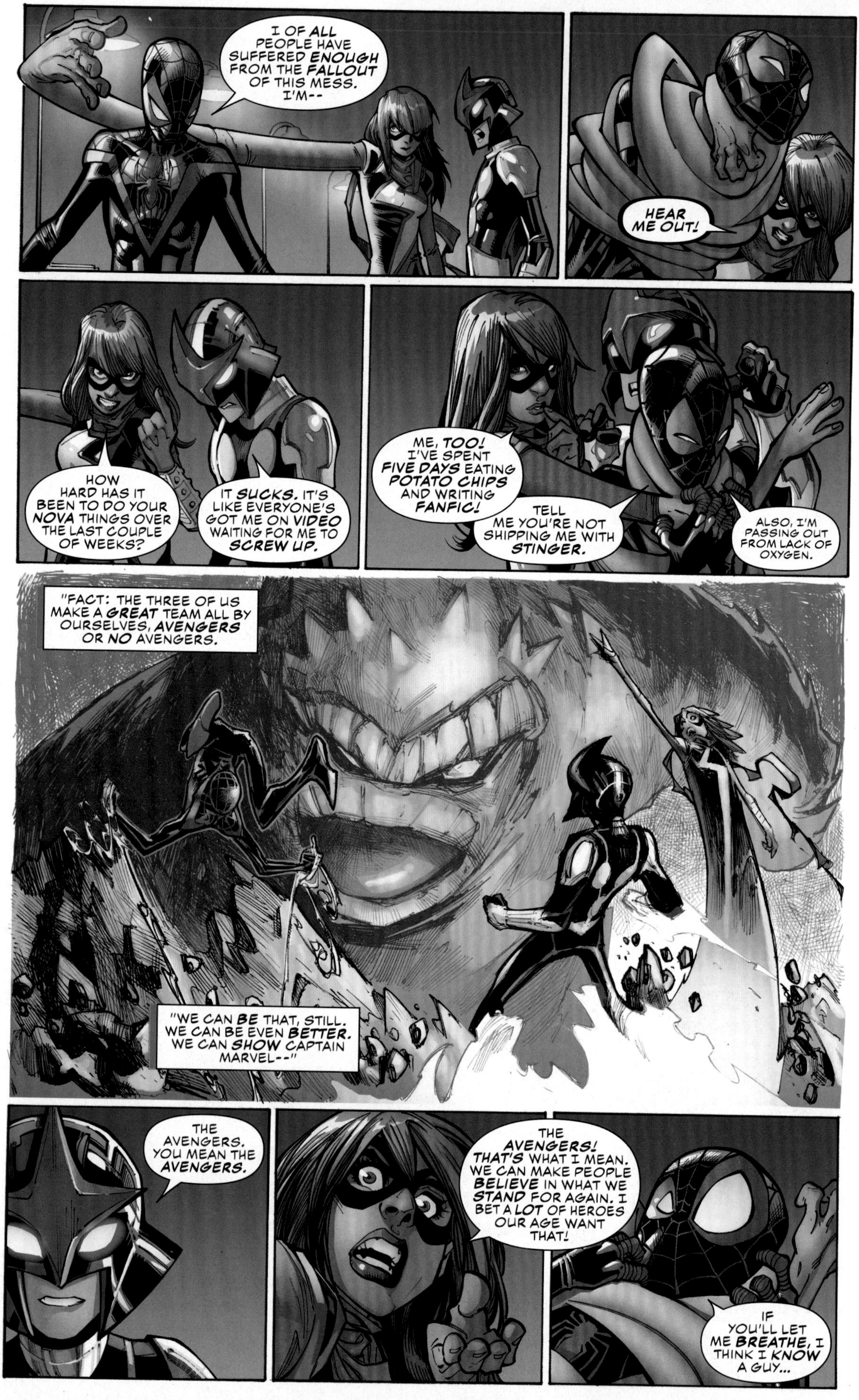
I OF ALL PEOPLE HAVE SUFFERED ENOUGH FROM THE FALLOUT OF THIS MESS. I'M--
HEAR ME OUT!
HOW HARD HAS IT BEEN TO DO YOUR NOVA THINGS OVER THE LAST COUPLE OF WEEKS?
IT SUCKS. IT'S LIKE EVERYONE'S GOT ME ON VIDEO WAITING FOR ME TO SCREW UP.
ME, TOO! I'VE SPENT FIVE DAYS EATING POTATO CHIPS AND WRITING FANFIC!
TELL ME YOU'RE NOT SHIPPING ME WITH STINGER.
ALSO, I'M PASSING OUT FROM LACK OF OXYGEN.
"FACT: THE THREE OF US MAKE A GREAT TEAM ALL BY OURSELVES, AVENGERS OR NO AVENGERS.
"WE CAN BE THAT, STILL. WE CAN BE EVEN BETTER. WE CAN SHOW CAPTAIN MARVEL--"
THE AVENGERS. YOU MEAN THE AVENGERS.
THE AVENGERS! THAT'S WHAT I MEAN. WE CAN MAKE PEOPLE BELIEVE IN WHAT WE STAND FOR AGAIN. I BET A LOT OF HEROES OUR AGE WANT THAT!
IF YOU'LL LET ME BREATHE, I THINK I KNOW A GUY...

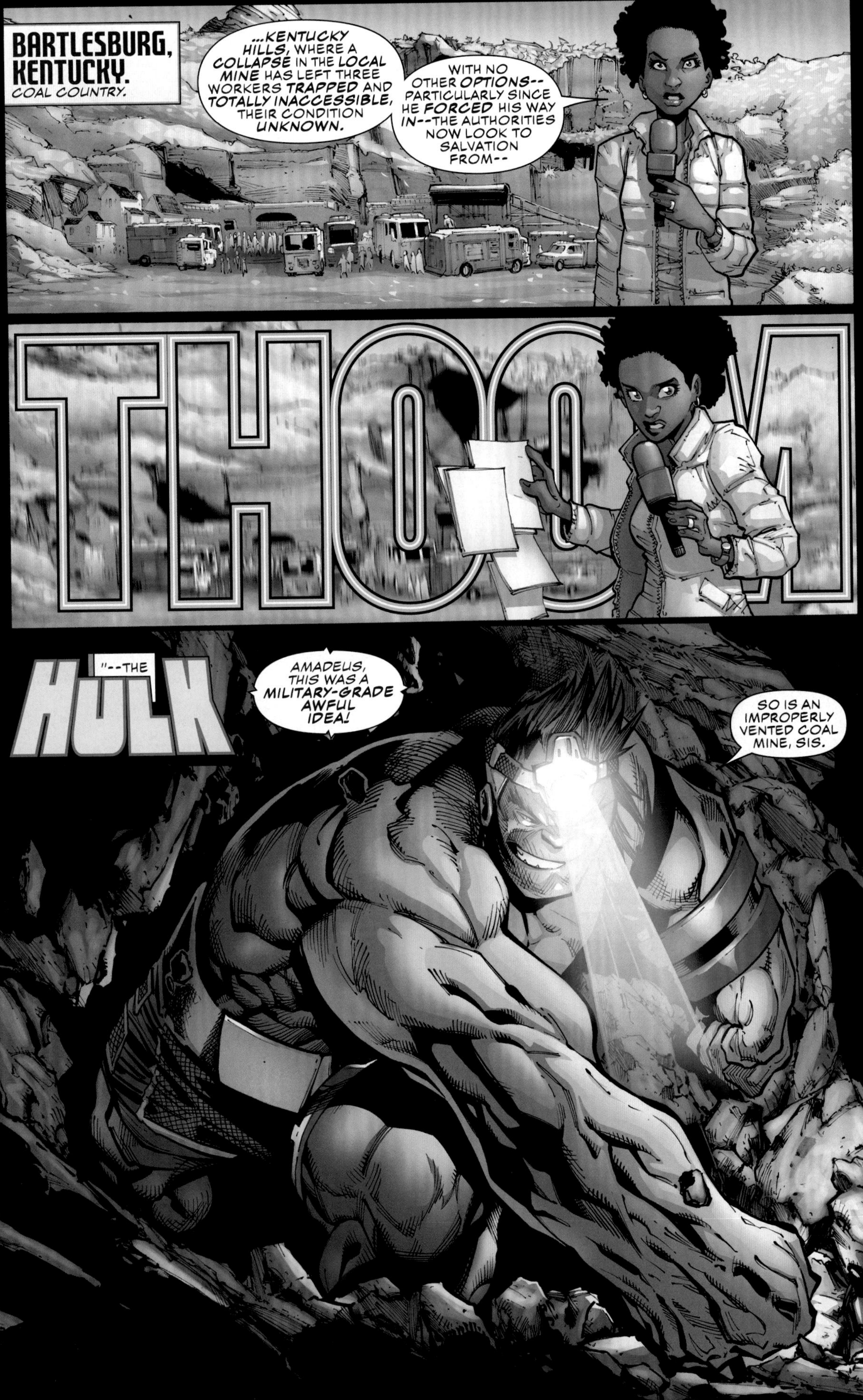
BARTLESBURG, KENTUCKY.
COAL COUNTRY.
...KENTUCKY HILLS, WHERE A COLLAPSE IN THE LOCAL MINE HAS LEFT THREE WORKERS TRAPPED AND TOTALLY INACCESSIBLE, THEIR CONDITION UNKNOWN.
WITH NO OTHER OPTIONS--PARTICULARLY SINCE HE FORCED HIS WAY IN--THE AUTHORITIES NOW LOOK TO SALVATION FROM--
THOOM
"--THE HULK
AMADEUS, THIS WAS A MILITARY-GRADE AWFUL IDEA!
SO IS AN IMPROPERLY VENTED COAL MINE, SIS.

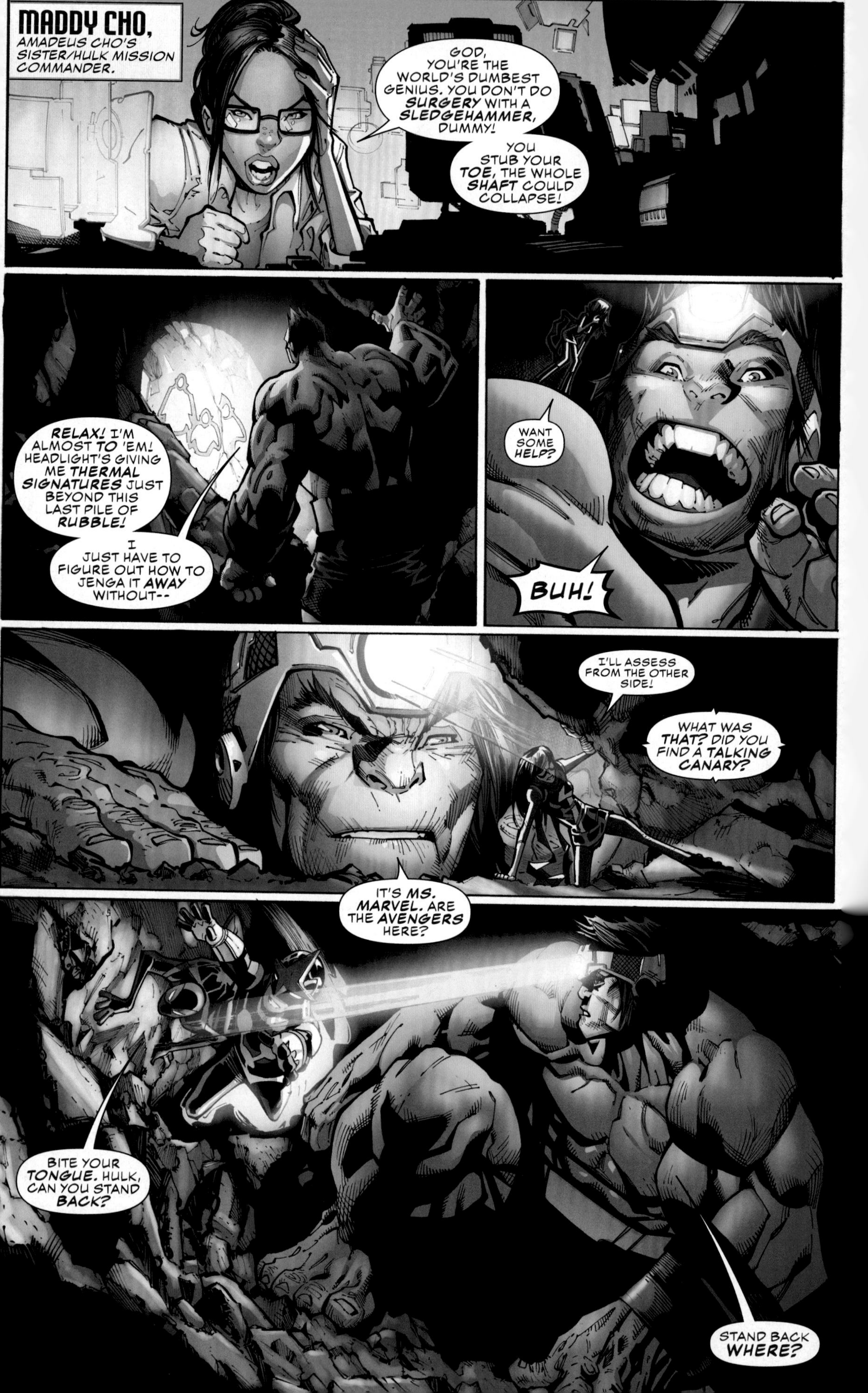
MADDY CHO, AMADEUS CHO'S SISTER/HULK MISSION COMMANDER.
GOD, YOU'RE THE WORLD'S DUMBEST GENIUS. YOU DON'T DO SURGERY WITH A SLEDGEHAMMER, DUMMY!
YOU STUB YOUR TOE, THE WHOLE SHAFT COULD COLLAPSE!
RELAX! I'M ALMOST TO 'EM! HEADLIGHT'S GIVING ME THERMAL SIGNATURES JUST BEYOND THIS LAST PILE OF RUBBLE!
I JUST HAVE TO FIGURE OUT HOW TO JENGA IT AWAY WITHOUT--
WANT SOME HELP?
BUH!
I'LL ASSESS FROM THE OTHER SIDE!
WHAT WAS THAT? DID YOU FIND A TALKING CANARY?
IT'S MS. MARVEL. ARE THE AVENGERS HERE?
BITE YOUR TONGUE. HULK, CAN YOU STAND BACK?
STAND BACK WHERE?

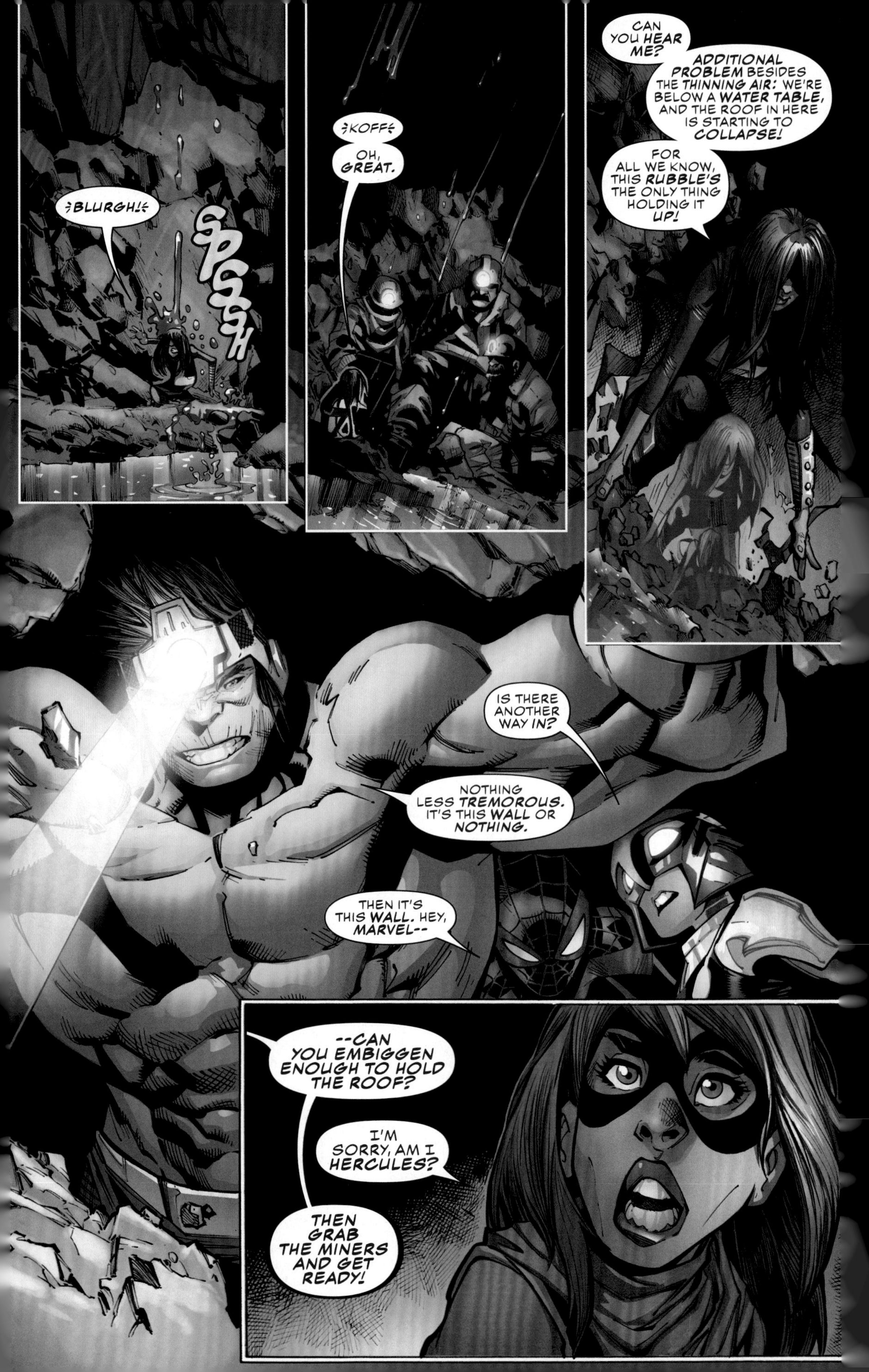

‹BLURGH!›
SPSSH
‹KOFF›
OH, GREAT.
CAN YOU HEAR ME?
ADDITIONAL PROBLEM BESIDES THE THINNING AIR: WE'RE BELOW A WATER TABLE, AND THE ROOF IN HERE IS STARTING TO COLLAPSE!
FOR ALL WE KNOW, THIS RUBBLE'S THE ONLY THING HOLDING IT UP!
IS THERE ANOTHER WAY IN?
NOTHING LESS TREMOROUS. IT'S THIS WALL OR NOTHING.
THEN IT'S THIS WALL. HEY, MARVEL--
--CAN YOU EMBIGGEN ENOUGH TO HOLD THE ROOF?
I'M SORRY, AM I HERCULES?
THEN GRAB THE MINERS AND GET READY!

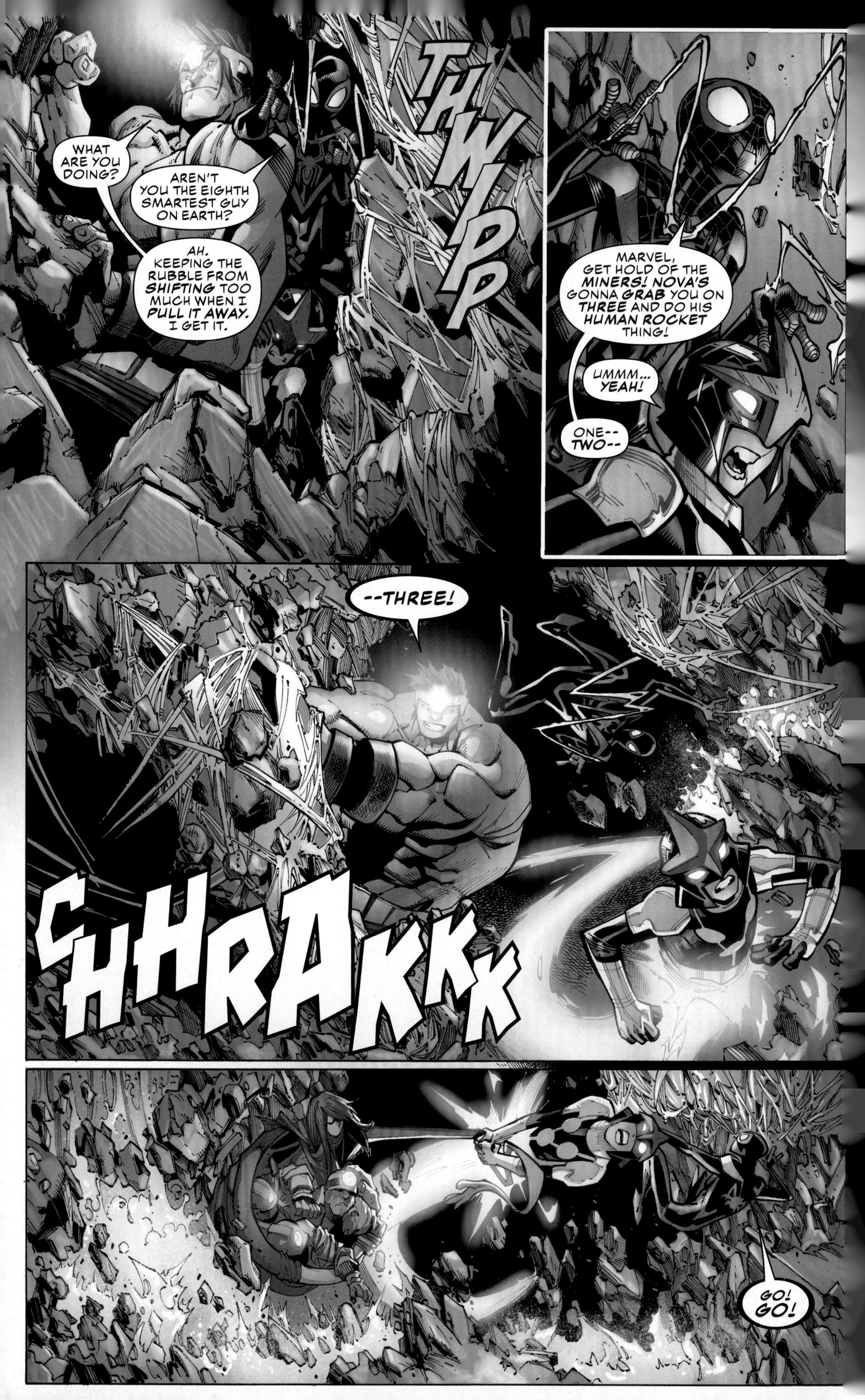
WHAT ARE YOU DOING?
AREN'T YOU THE EIGHTH SMARTEST GUY ON EARTH?
AH. KEEPING THE RUBBLE FROM SHIFTING TOO MUCH WHEN I PULL IT AWAY. I GET IT.
THWIPP
MARVEL, GET HOLD OF THE MINERS! NOVA'S GONNA GRAB YOU ON THREE AND DO HIS HUMAN ROCKET THING!
UMMM... YEAH!
ONE-- TWO--
--THREE!
CHHRAKKK
GO! GO!

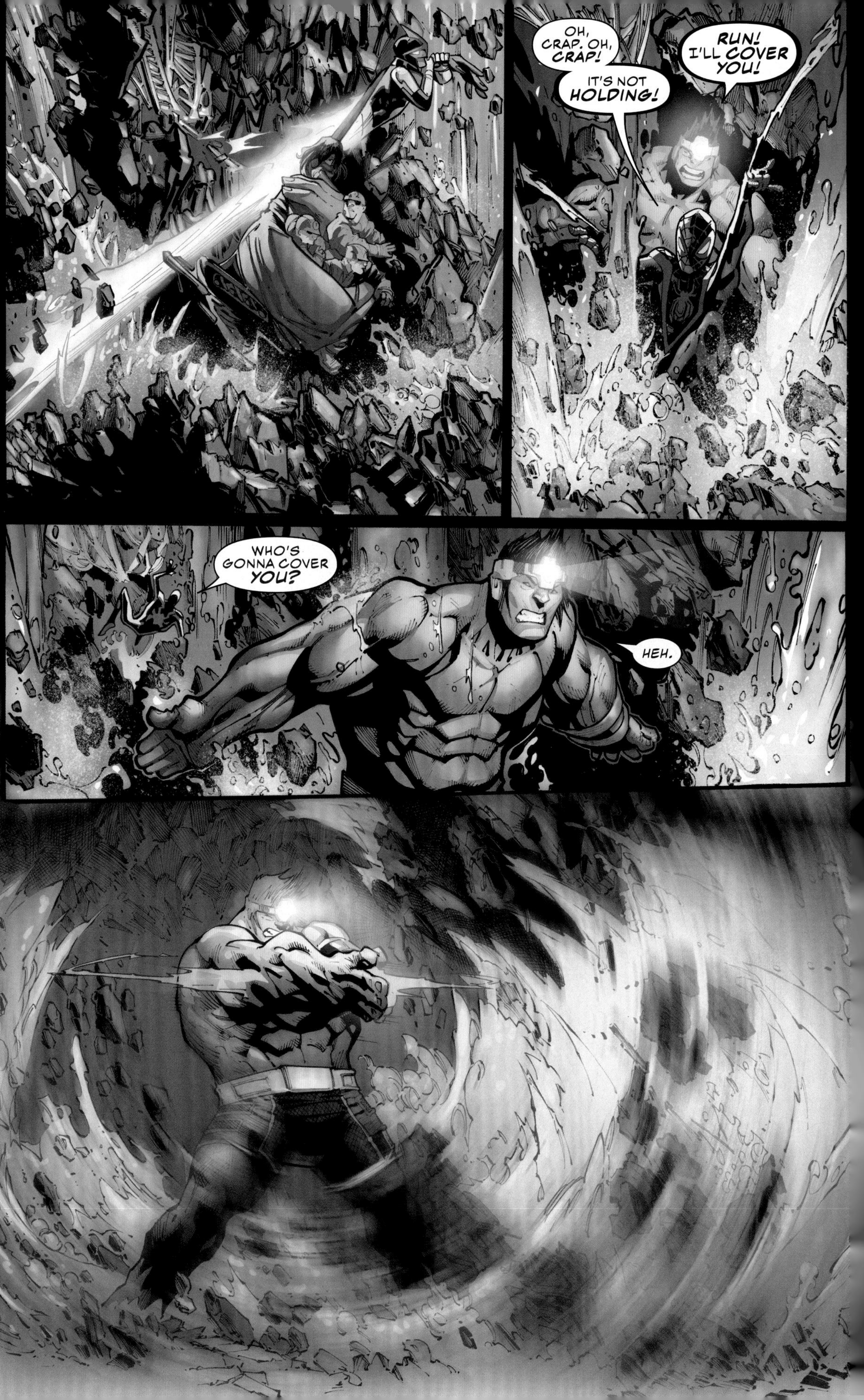
OH, CRAP. OH, CRAP!
IT'S NOT HOLDING!
RUN! I'LL COVER YOU!
WHO'S GONNA COVER YOU?
HEH.

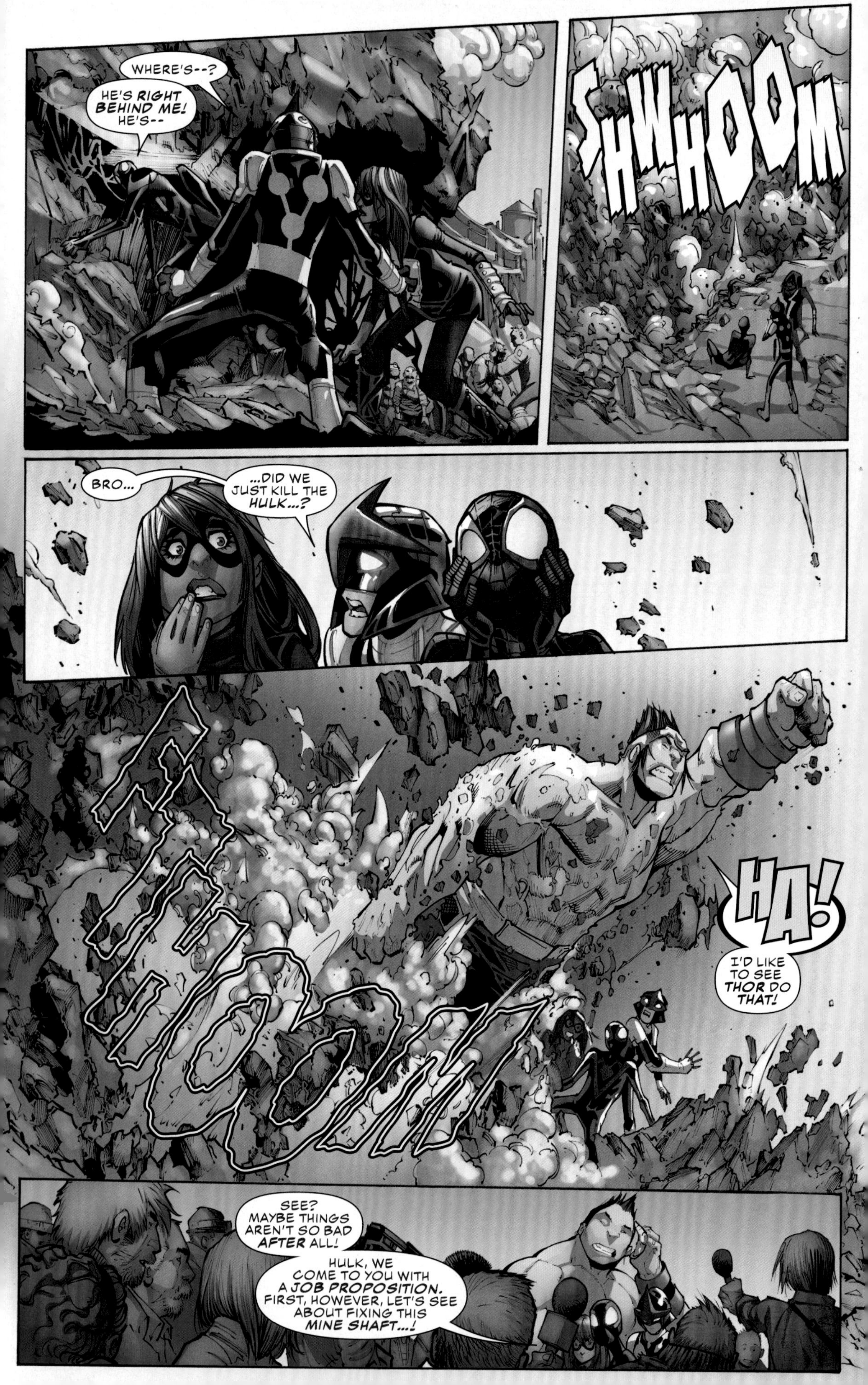
WHERE'S--?
HE'S RIGHT BEHIND ME! HE'S--
SHWHOOM
BRO...
...DID WE JUST KILL THE HULK...?
HA!
I'D LIKE TO SEE THOR DO THAT!
SEE? MAYBE THINGS AREN'T SO BAD AFTER ALL!
HULK, WE COME TO YOU WITH A JOB PROPOSITION. FIRST, HOWEVER, LET'S SEE ABOUT FIXING THIS MINE SHAFT...!

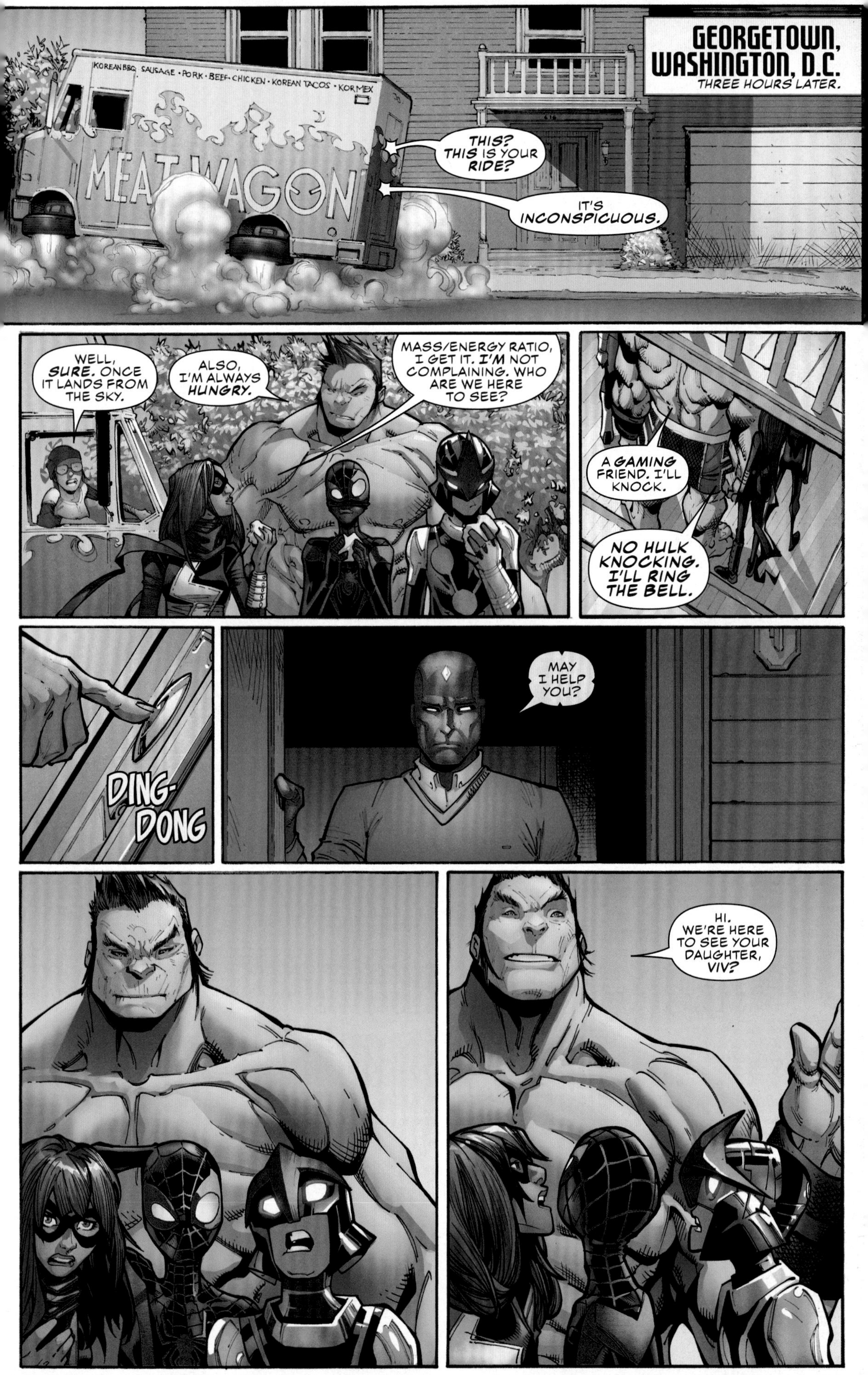
GEORGETOWN, WASHINGTON, D.C.
THREE HOURS LATER.
KOREAN BBQ SAUSAGE • PORK • BEEF • CHICKEN • KOREAN TACOS • KOR MEX
MEAT WAGON
THIS? THIS IS YOUR RIDE?
IT'S INCONSPICUOUS.
WELL, SURE. ONCE IT LANDS FROM THE SKY.
ALSO, I'M ALWAYS HUNGRY.
MASS/ENERGY RATIO, I GET IT. I'M NOT COMPLAINING. WHO ARE WE HERE TO SEE?
A GAMING FRIEND. I'LL KNOCK.
NO HULK KNOCKING. I'LL RING THE BELL.
DING-DONG
MAY I HELP YOU?
HI. WE'RE HERE TO SEE YOUR DAUGHTER, VIV?

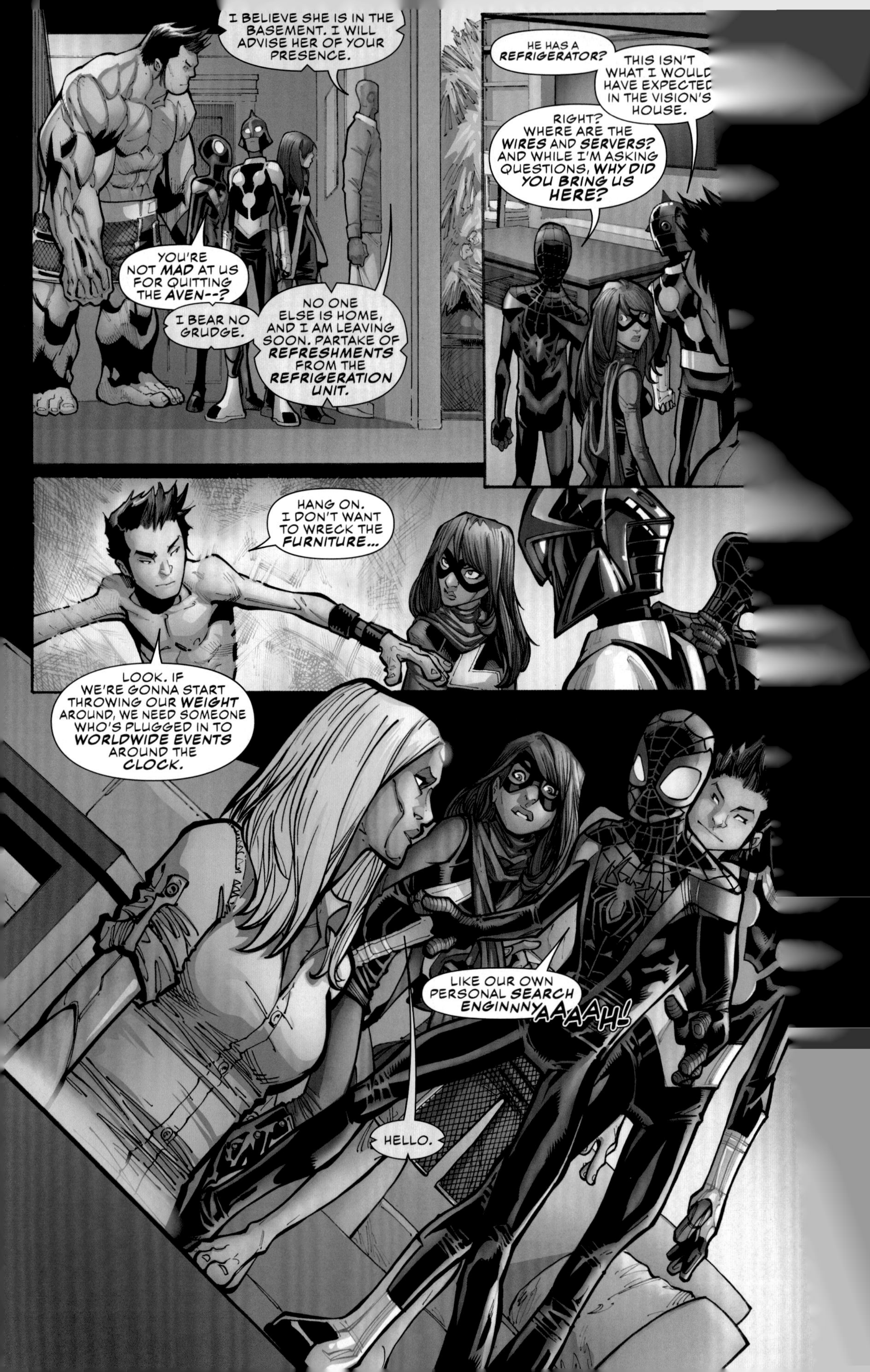
I BELIEVE SHE IS IN THE BASEMENT. I WILL ADVISE HER OF YOUR PRESENCE.
YOU'RE NOT MAD AT US FOR QUITTING THE AVEN--?
I BEAR NO GRUDGE.
NO ONE ELSE IS HOME, AND I AM LEAVING SOON. PARTAKE OF REFRESHMENTS FROM THE REFRIGERATION UNIT.
HE HAS A REFRIGERATOR?
THIS ISN'T WHAT I WOULD HAVE EXPECTED IN THE VISION'S HOUSE.
RIGHT? WHERE ARE THE WIRES AND SERVERS? AND WHILE I'M ASKING QUESTIONS, WHY DID YOU BRING US HERE?
HANG ON. I DON'T WANT TO WRECK THE FURNITURE...
LOOK. IF WE'RE GONNA START THROWING OUR WEIGHT AROUND, WE NEED SOMEONE WHO'S PLUGGED IN TO WORLDWIDE EVENTS AROUND THE CLOCK.
LIKE OUR OWN PERSONAL SEARCH ENGINNNYAAAAH!
HELLO.

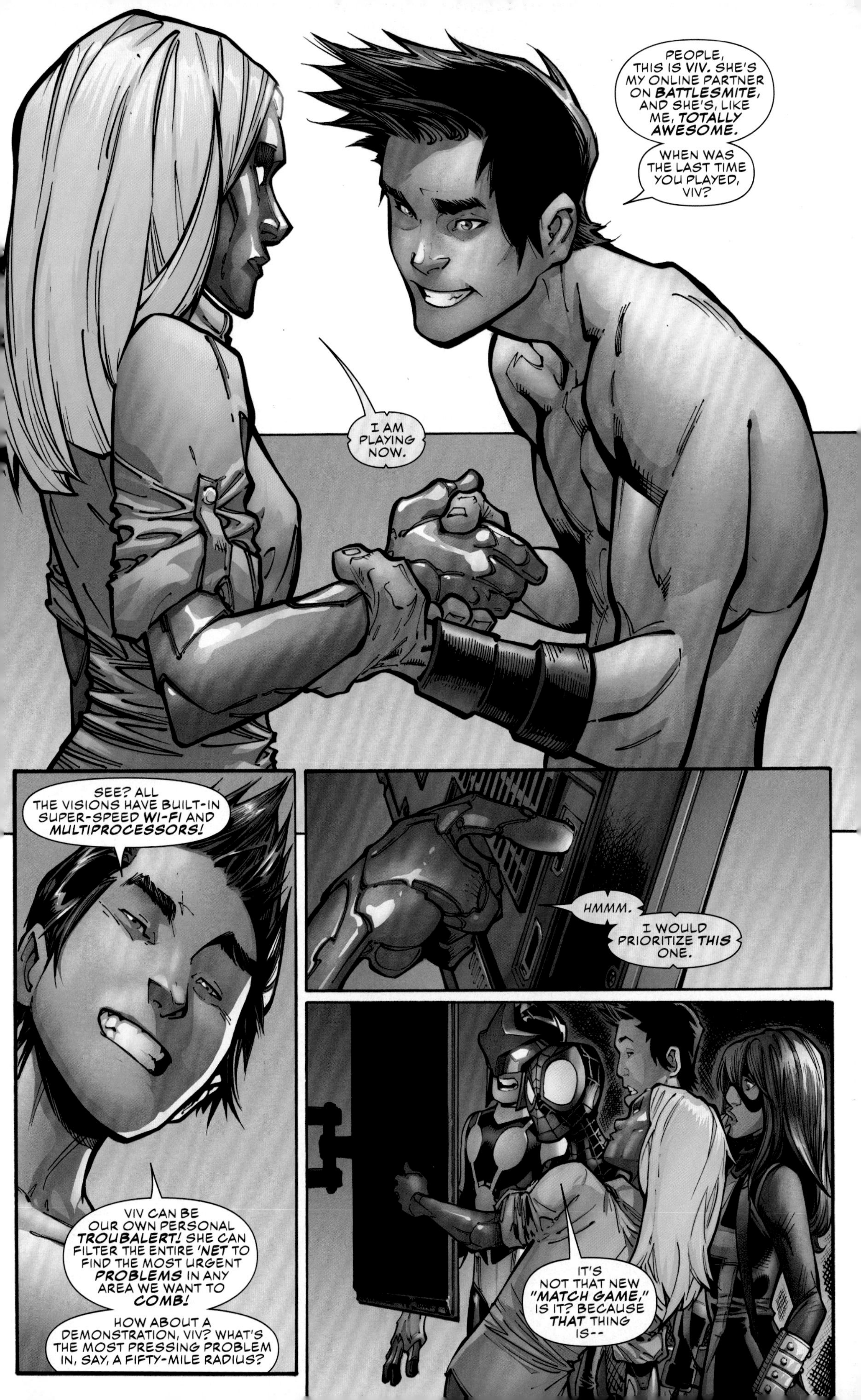
PEOPLE, THIS IS VIV. SHE'S MY ONLINE PARTNER ON BATTLESMITE, AND SHE'S, LIKE ME, TOTALLY AWESOME.
WHEN WAS THE LAST TIME YOU PLAYED, VIV?
I AM PLAYING NOW.
SEE? ALL THE VISIONS HAVE BUILT-IN SUPER-SPEED WI-FI AND MULTIPROCESSORS!
VIV CAN BE OUR OWN PERSONAL TROUBALERT! SHE CAN FILTER THE ENTIRE 'NET TO FIND THE MOST URGENT PROBLEMS IN ANY AREA WE WANT TO COMB!
HOW ABOUT A DEMONSTRATION, VIV? WHAT'S THE MOST PRESSING PROBLEM IN, SAY, A FIFTY-MILE RADIUS?
HMMM.
I WOULD PRIORITIZE THIS ONE.
IT'S NOT THAT NEW "MATCH GAME," IS IT? BECAUSE THAT THING IS--

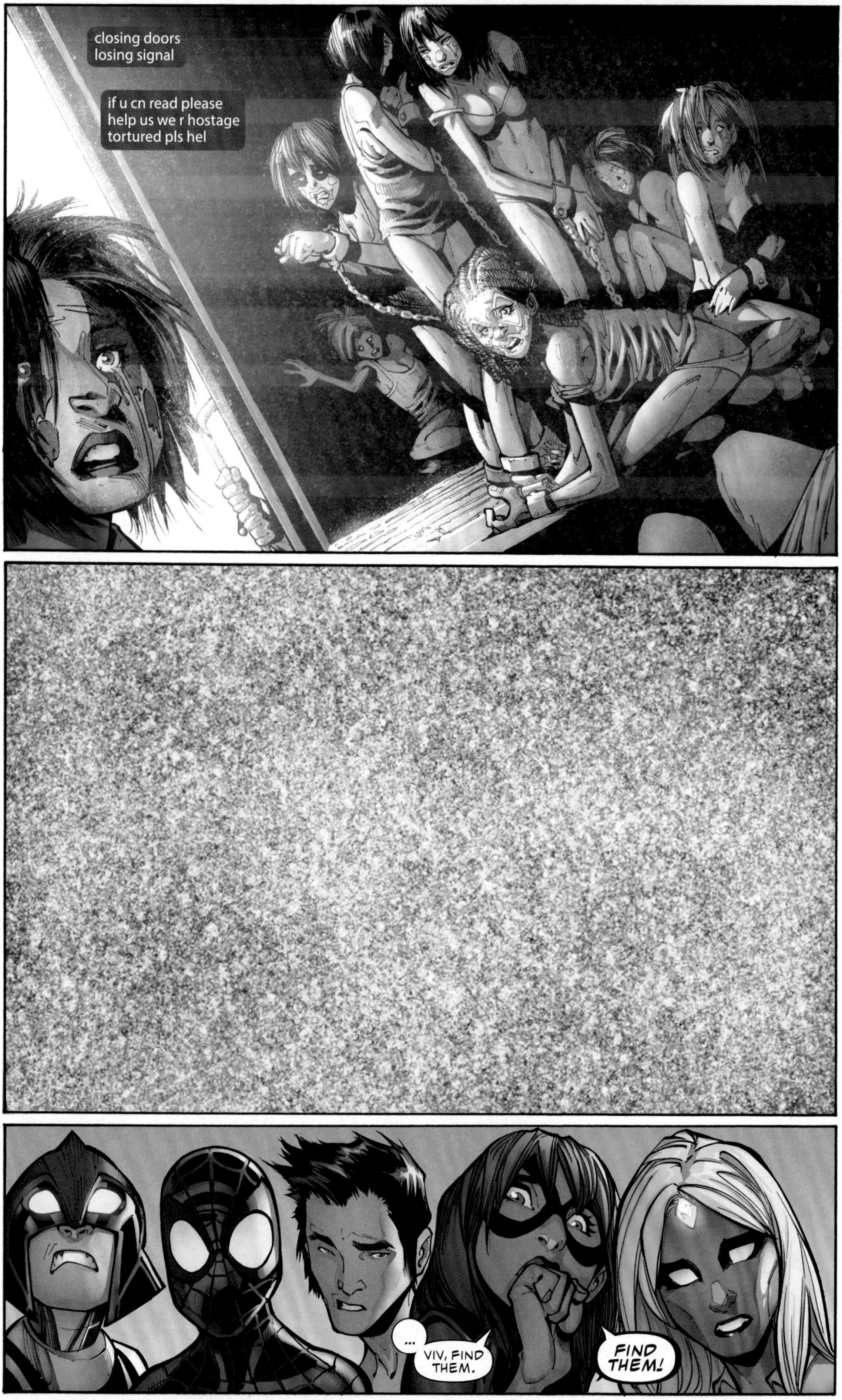
closing doors
losing signal
if u cn read please
help us we r hostage
tortured pls hel
...
VIV, FIND THEM.
FIND THEM!

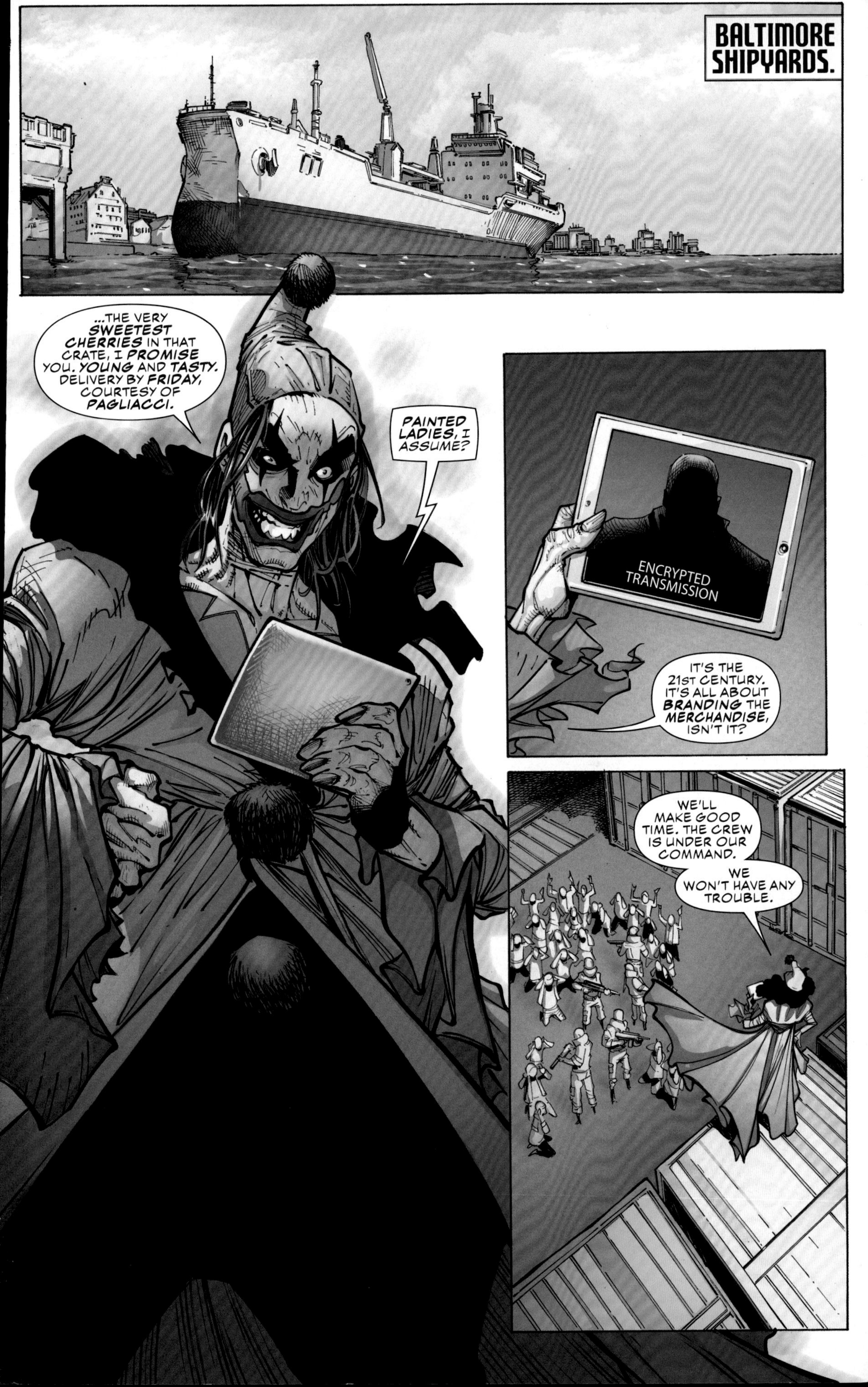
BALTIMORE SHIPYARDS.
...THE VERY SWEETEST CHERRIES IN THAT CRATE, I PROMISE YOU. YOUNG AND TASTY. DELIVERY BY FRIDAY, COURTESY OF PAGLIACCI.
PAINTED LADIES, I ASSUME?
ENCRYPTED TRANSMISSION
IT'S THE 21ST CENTURY. IT'S ALL ABOUT BRANDING THE MERCHANDISE, ISN'T IT?
WE'LL MAKE GOOD TIME. THE CREW IS UNDER OUR COMMAND.
WE WON'T HAVE ANY TROUBLE.

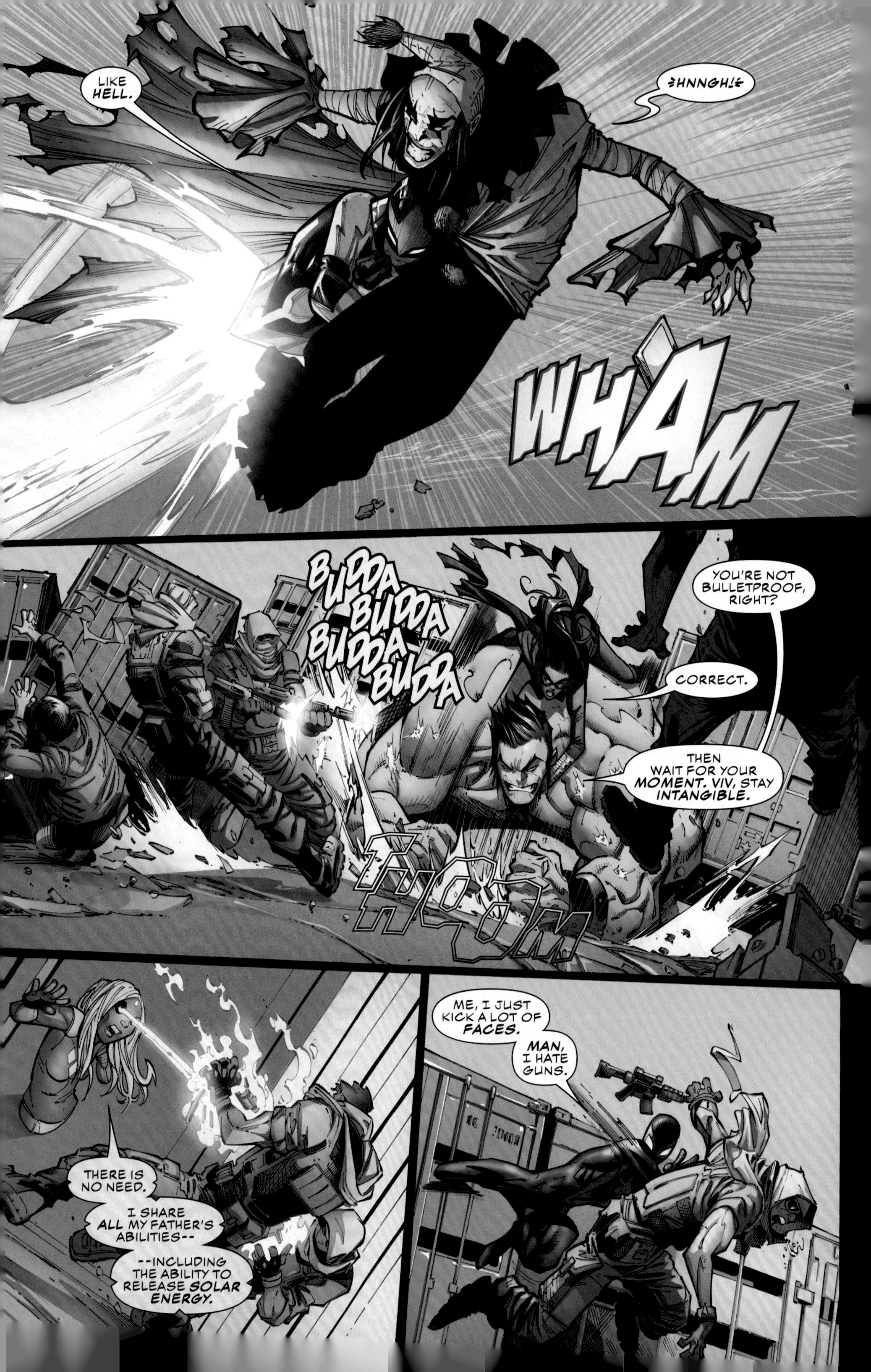
LIKE HELL.
HNNGH!
WHAM
BUDDA BUDDA BUDDA BUDDA
YOU'RE NOT BULLETPROOF, RIGHT?
CORRECT.
THEN WAIT FOR YOUR MOMENT. VIV, STAY INTANGIBLE.
FWOOM
THERE IS NO NEED.
I SHARE ALL MY FATHER'S ABILITIES--
--INCLUDING THE ABILITY TO RELEASE SOLAR ENERGY.
ME, I JUST KICK A LOT OF FACES.
MAN, I HATE GUNS.

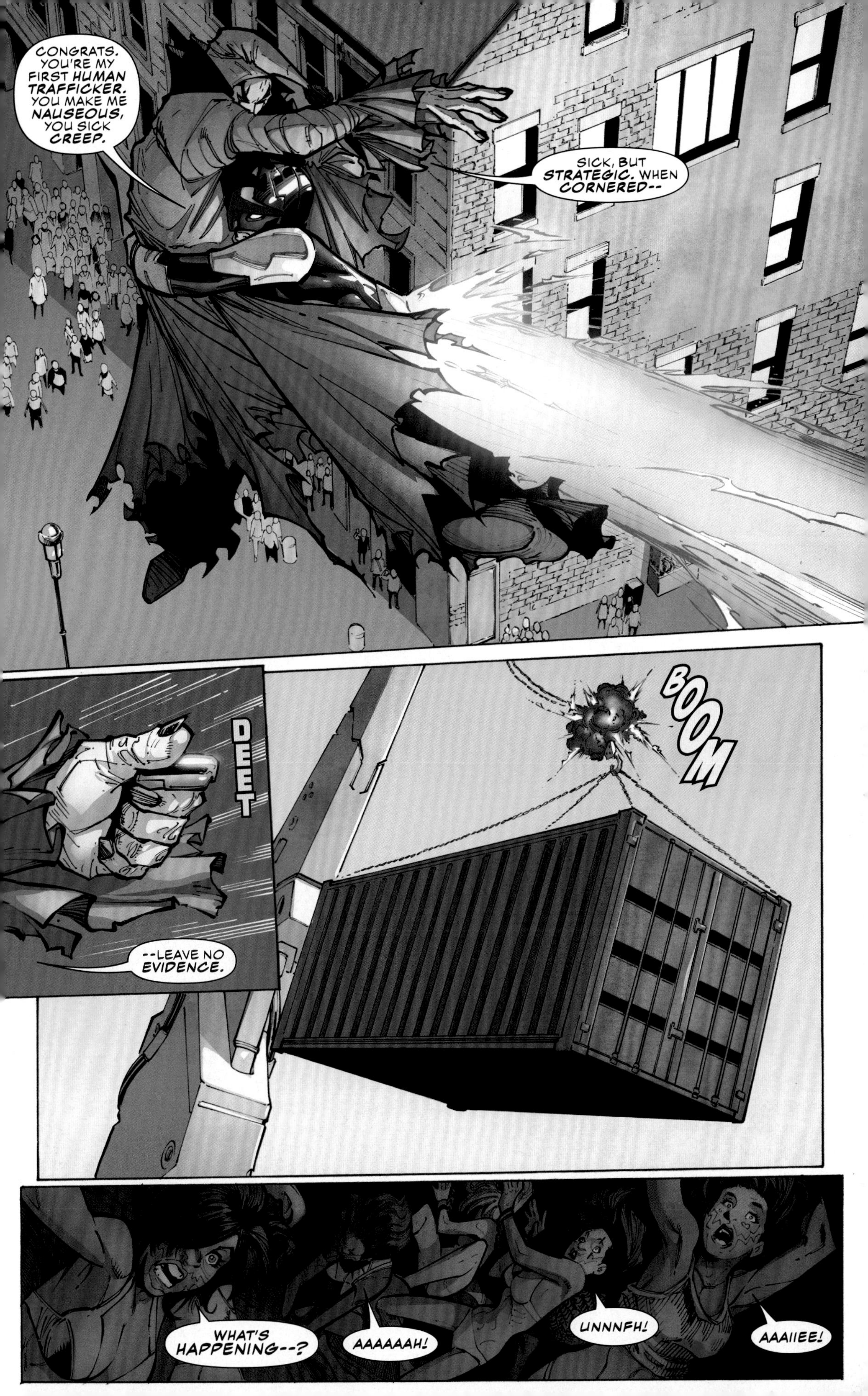
CONGRATS. YOU'RE MY FIRST HUMAN TRAFFICKER. YOU MAKE ME NAUSEOUS, YOU SICK CREEP.
SICK, BUT STRATEGIC. WHEN CORNERED--
DEET
--LEAVE NO EVIDENCE.
BOOM
WHAT'S HAPPENING--?
AAAAAAH!
UNNNFH!
AAAIIEE!

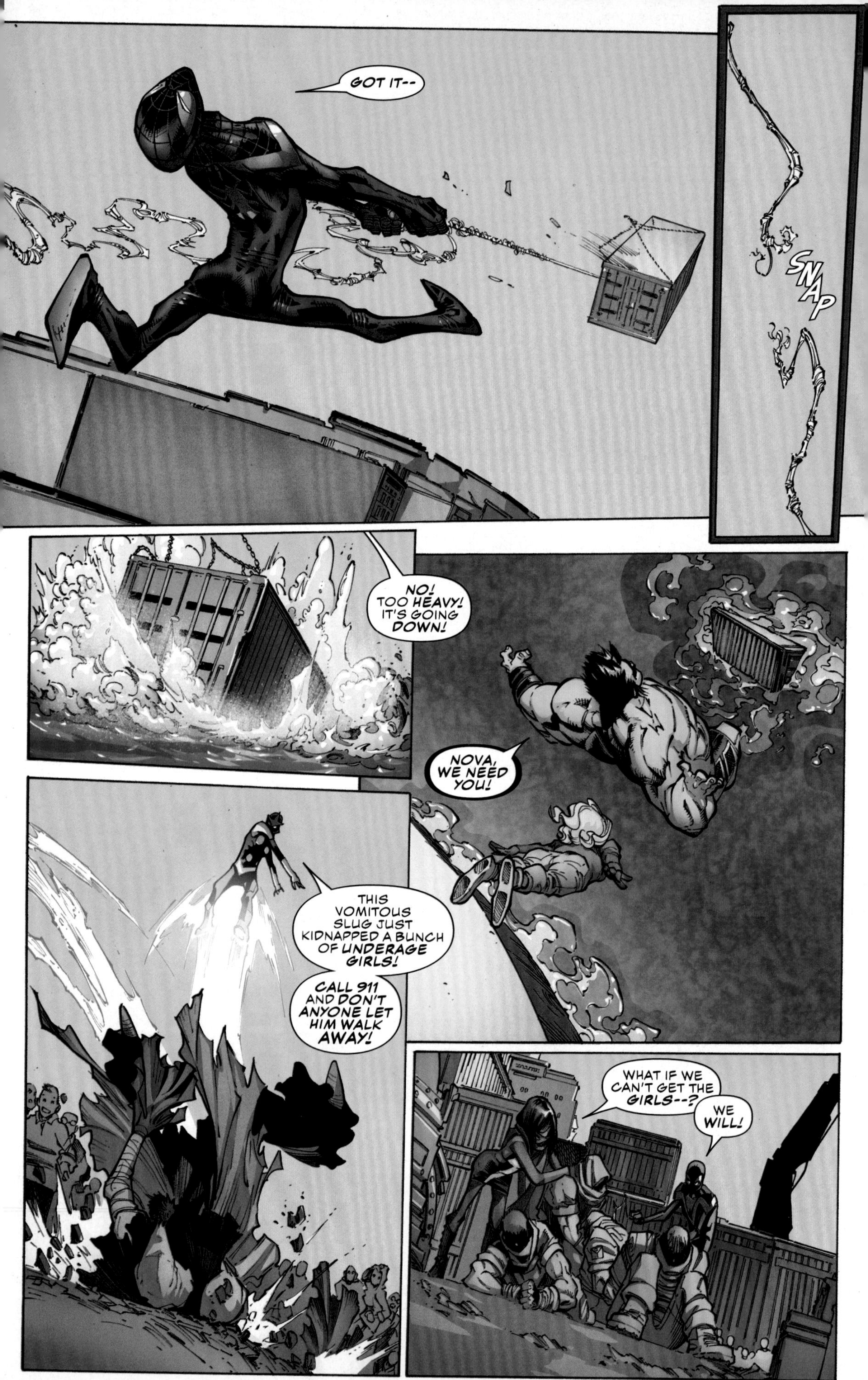
GOT IT--
SNAP
NO! TOO HEAVY! IT'S GOING DOWN!
NOVA, WE NEED YOU!
THIS VOMITOUS SLUG JUST KIDNAPPED A BUNCH OF UNDERAGE GIRLS!
CALL 911 AND DON'T ANYONE LET HIM WALK AWAY!
WHAT IF WE CAN'T GET THE GIRLS--?
WE WILL!

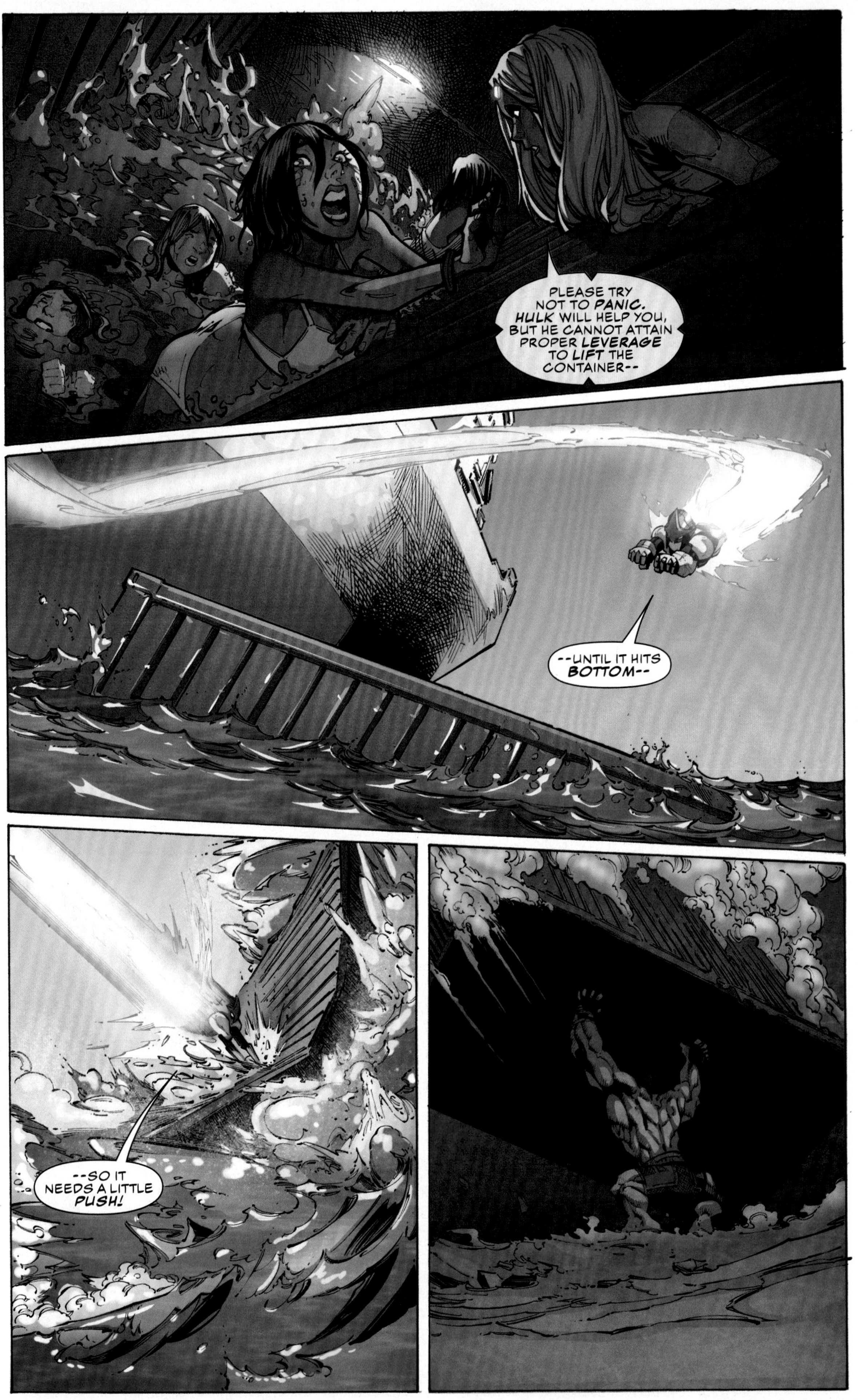
PLEASE TRY NOT TO PANIC. HULK WILL HELP YOU, BUT HE CANNOT ATTAIN PROPER LEVERAGE TO LIFT THE CONTAINER--
--UNTIL IT HITS BOTTOM--
--SO IT NEEDS A LITTLE PUSH!

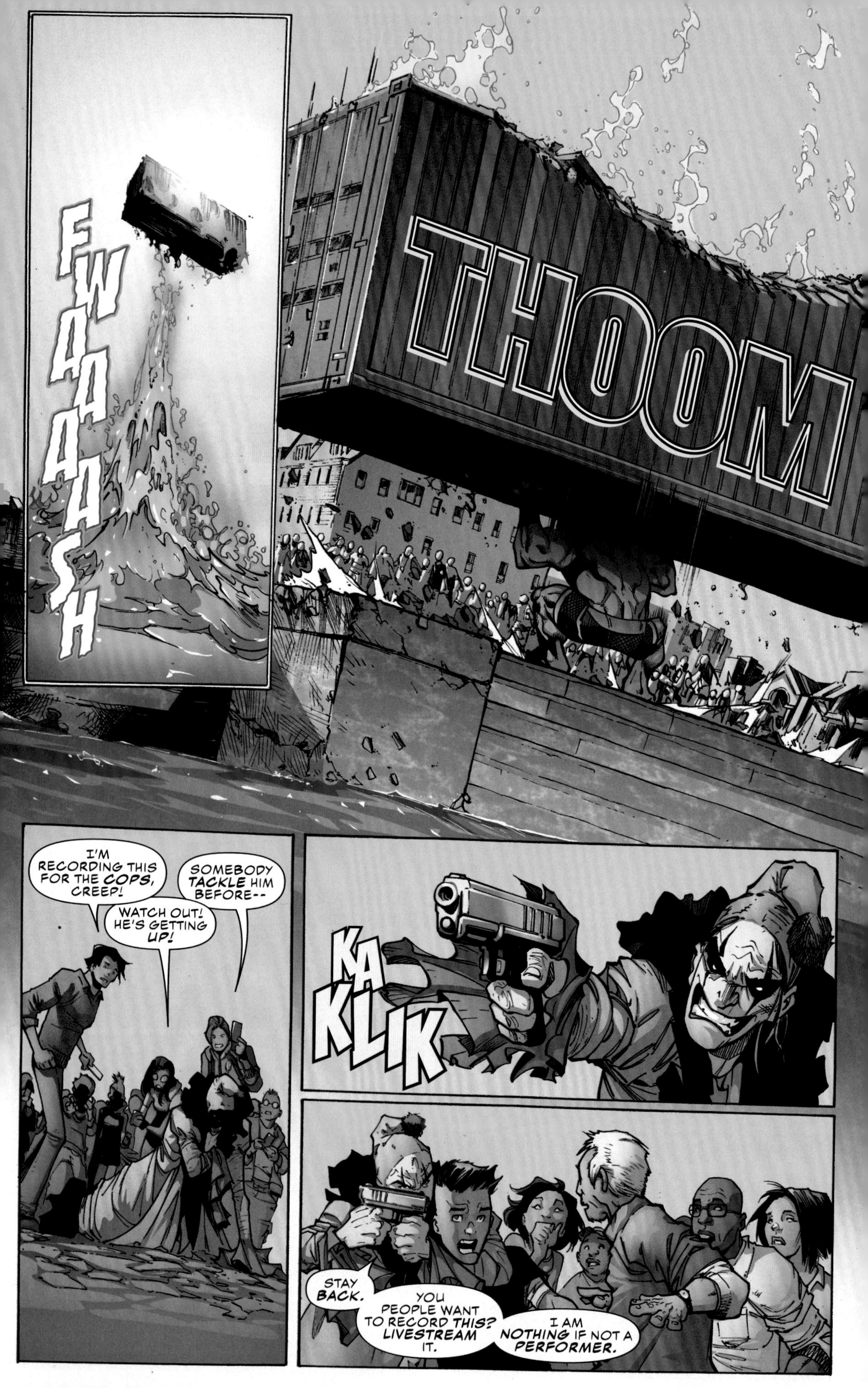
FWAAAASH
THOOM
I'M RECORDING THIS FOR THE COPS, CREEP!
WATCH OUT! HE'S GETTING UP!
SOMEBODY TACKLE HIM BEFORE--
KA KLIK
STAY BACK.
YOU PEOPLE WANT TO RECORD THIS? LIVESTREAM IT.
I AM NOTHING IF NOT A PERFORMER.

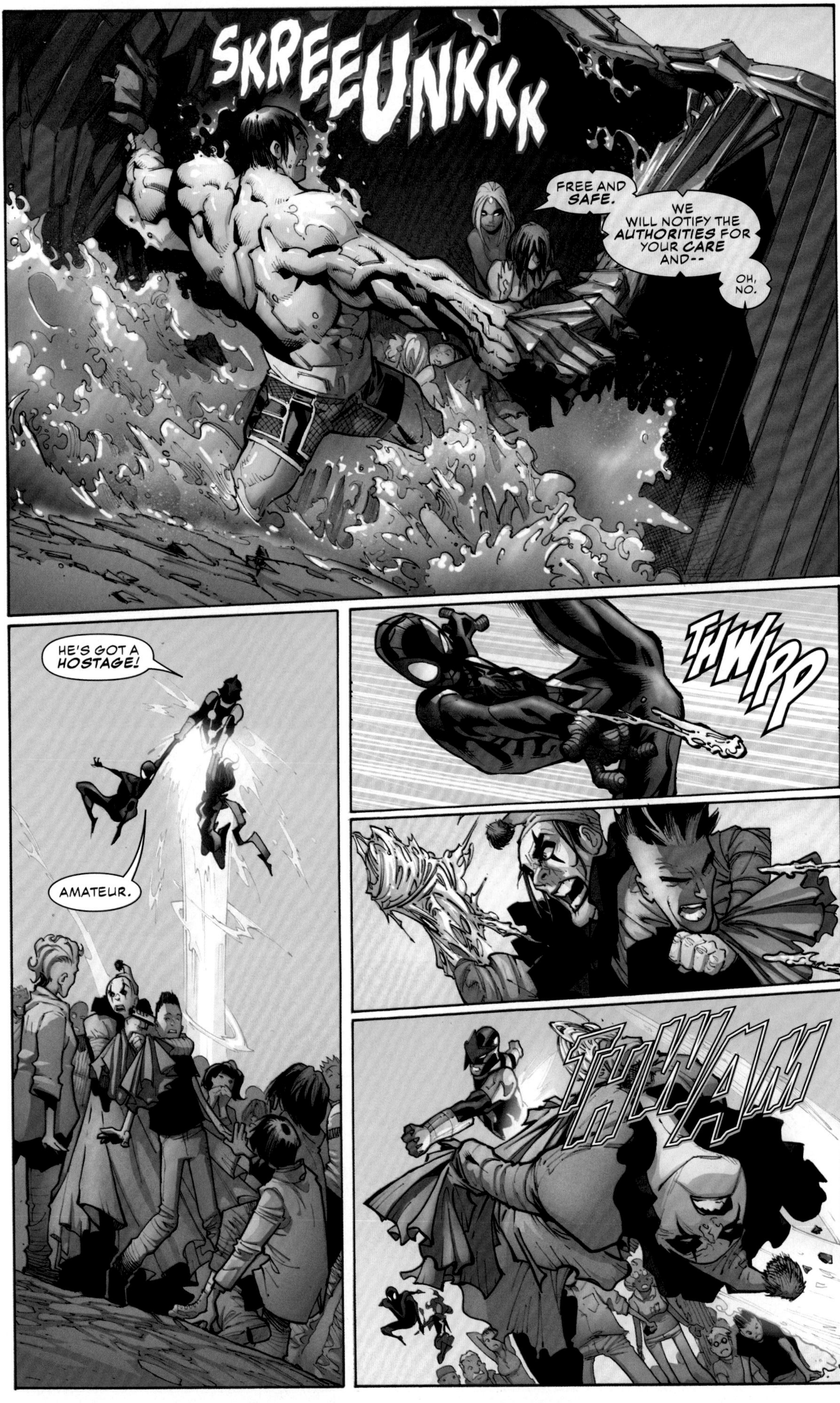
SKREEUNKKK
FREE AND SAFE.
WE WILL NOTIFY THE AUTHORITIES FOR YOUR CARE AND--
OH, NO.
HE'S GOT A HOSTAGE!
AMATEUR.
THWIPP
THWAM

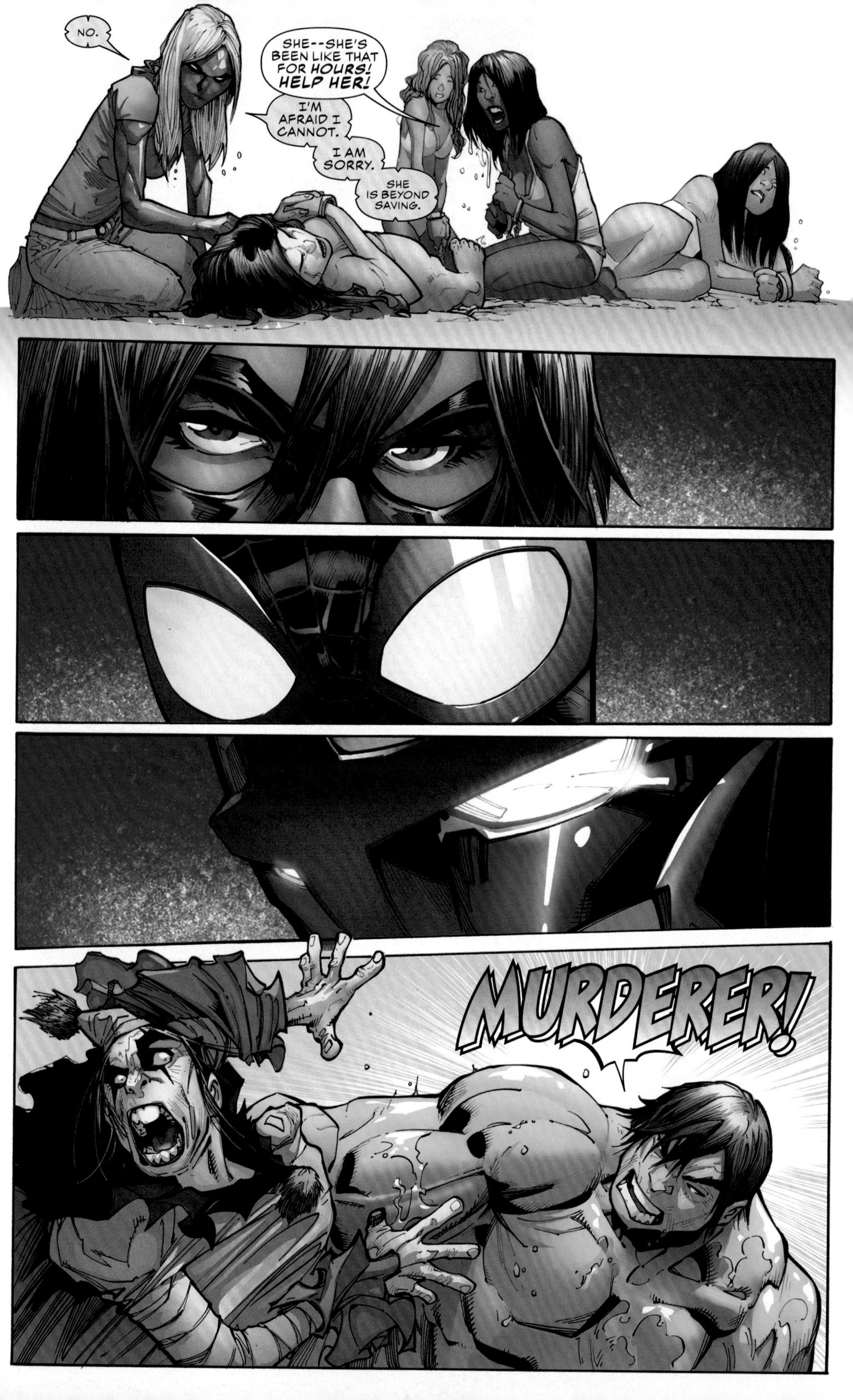
NO.
SHE--SHE'S BEEN LIKE THAT FOR HOURS! HELP HER!
I'M AFRAID I CANNOT.
I AM SORRY.
SHE IS BEYOND SAVING.
MURDERER!

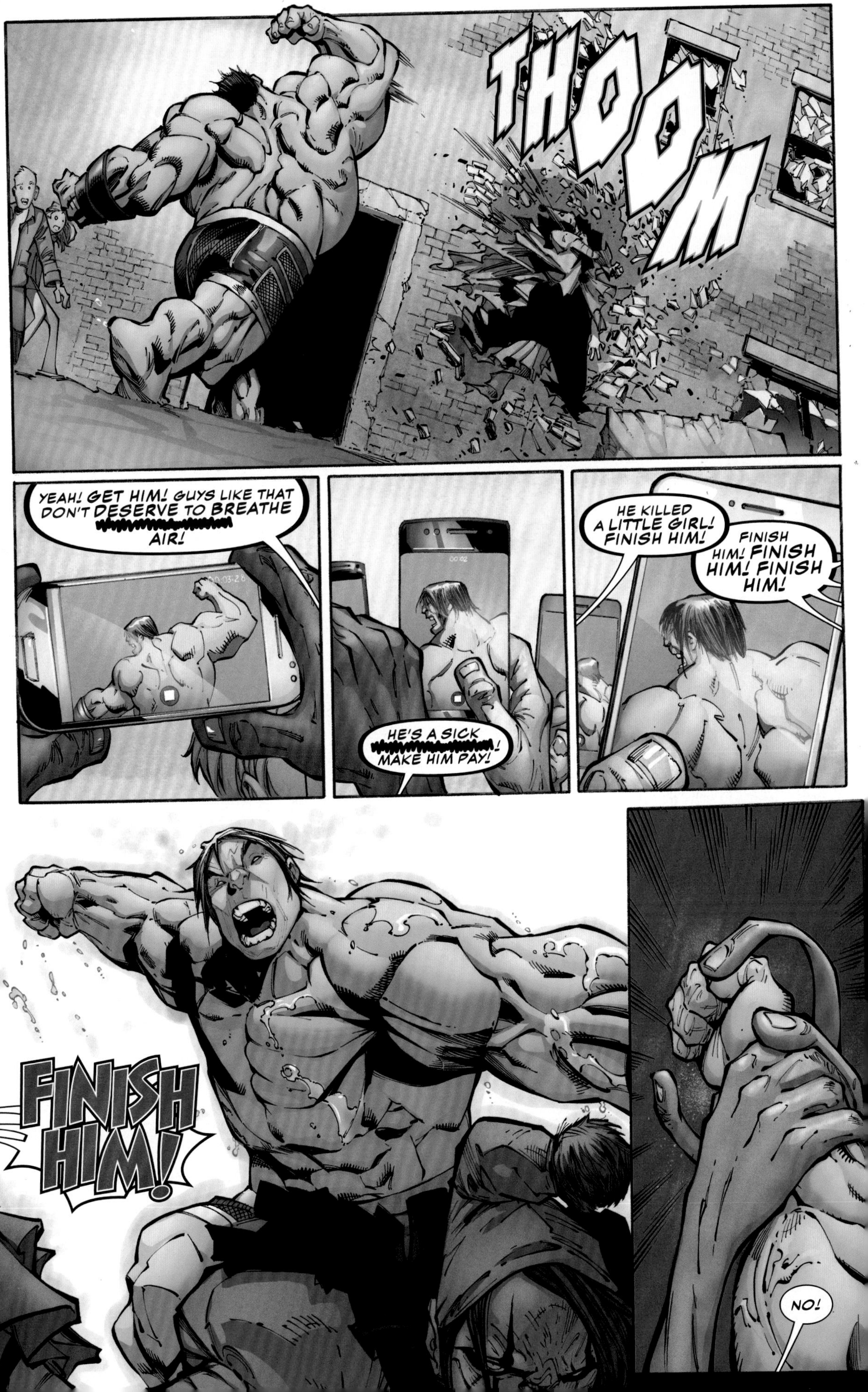
THOOM
YEAH! GET HIM! GUYS LIKE THAT DON'T DESERVE TO BREATHE AIR!
HE'S A SICK ! MAKE HIM PAY!
HE KILLED A LITTLE GIRL! FINISH HIM!
FINISH HIM! FINISH HIM! FINISH HIM!
FINISH HIM!
NO!

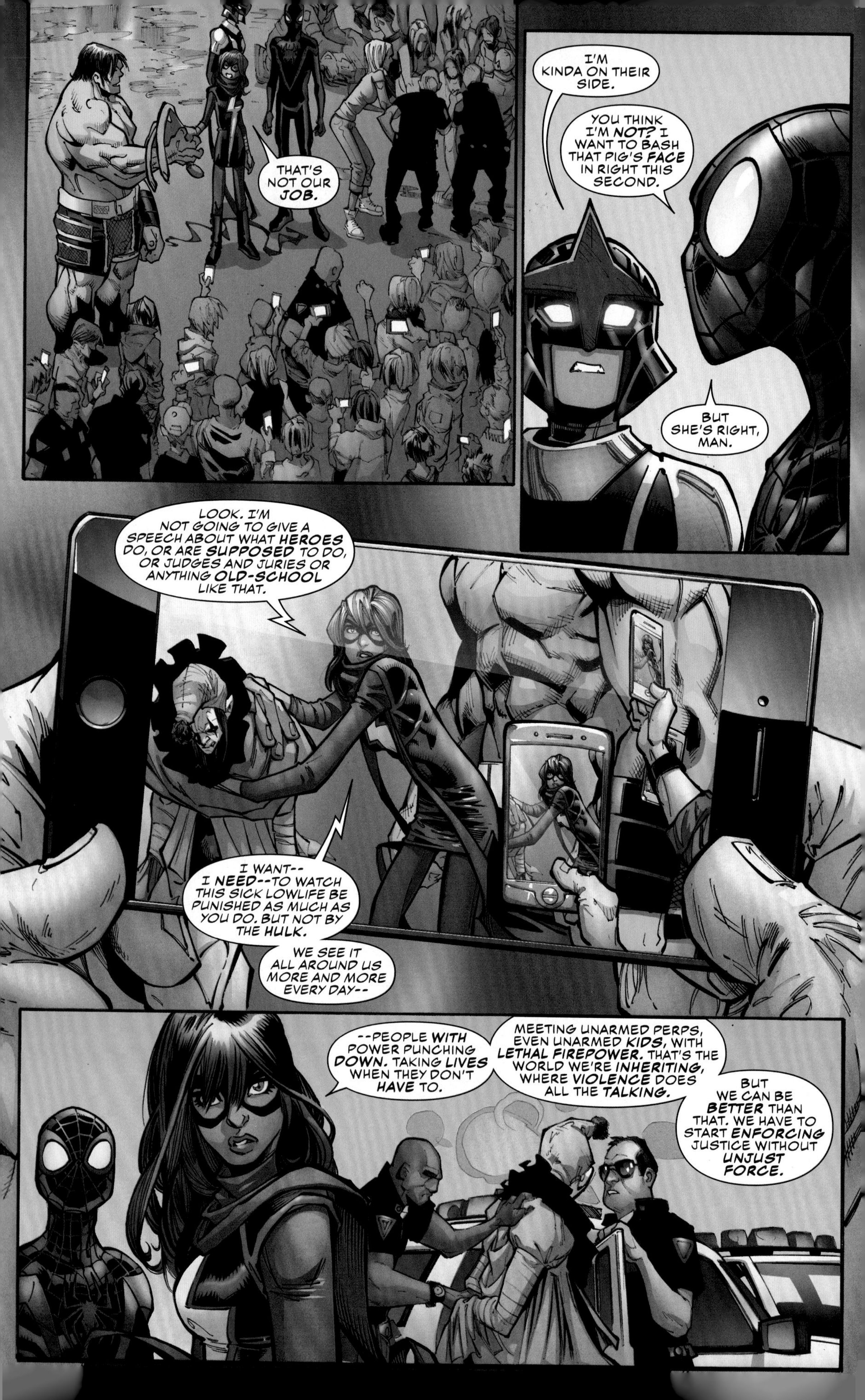
THAT'S NOT OUR JOB.
I'M KINDA ON THEIR SIDE.
YOU THINK I'M NOT? I WANT TO BASH THAT PIG'S FACE IN RIGHT THIS SECOND.
BUT SHE'S RIGHT, MAN.
LOOK. I'M NOT GOING TO GIVE A SPEECH ABOUT WHAT HEROES DO, OR ARE SUPPOSED TO DO, OR JUDGES AND JURIES OR ANYTHING OLD-SCHOOL LIKE THAT.
I WANT-- I NEED--TO WATCH THIS SICK LOWLIFE BE PUNISHED AS MUCH AS YOU DO. BUT NOT BY THE HULK.
WE SEE IT ALL AROUND US MORE AND MORE EVERY DAY--
--PEOPLE WITH POWER PUNCHING DOWN. TAKING LIVES WHEN THEY DON'T HAVE TO.
MEETING UNARMED PERPS, EVEN UNARMED KIDS, WITH LETHAL FIREPOWER. THAT'S THE WORLD WE'RE INHERITING, WHERE VIOLENCE DOES ALL THE TALKING.
BUT WE CAN BE BETTER THAN THAT. WE HAVE TO START ENFORCING JUSTICE WITHOUT UNJUST FORCE.

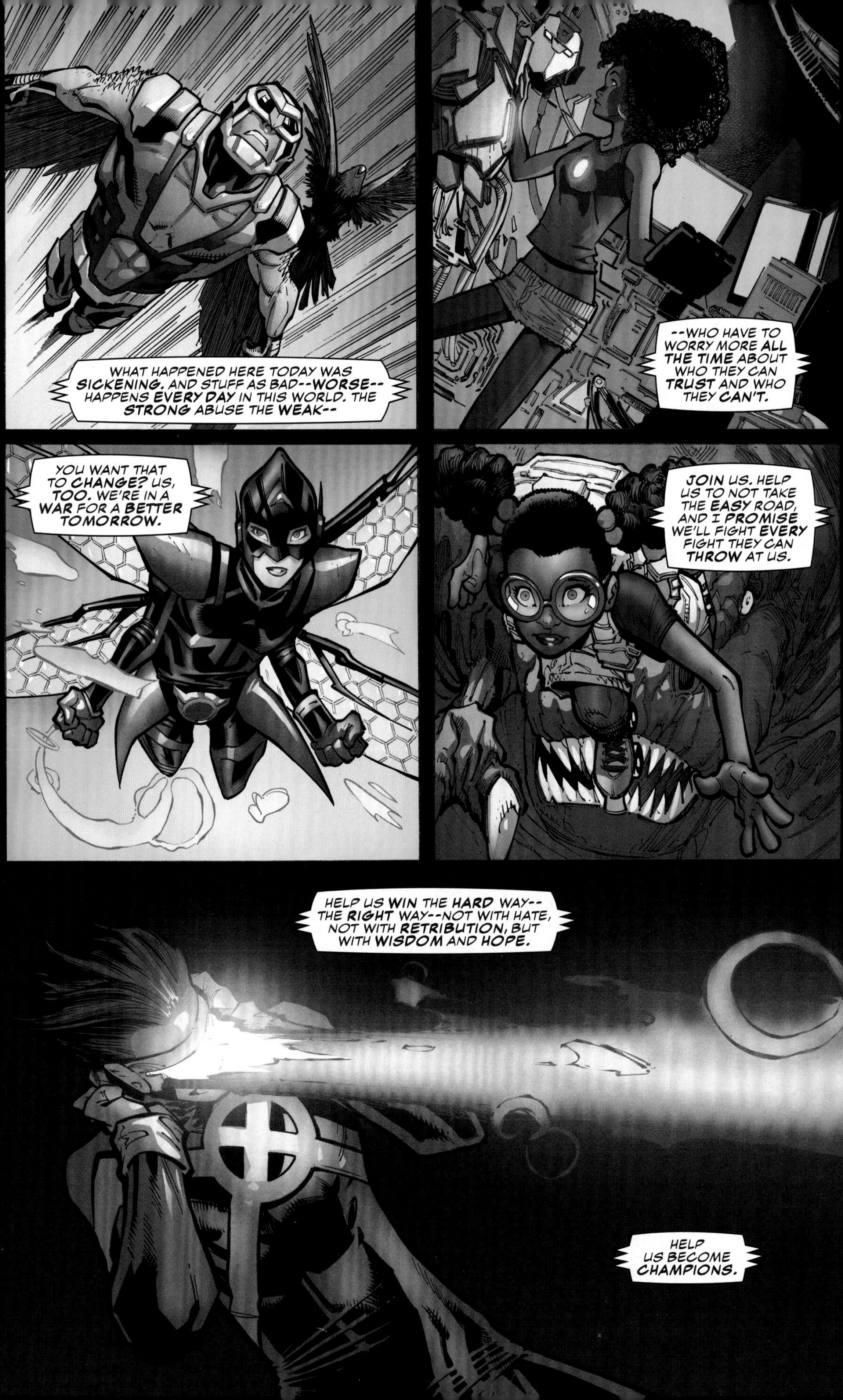
WHAT HAPPENED HERE TODAY WAS SICKENING. AND STUFF AS BAD--WORSE--HAPPENS EVERY DAY IN THIS WORLD. THE STRONG ABUSE THE WEAK--
--WHO HAVE TO WORRY MORE ALL THE TIME ABOUT WHO THEY CAN TRUST AND WHO THEY CAN'T.
YOU WANT THAT TO CHANGE? US, TOO. WE'RE IN A WAR FOR A BETTER TOMORROW.
JOIN US. HELP US TO NOT TAKE THE EASY ROAD, AND I PROMISE WE'LL FIGHT EVERY FIGHT THEY CAN THROW AT US.
HELP US WIN THE HARD WAY--THE RIGHT WAY--NOT WITH HATE, NOT WITH RETRIBUTION, BUT WITH WISDOM AND HOPE.
HELP US BECOME CHAMPIONS.

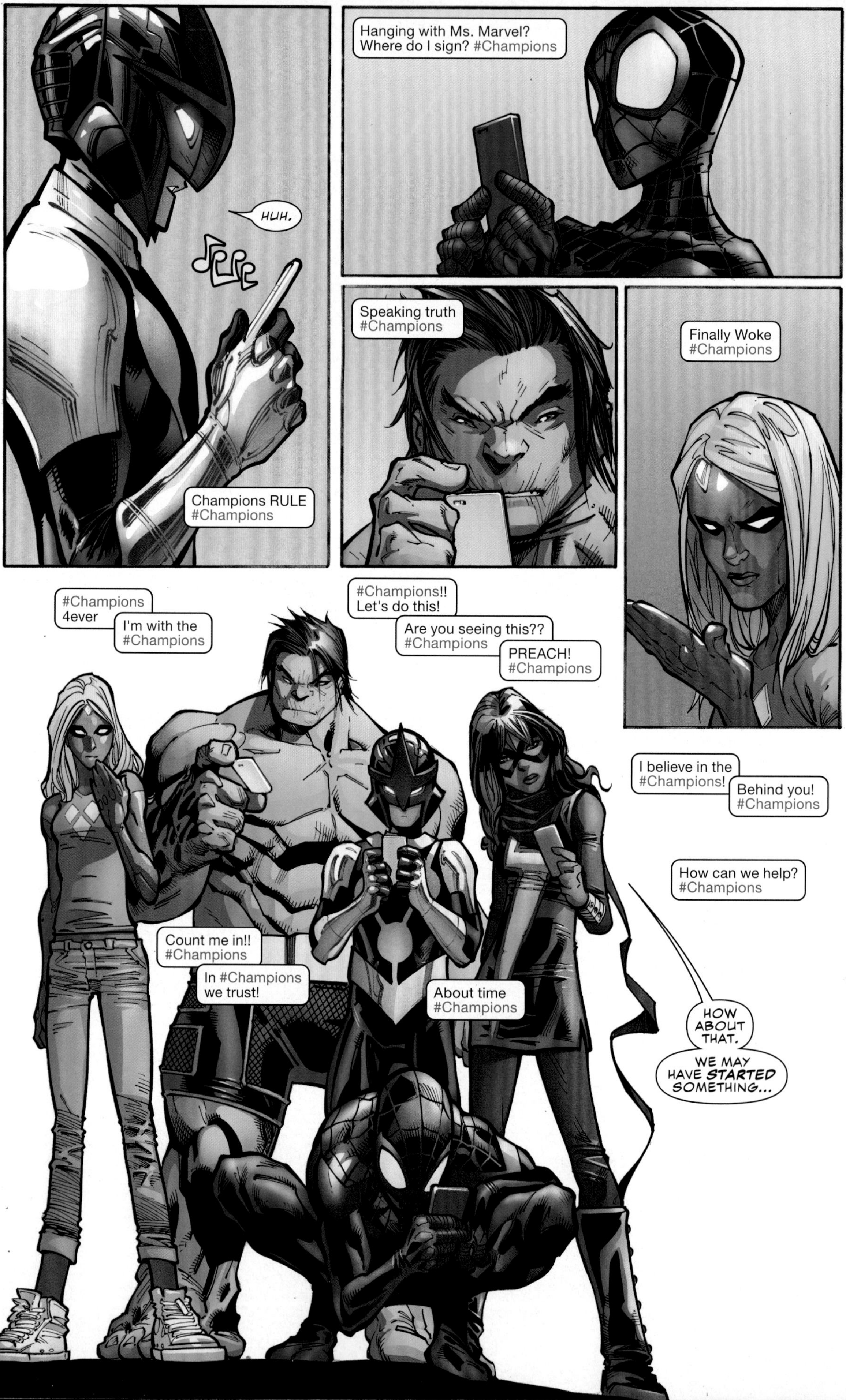
HUH.
SPLRRE
Champions RULE #Champions
Hanging with Ms. Marvel? Where do I sign? #Champions
Speaking truth #Champions
Finally Woke #Champions
#Champions 4ever
I'm with the #Champions
#Champions!! Let's do this!
Are you seeing this?? #Champions
PREACH! #Champions
I believe in the #Champions!
Behind you! #Champions
How can we help? #Champions
Count me in!! #Champions
In #Champions we trust!
About time #Champions
HOW ABOUT THAT.
WE MAY HAVE STARTED SOMETHING...

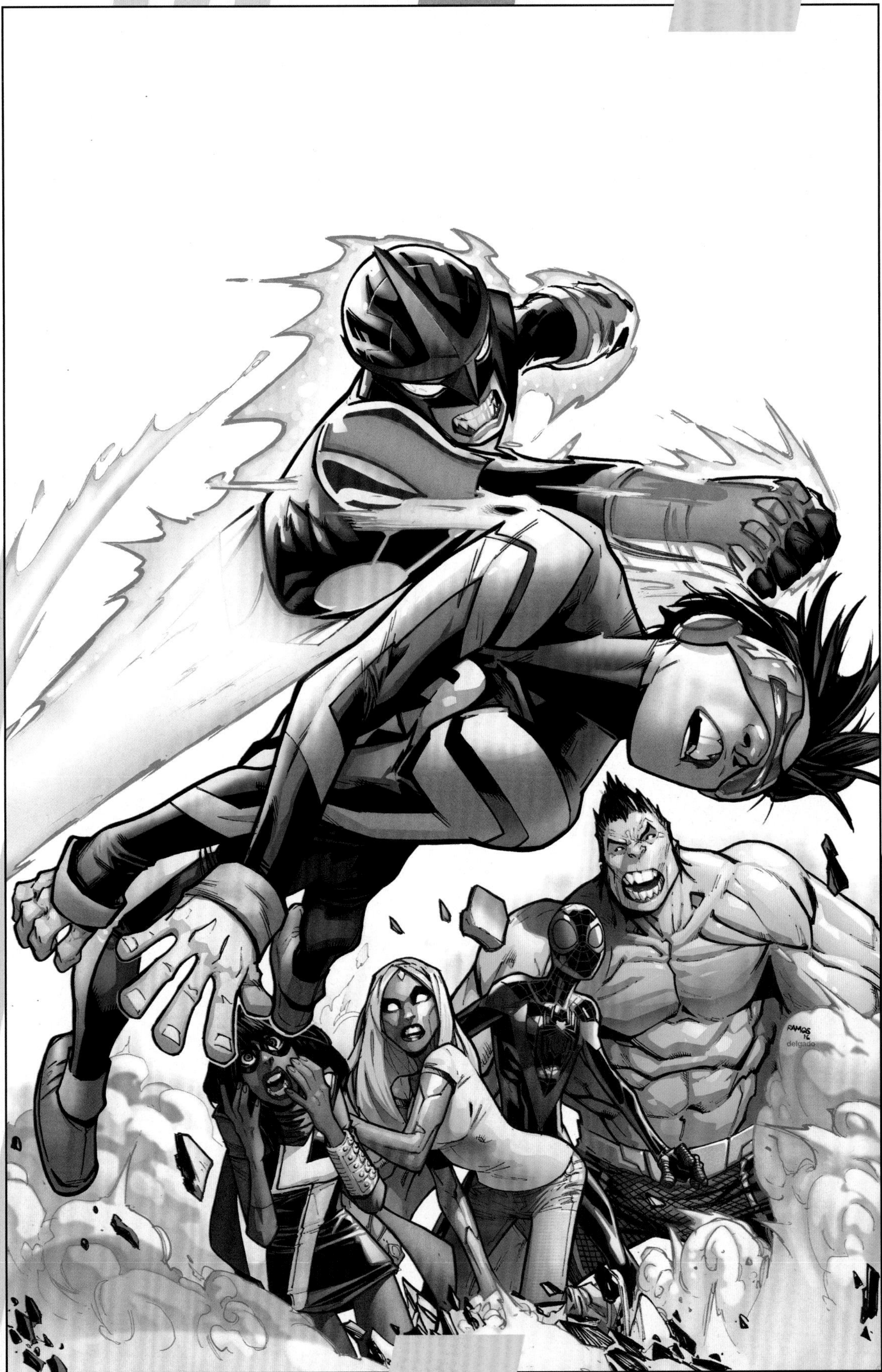
RAMOS 16
delgado

2

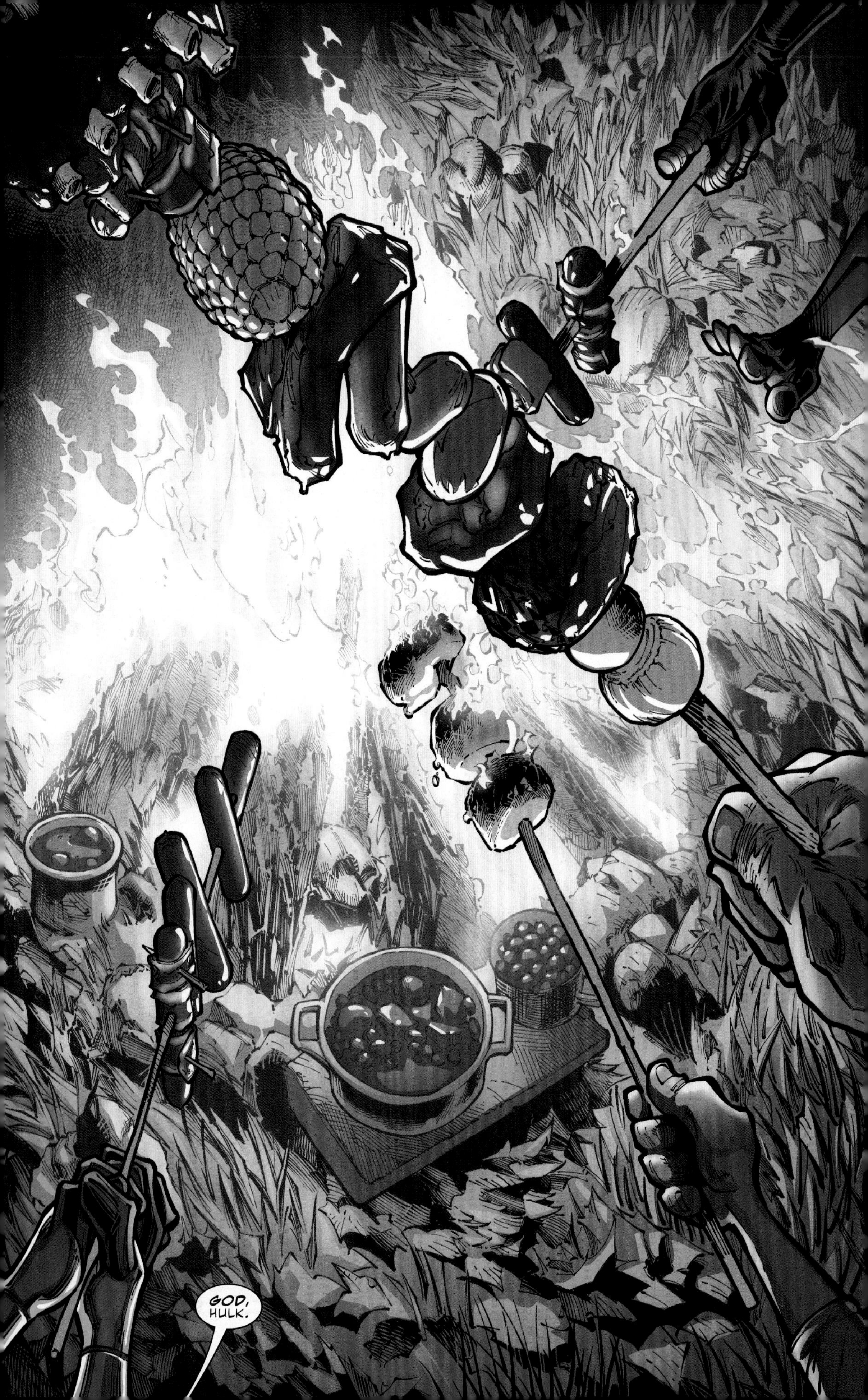
GOD, HULK.

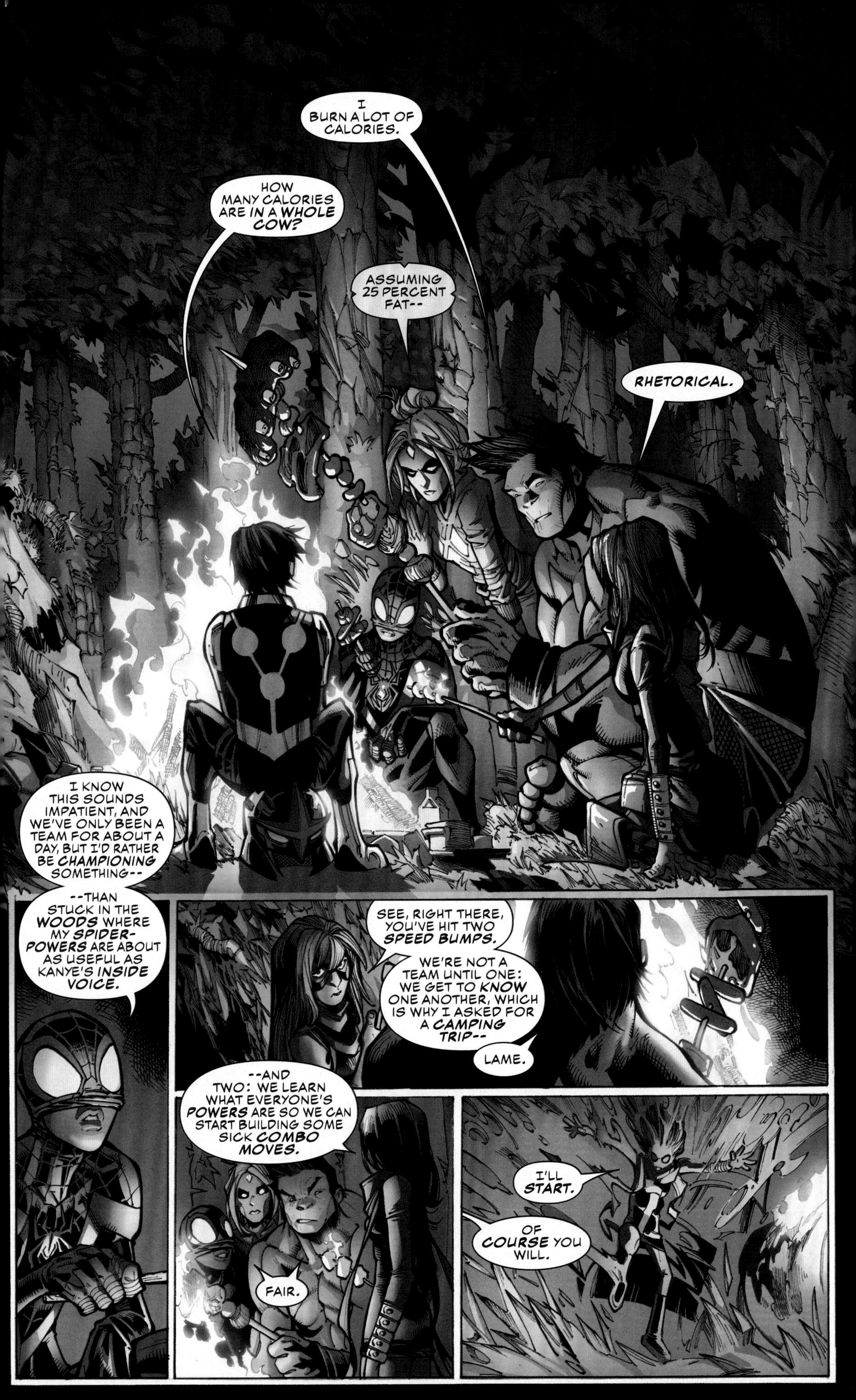
HOW MANY CALORIES ARE IN A WHOLE COW?
I BURN A LOT OF CALORIES.
ASSUMING 25 PERCENT FAT--
RHETORICAL.
I KNOW THIS SOUNDS IMPATIENT, AND WE'VE ONLY BEEN A TEAM FOR ABOUT A DAY, BUT I'D RATHER BE CHAMPIONING SOMETHING--
--THAN STUCK IN THE WOODS WHERE MY SPIDER-POWERS ARE ABOUT AS USEFUL AS KANYE'S INSIDE VOICE.
SEE, RIGHT THERE, YOU'VE HIT TWO SPEED BUMPS.
WE'RE NOT A TEAM UNTIL ONE: WE GET TO KNOW ONE ANOTHER, WHICH IS WHY I ASKED FOR A CAMPING TRIP--
LAME.
--AND TWO: WE LEARN WHAT EVERYONE'S POWERS ARE SO WE CAN START BUILDING SOME SICK COMBO MOVES.
FAIR.
I'LL START.
OF COURSE YOU WILL.

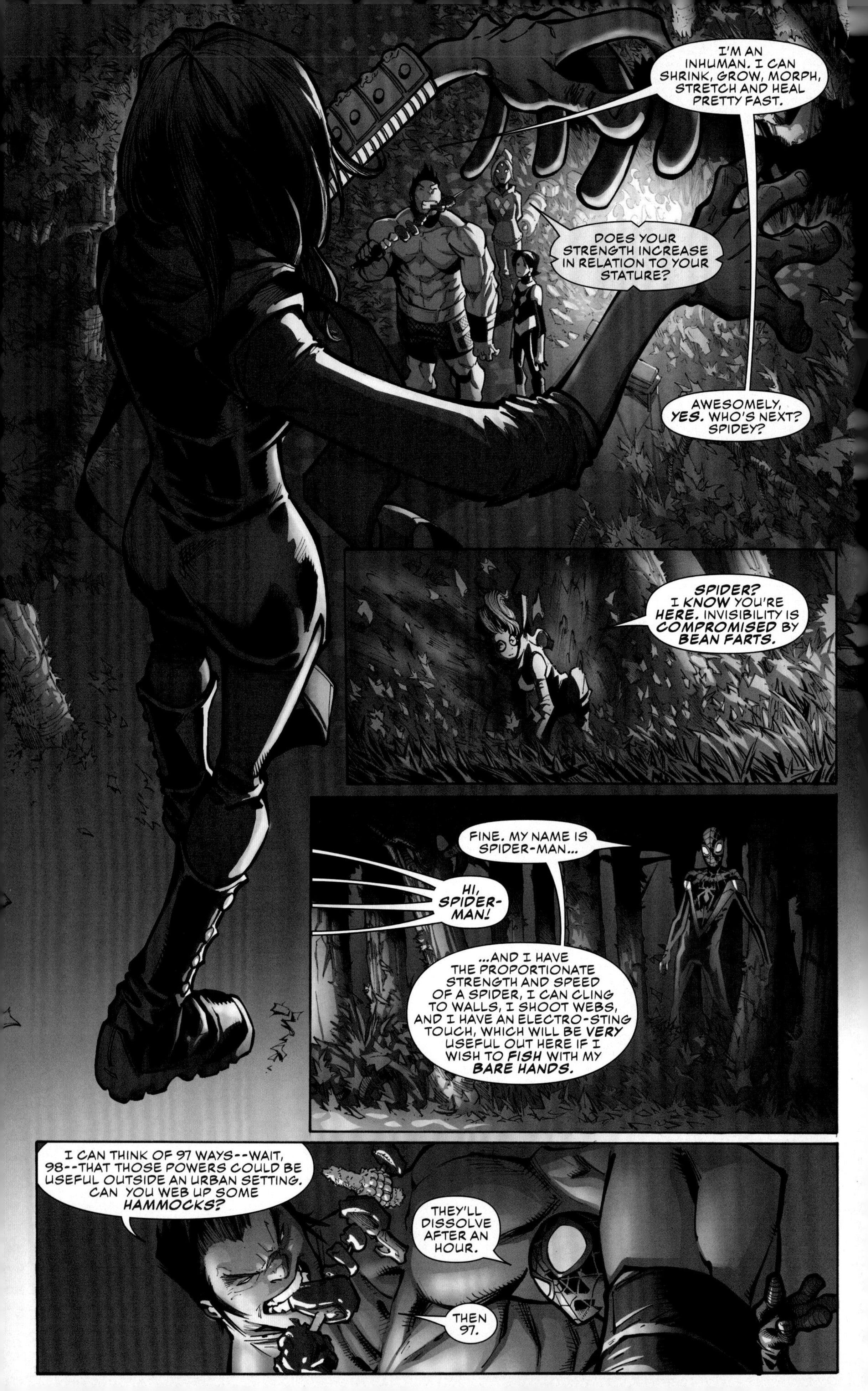
I'M AN INHUMAN. I CAN SHRINK, GROW, MORPH, STRETCH AND HEAL PRETTY FAST.
DOES YOUR STRENGTH INCREASE IN RELATION TO YOUR STATURE?
AWESOMELY, YES. WHO'S NEXT? SPIDEY?
SPIDER? I KNOW YOU'RE HERE. INVISIBILITY IS COMPROMISED BY BEAN FARTS.
FINE. MY NAME IS SPIDER-MAN...
HI, SPIDER-MAN!
...AND I HAVE THE PROPORTIONATE STRENGTH AND SPEED OF A SPIDER, I CAN CLING TO WALLS, I SHOOT WEBS, AND I HAVE AN ELECTRO-STING TOUCH, WHICH WILL BE VERY USEFUL OUT HERE IF I WISH TO FISH WITH MY BARE HANDS.
I CAN THINK OF 97 WAYS--WAIT, 98--THAT THOSE POWERS COULD BE USEFUL OUTSIDE AN URBAN SETTING. CAN YOU WEB UP SOME HAMMOCKS?
THEY'LL DISSOLVE AFTER AN HOUR.
THEN 97.

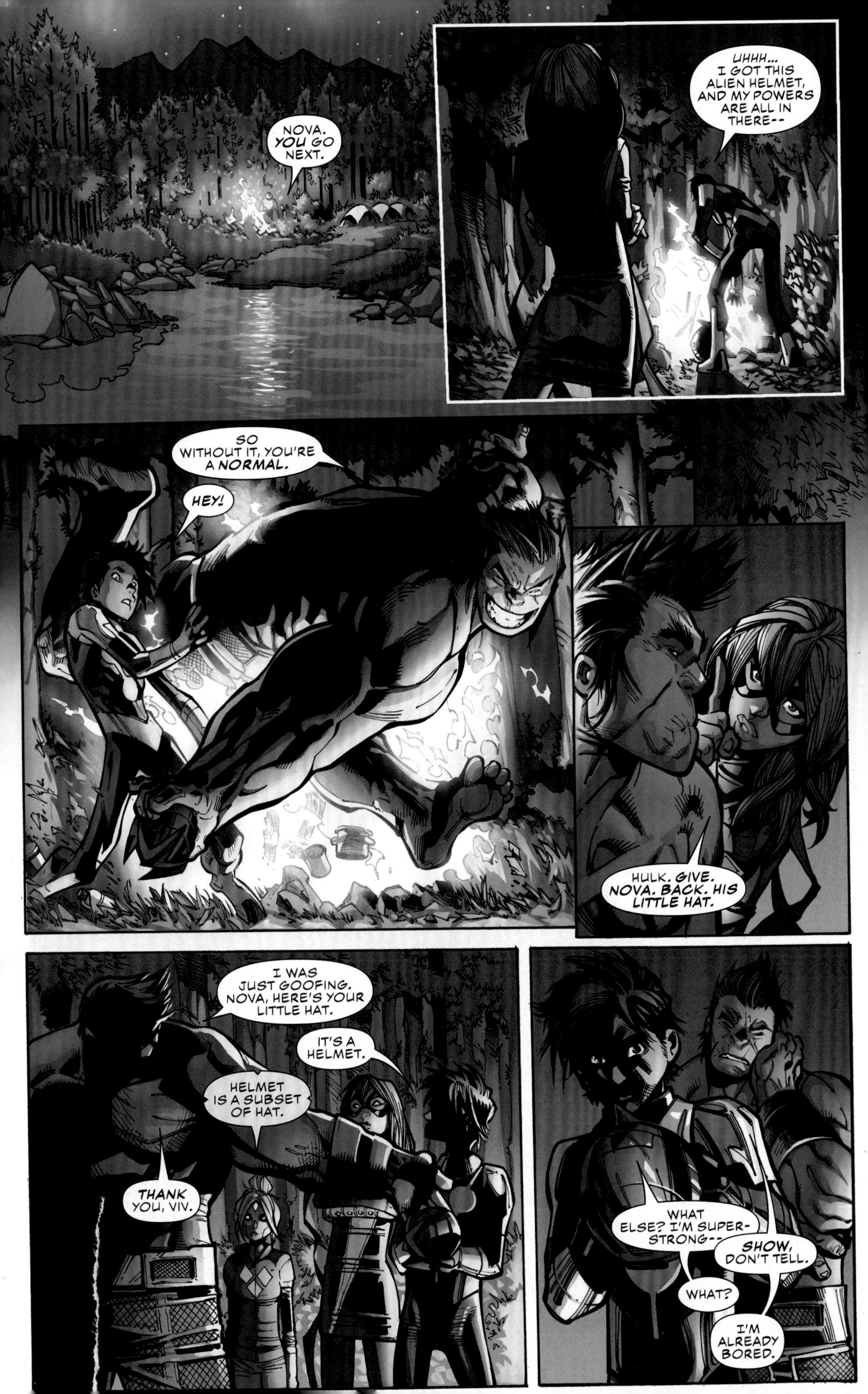

NOVA. YOU GO NEXT.
UHHH... I GOT THIS ALIEN HELMET, AND MY POWERS ARE ALL IN THERE--
SO WITHOUT IT, YOU'RE A NORMAL.
HEY!
HULK. GIVE. NOVA. BACK. HIS LITTLE HAT.
I WAS JUST GOOFING. NOVA, HERE'S YOUR LITTLE HAT.
IT'S A HELMET.
HELMET IS A SUBSET OF HAT.
THANK YOU, VIV.
WHAT ELSE? I'M SUPER-STRONG--
SHOW, DON'T TELL.
WHAT?
I'M ALREADY BORED.

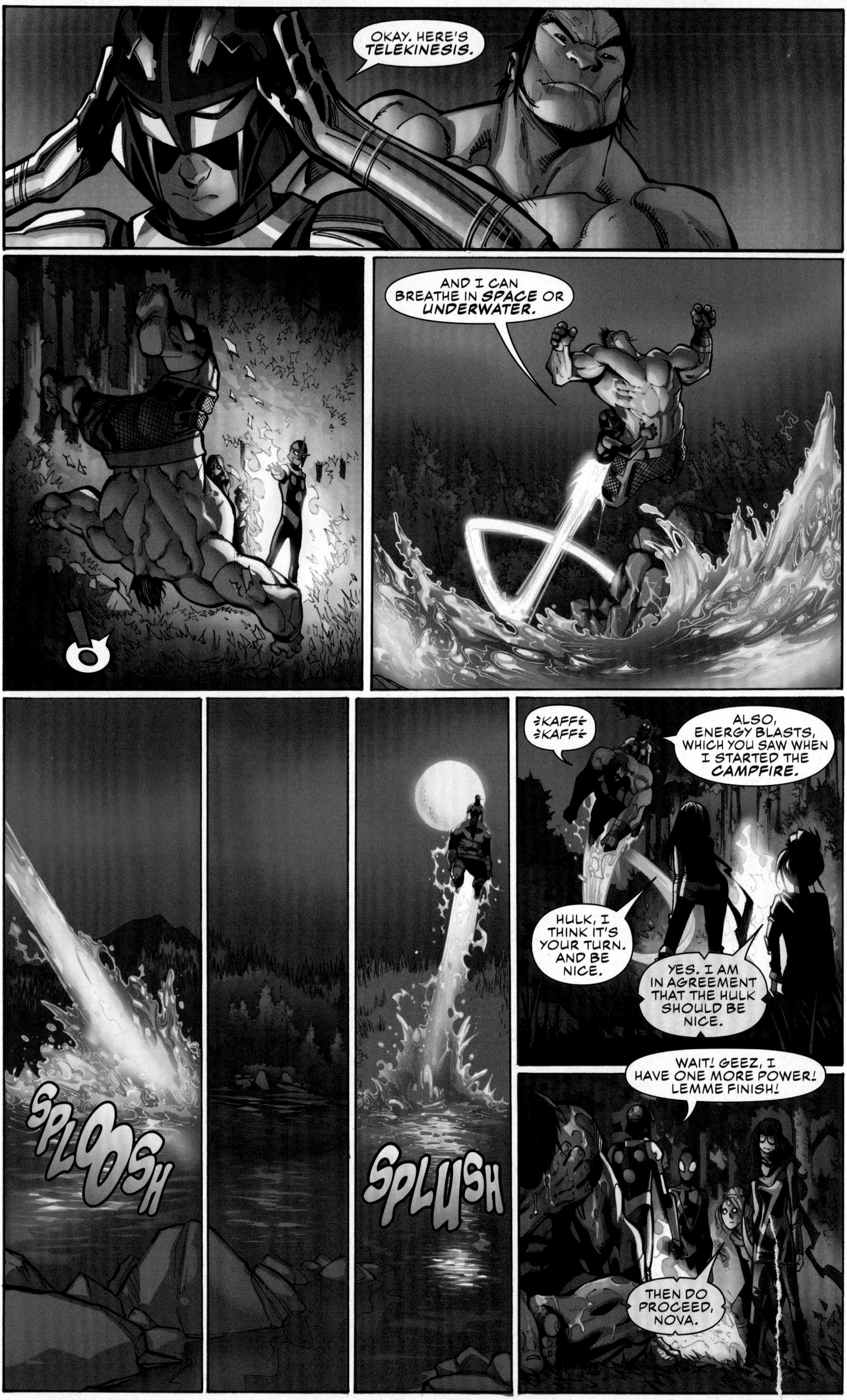
OKAY. HERE'S TELEKINESIS.
AND I CAN BREATHE IN SPACE OR UNDERWATER.
SPLOOSH
SPLUSH
KAFF KAFF
ALSO, ENERGY BLASTS, WHICH YOU SAW WHEN I STARTED THE CAMPFIRE.
HULK, I THINK IT'S YOUR TURN. AND BE NICE.
YES. I AM IN AGREEMENT THAT THE HULK SHOULD BE NICE.
WAIT! GEEZ, I HAVE ONE MORE POWER! LEMME FINISH!
THEN DO PROCEED, NOVA.

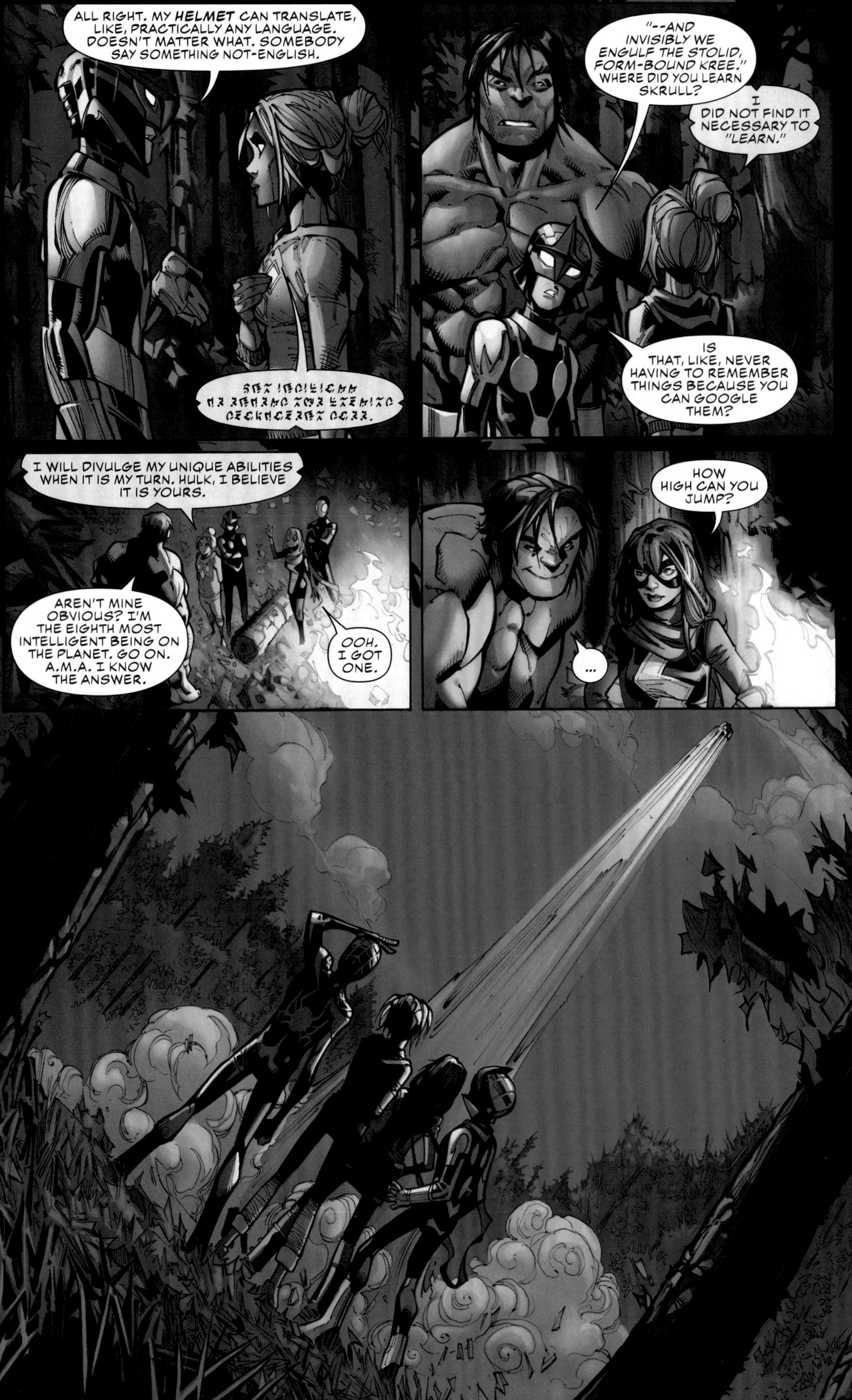
ALL RIGHT. MY HELMET CAN TRANSLATE, LIKE, PRACTICALLY ANY LANGUAGE. DOESN'T MATTER WHAT. SOMEBODY SAY SOMETHING NOT-ENGLISH.
"--AND INVISIBLY WE ENGULF THE STOLID, FORM-BOUND KREE." WHERE DID YOU LEARN SKRULL?
I DID NOT FIND IT NECESSARY TO "LEARN."
IS THAT, LIKE, NEVER HAVING TO REMEMBER THINGS BECAUSE YOU CAN GOOGLE THEM?
I WILL DIVULGE MY UNIQUE ABILITIES WHEN IT IS MY TURN. HULK, I BELIEVE IT IS YOURS.
AREN'T MINE OBVIOUS? I'M THE EIGHTH MOST INTELLIGENT BEING ON THE PLANET. GO ON. A.M.A. I KNOW THE ANSWER.
OOH. I GOT ONE.
HOW HIGH CAN YOU JUMP?
...

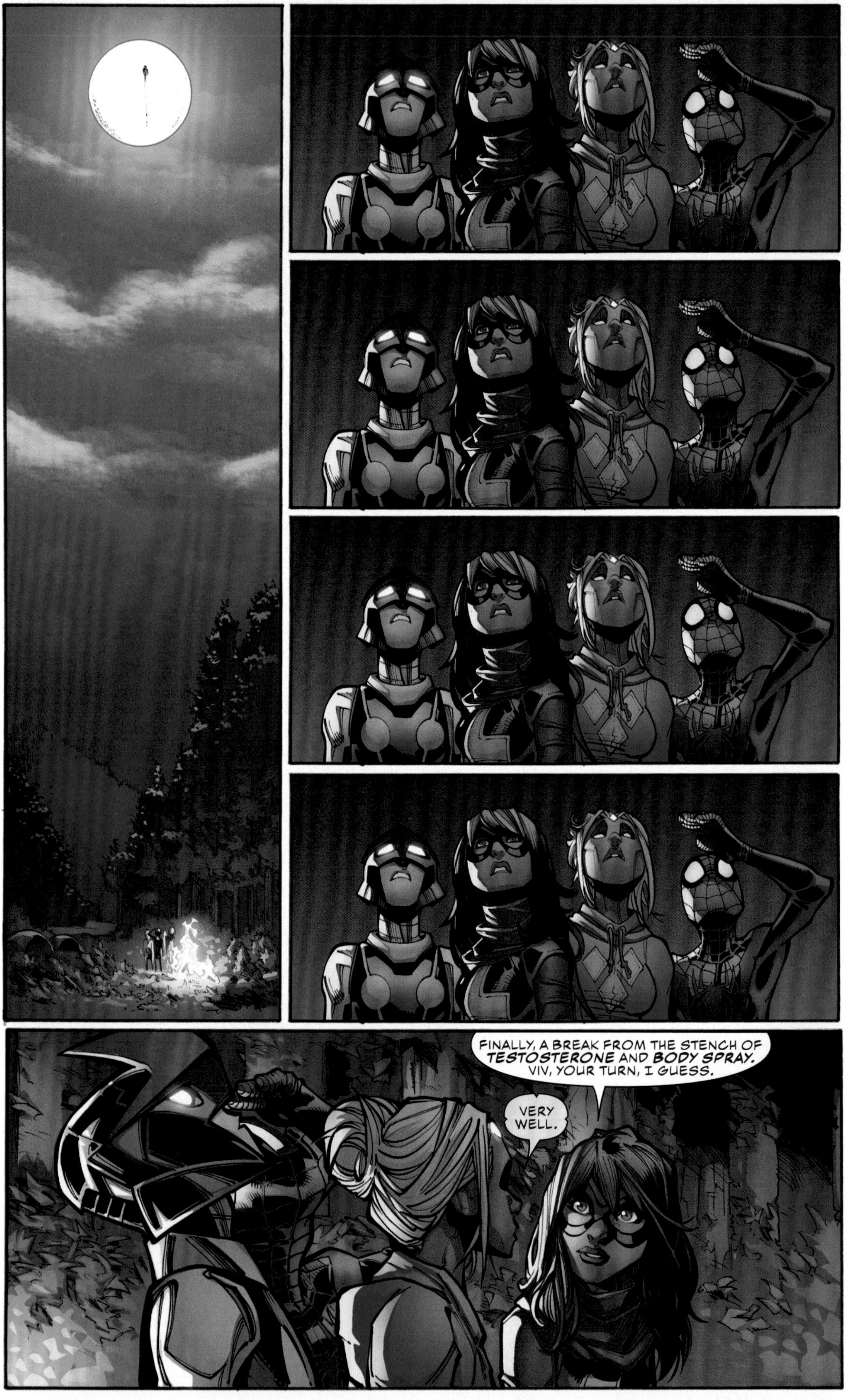
FINALLY, A BREAK FROM THE STENCH OF TESTOSTERONE AND BODY SPRAY. VIV, YOUR TURN, I GUESS.
VERY WELL.

I AM A SYNTHEZOID--AN ANDROID COMPOSED OF SYNTHETIC ORGANS, MUSCLE AND FLESH.

I POSSESS INTERNAL SERVERS AND A COMPUTER MIND. I AM ABLE TO FLY AND ALTER MY DENSITY, FROM DIAMOND-HARD TO INSUBSTAN--

WAIT. BACK UP. INTERNAL SERVERS? YOU HAVE WIFI?

AFFIRMATIVE.

WHY DIDN'T YOU *SAY* SO? WE'RE, LIKE, A MILLION MILES FROM ANY SIGNAL AT ALL. WHAT'S YOUR PASSWORD?

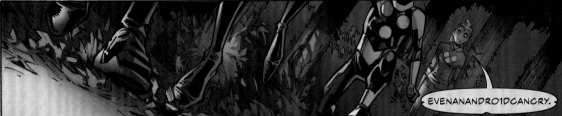

EVENANANDRO1DCANCRY.

ALL RIGHT, NOW THAT WE KNOW EACH OTHER'S POWERS, I READ ABOUT SOME EXERCISES--

IN A MINUTE.

NO.

NO.

DON'T YOU *DO* THIS.

DO WHAT?

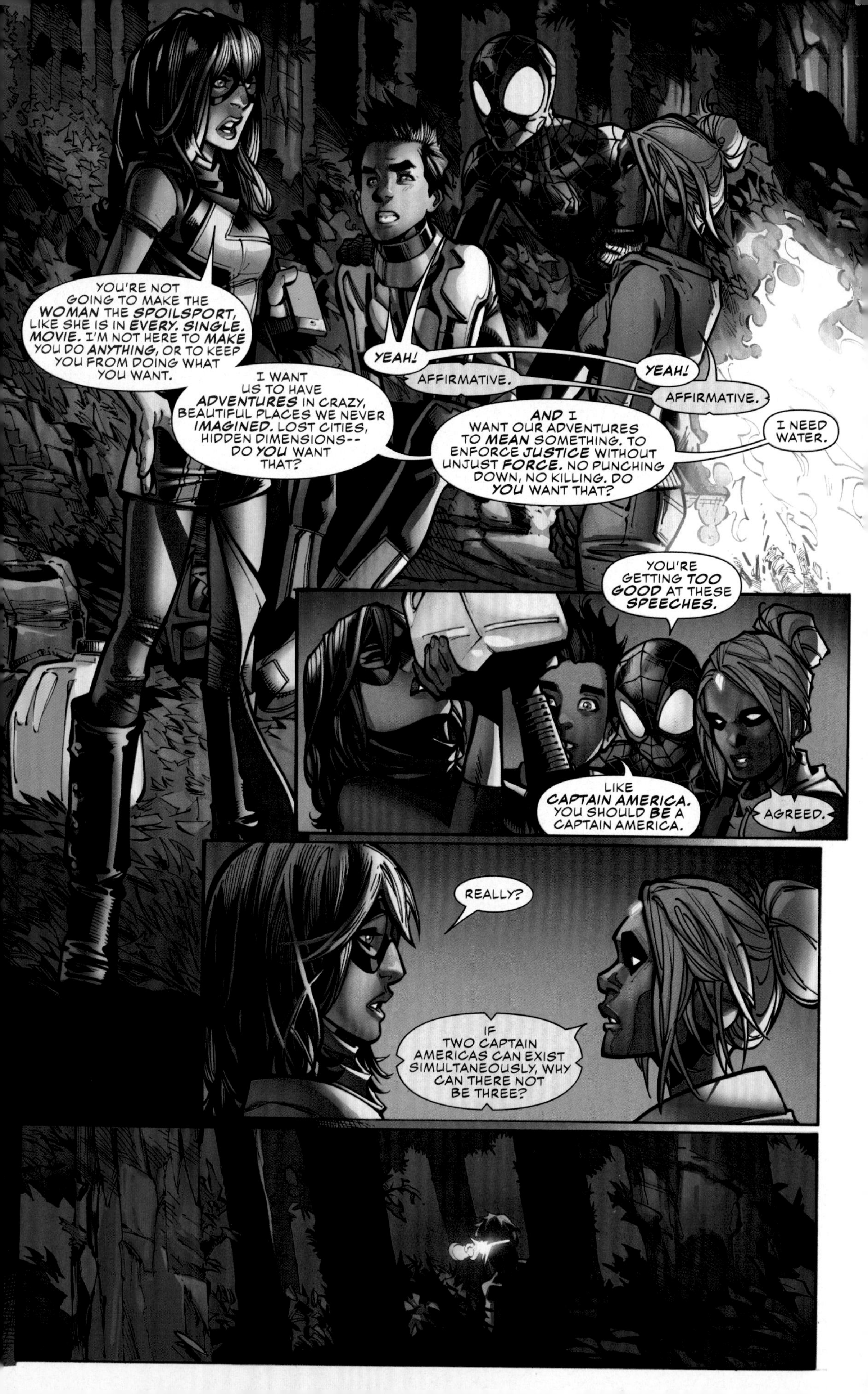
YOU'RE NOT GOING TO MAKE THE WOMAN THE SPOILSPORT, LIKE SHE IS IN EVERY. SINGLE. MOVIE. I'M NOT HERE TO MAKE YOU DO ANYTHING, OR TO KEEP YOU FROM DOING WHAT YOU WANT.
I WANT US TO HAVE ADVENTURES IN CRAZY, BEAUTIFUL PLACES WE NEVER IMAGINED. LOST CITIES, HIDDEN DIMENSIONS-- DO YOU WANT THAT?
YEAH!
AFFIRMATIVE.
AND I WANT OUR ADVENTURES TO MEAN SOMETHING. TO ENFORCE JUSTICE WITHOUT UNJUST FORCE. NO PUNCHING DOWN, NO KILLING. DO YOU WANT THAT?
YEAH!
AFFIRMATIVE.
I NEED WATER.
YOU'RE GETTING TOO GOOD AT THESE SPEECHES.
LIKE CAPTAIN AMERICA. YOU SHOULD BE A CAPTAIN AMERICA.
AGREED.
REALLY?
IF TWO CAPTAIN AMERICAS CAN EXIST SIMULTANEOUSLY, WHY CAN THERE NOT BE THREE?

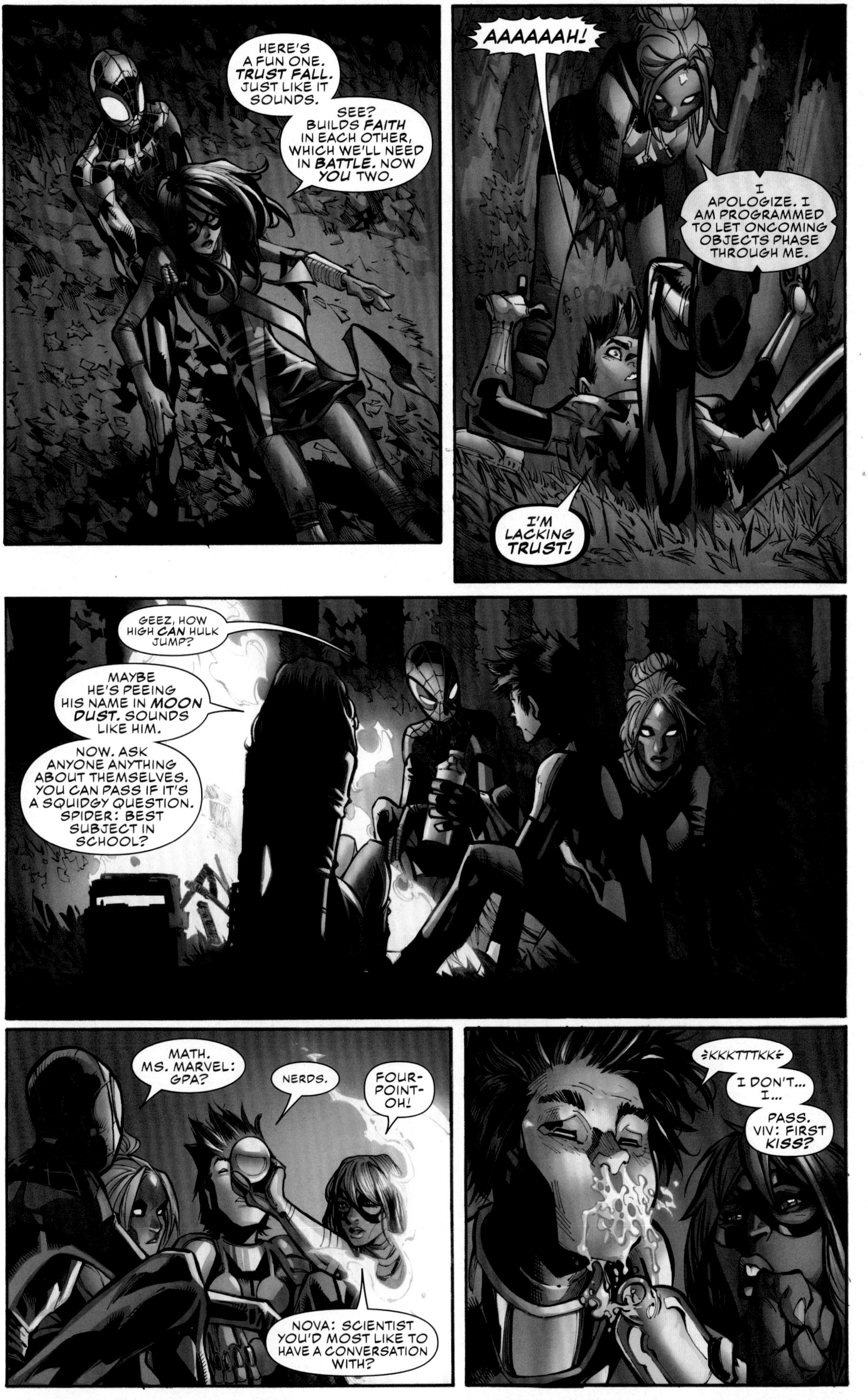
HERE'S A FUN ONE. TRUST FALL. JUST LIKE IT SOUNDS.
SEE? BUILDS FAITH IN EACH OTHER, WHICH WE'LL NEED IN BATTLE. NOW YOU TWO.
AAAAAAH!
I APOLOGIZE. I AM PROGRAMMED TO LET ONCOMING OBJECTS PHASE THROUGH ME.
I'M LACKING TRUST!
GEEZ, HOW HIGH CAN HULK JUMP?
MAYBE HE'S PEEING HIS NAME IN MOON DUST. SOUNDS LIKE HIM.
NOW. ASK ANYONE ANYTHING ABOUT THEMSELVES. YOU CAN PASS IF IT'S A SQUIDGY QUESTION. SPIDER: BEST SUBJECT IN SCHOOL?
MATH. MS. MARVEL: GPA?
NERDS.
FOUR-POINT-OH!
NOVA: SCIENTIST YOU'D MOST LIKE TO HAVE A CONVERSATION WITH?
KKKTTTKK
I DON'T... I...
PASS. VIV: FIRST KISS?

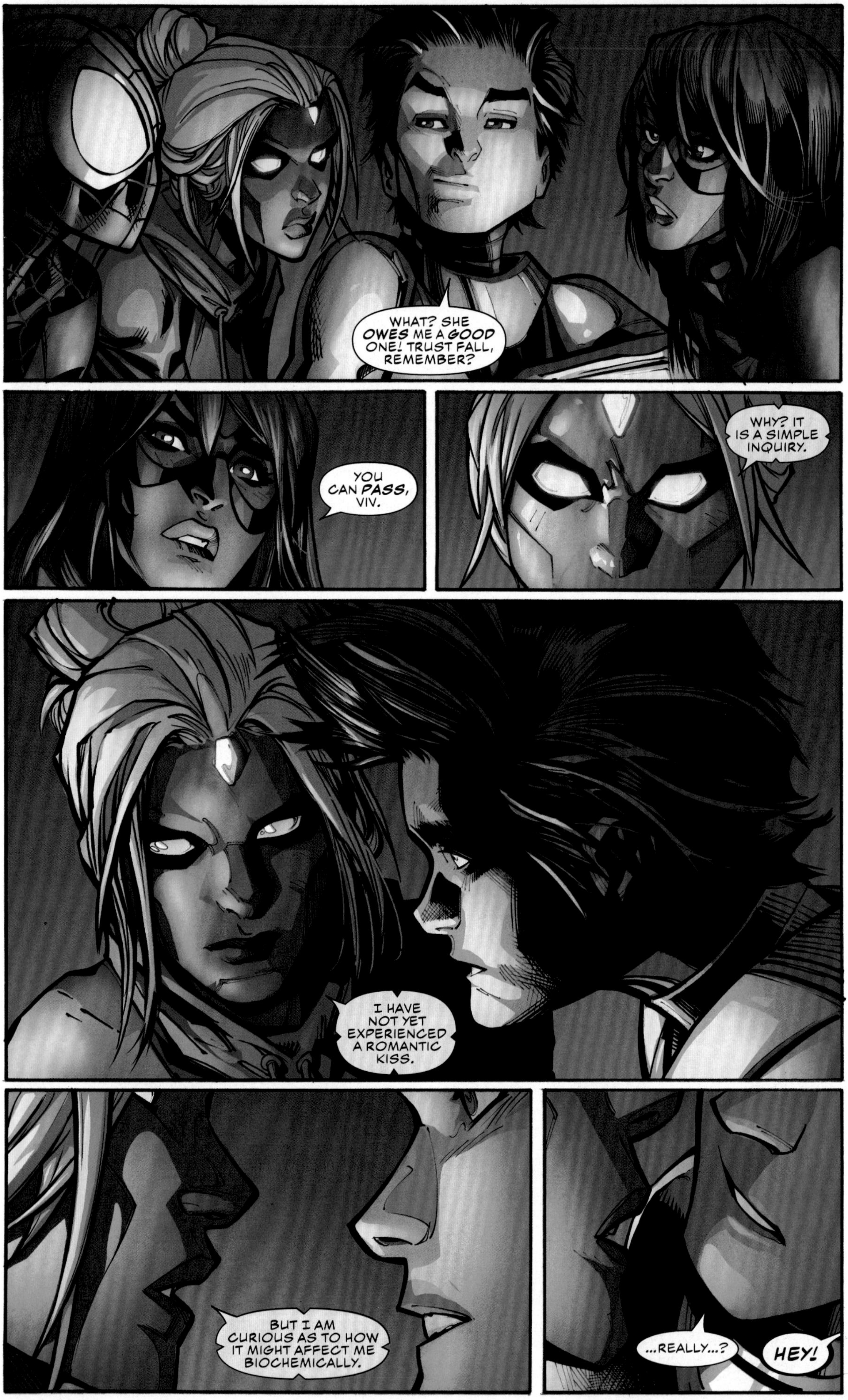
WHAT? SHE OWES ME A GOOD ONE! TRUST FALL, REMEMBER?
YOU CAN PASS, VIV.
WHY? IT IS A SIMPLE INQUIRY.
I HAVE NOT YET EXPERIENCED A ROMANTIC KISS.
BUT I AM CURIOUS AS TO HOW IT MIGHT AFFECT ME BIOCHEMICALLY.
...REALLY...?
HEY!

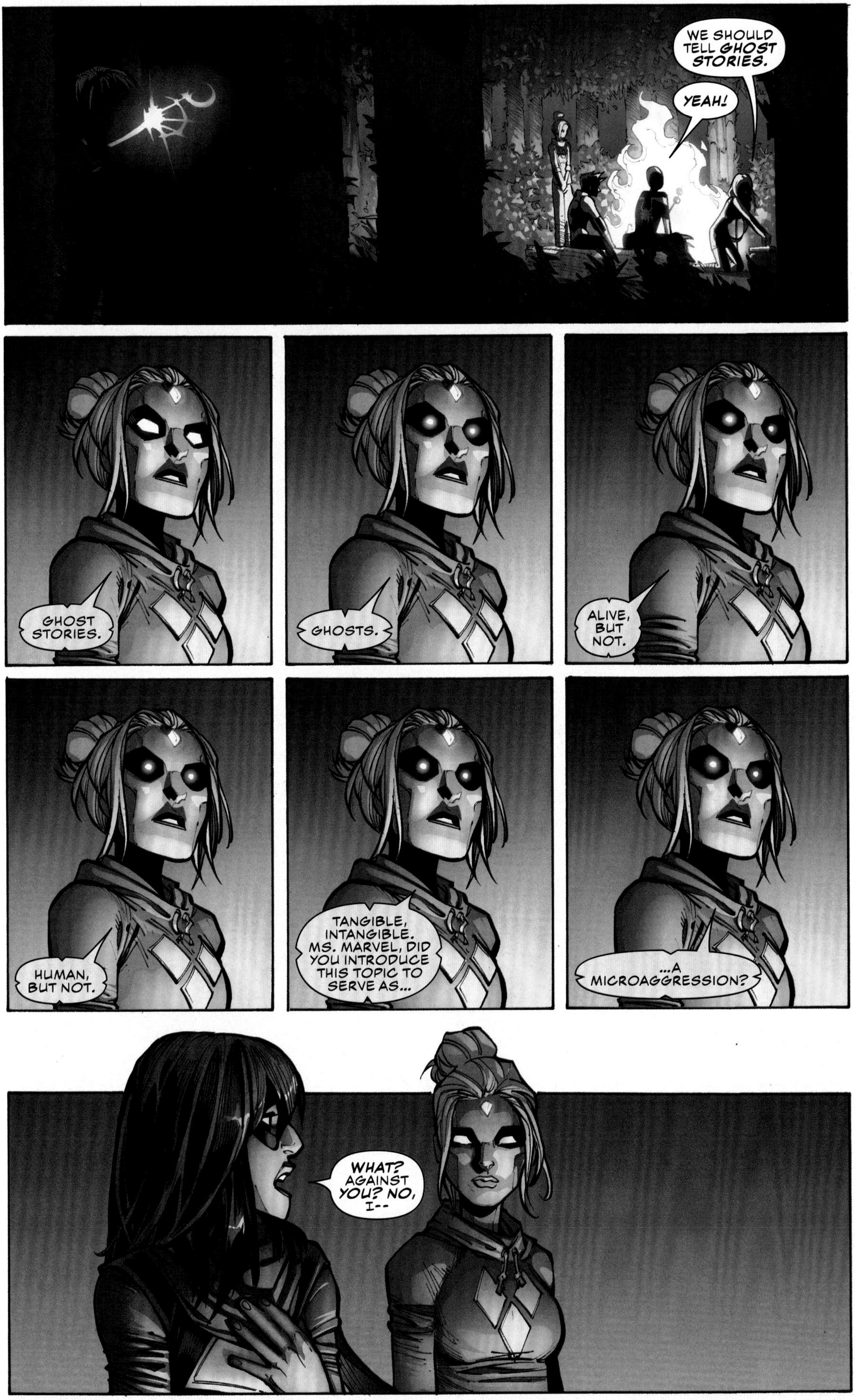
WE SHOULD TELL GHOST STORIES.
YEAH!
GHOST STORIES.
GHOSTS.
ALIVE, BUT NOT.
HUMAN, BUT NOT.
TANGIBLE, INTANGIBLE. MS. MARVEL, DID YOU INTRODUCE THIS TOPIC TO SERVE AS...
...A MICROAGGRESSION?
WHAT? AGAINST YOU? NO, I--

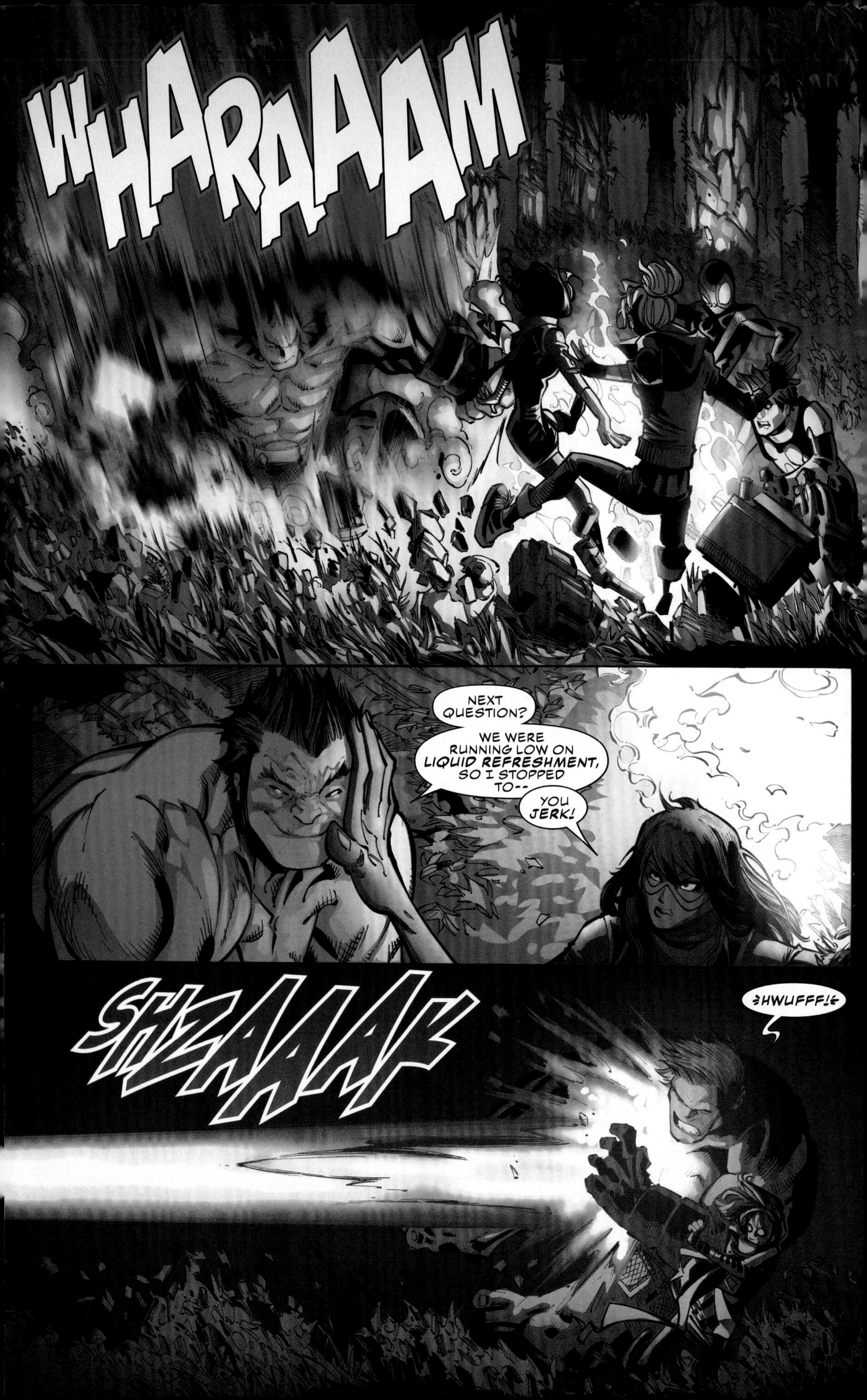
WHARAAAM
NEXT QUESTION?
WE WERE RUNNING LOW ON LIQUID REFRESHMENT, SO I STOPPED TO--
YOU JERK!
SHZAAAAK
HWUFFF!

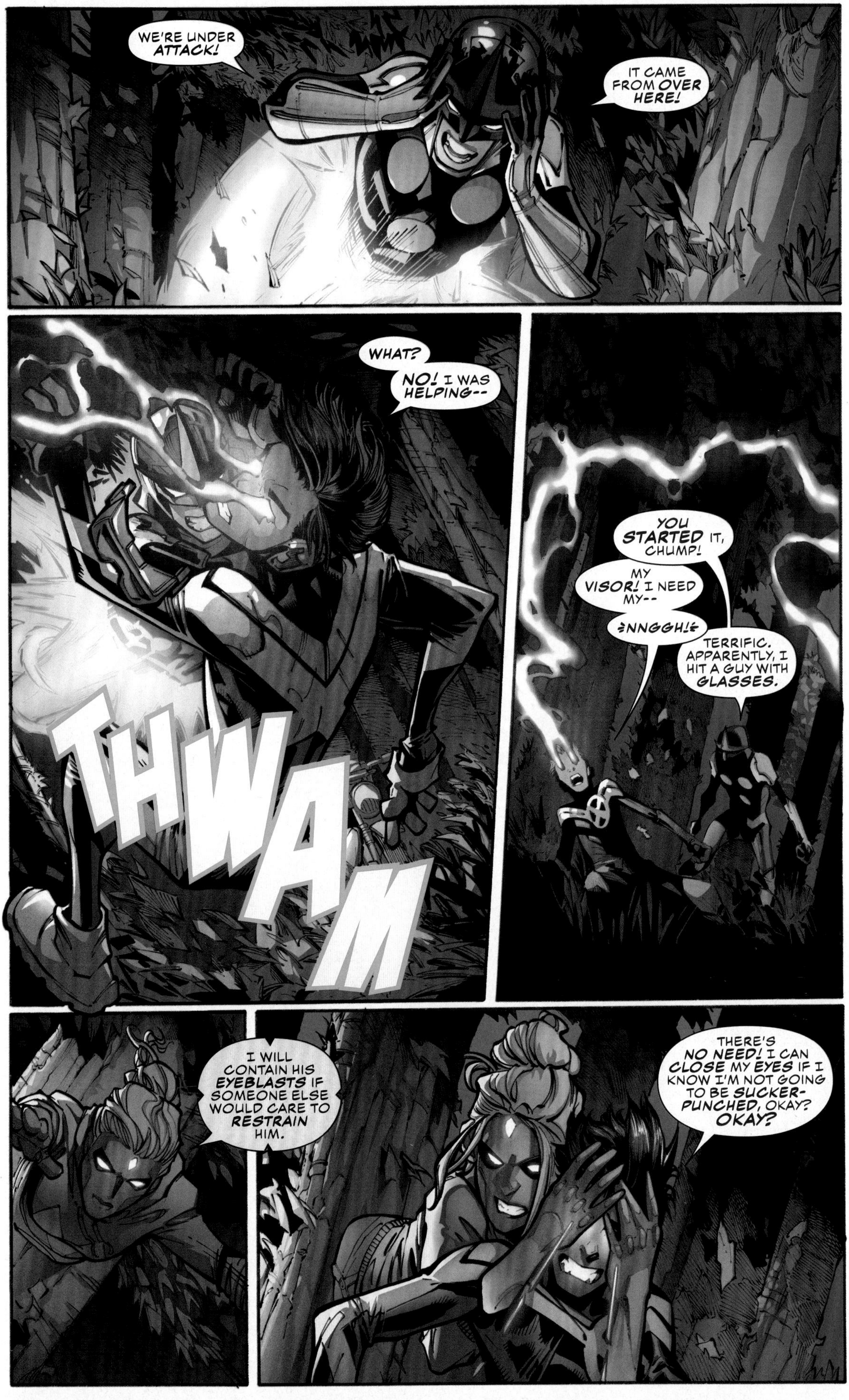

WE'RE UNDER ATTACK!
IT CAME FROM OVER HERE!
WHAT?
NO! I WAS HELPING--
THWAM
YOU STARTED IT, CHUMP!
MY VISOR! I NEED MY--
NNGGH!
TERRIFIC. APPARENTLY, I HIT A GUY WITH GLASSES.
I WILL CONTAIN HIS EYEBLASTS IF SOMEONE ELSE WOULD CARE TO RESTRAIN HIM.
THERE'S NO NEED! I CAN CLOSE MY EYES IF I KNOW I'M NOT GOING TO BE SUCKER-PUNCHED, OKAY? OKAY?

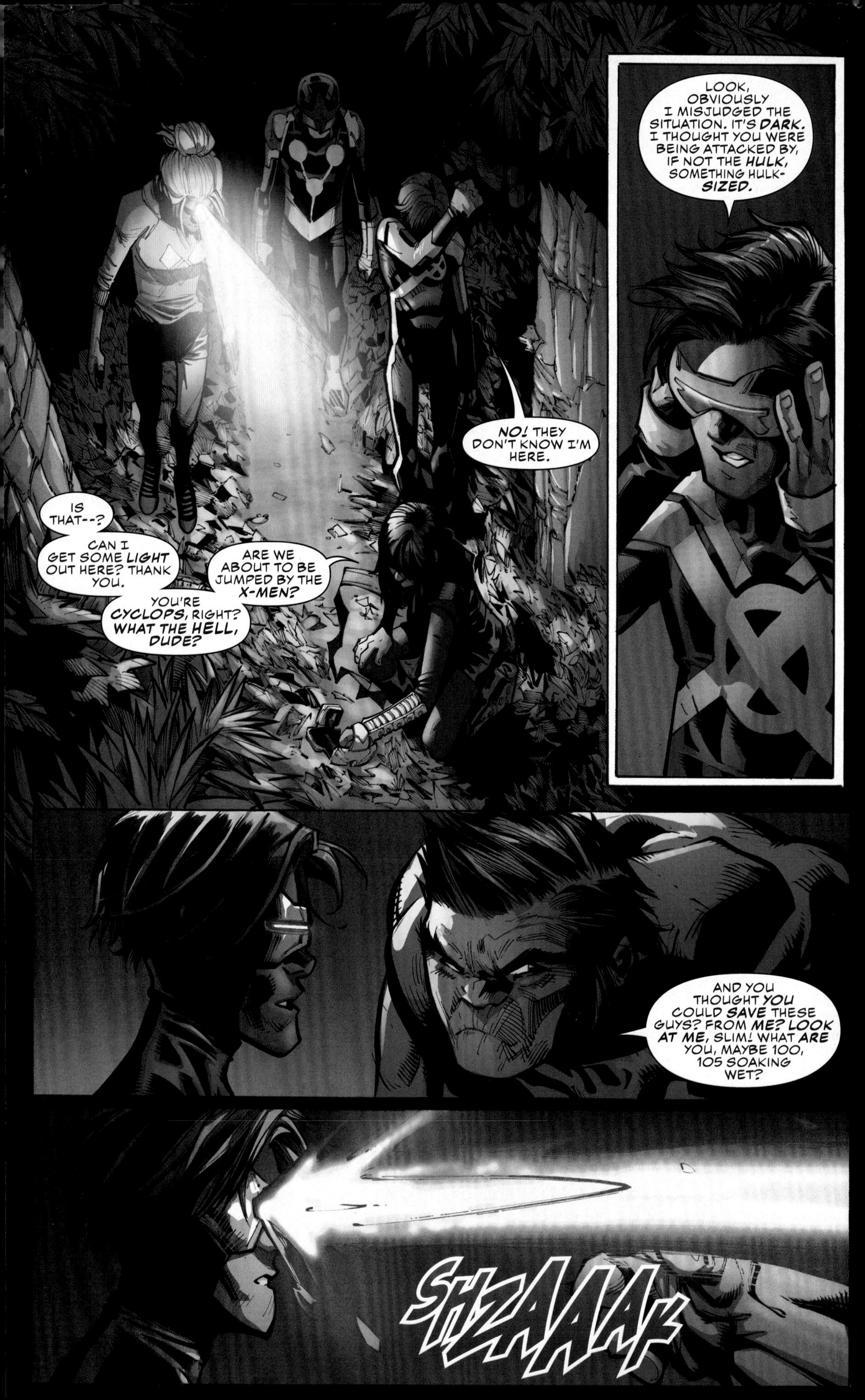

LOOK, OBVIOUSLY I MISJUDGED THE SITUATION. IT'S DARK. I THOUGHT YOU WERE BEING ATTACKED BY, IF NOT THE HULK, SOMETHING HULK-SIZED.
NO! THEY DON'T KNOW I'M HERE.
IS THAT--?
CAN I GET SOME LIGHT OUT HERE? THANK YOU.
ARE WE ABOUT TO BE JUMPED BY THE X-MEN?
YOU'RE CYCLOPS, RIGHT? WHAT THE HELL, DUDE?
AND YOU THOUGHT YOU COULD SAVE THESE GUYS? FROM ME? LOOK AT ME, SLIM! WHAT ARE YOU, MAYBE 100, 105 SOAKING WET?
SHZAAAK

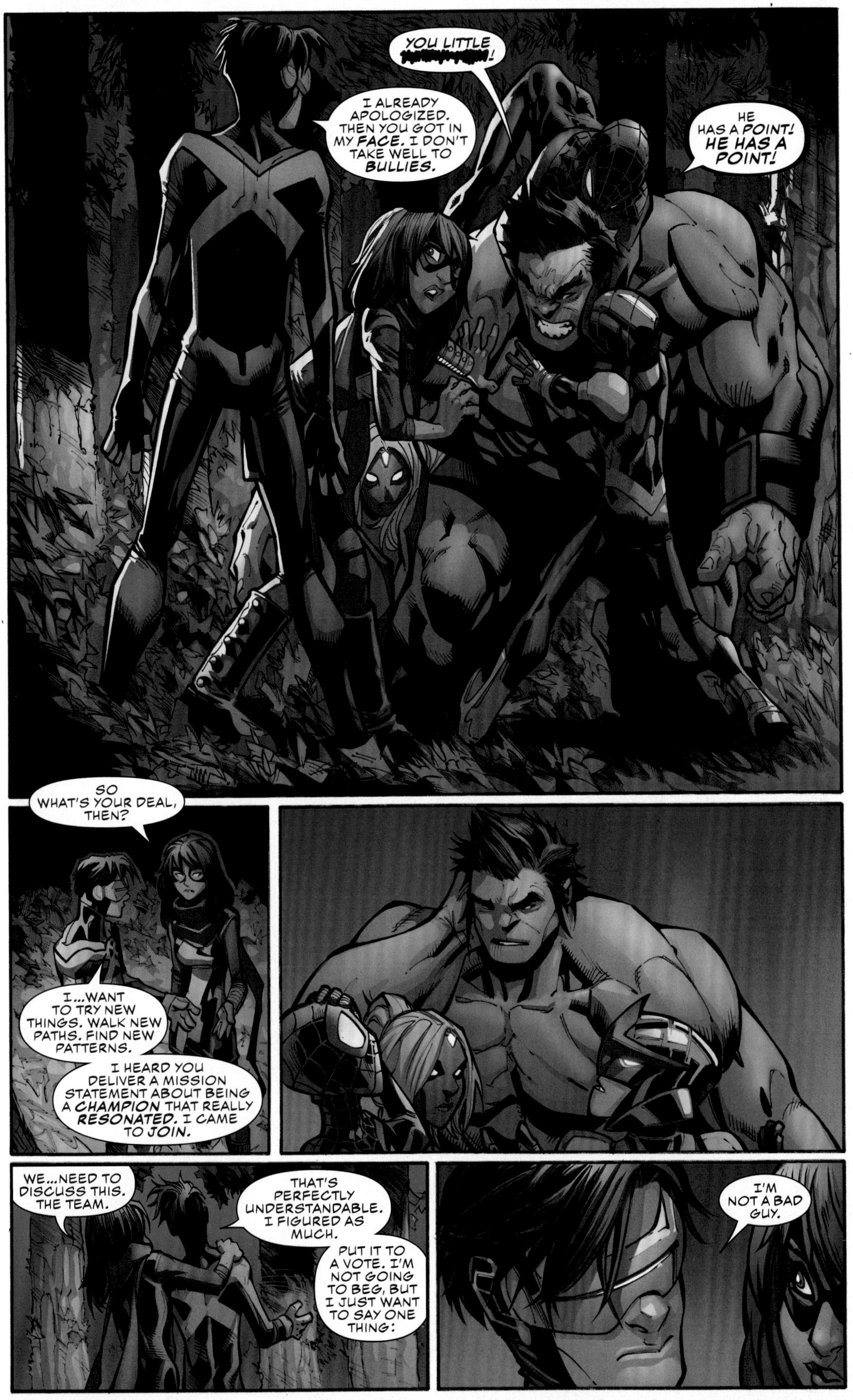
YOU LITTLE [redacted]!
I ALREADY APOLOGIZED. THEN YOU GOT IN MY FACE. I DON'T TAKE WELL TO BULLIES.
HE HAS A POINT! HE HAS A POINT!
SO WHAT'S YOUR DEAL, THEN?
I...WANT TO TRY NEW THINGS. WALK NEW PATHS. FIND NEW PATTERNS.
I HEARD YOU DELIVER A MISSION STATEMENT ABOUT BEING A CHAMPION THAT REALLY RESONATED. I CAME TO JOIN.
WE...NEED TO DISCUSS THIS. THE TEAM.
THAT'S PERFECTLY UNDERSTANDABLE. I FIGURED AS MUCH.
PUT IT TO A VOTE. I'M NOT GOING TO BEG, BUT I JUST WANT TO SAY ONE THING:
I'M NOT A BAD GUY.

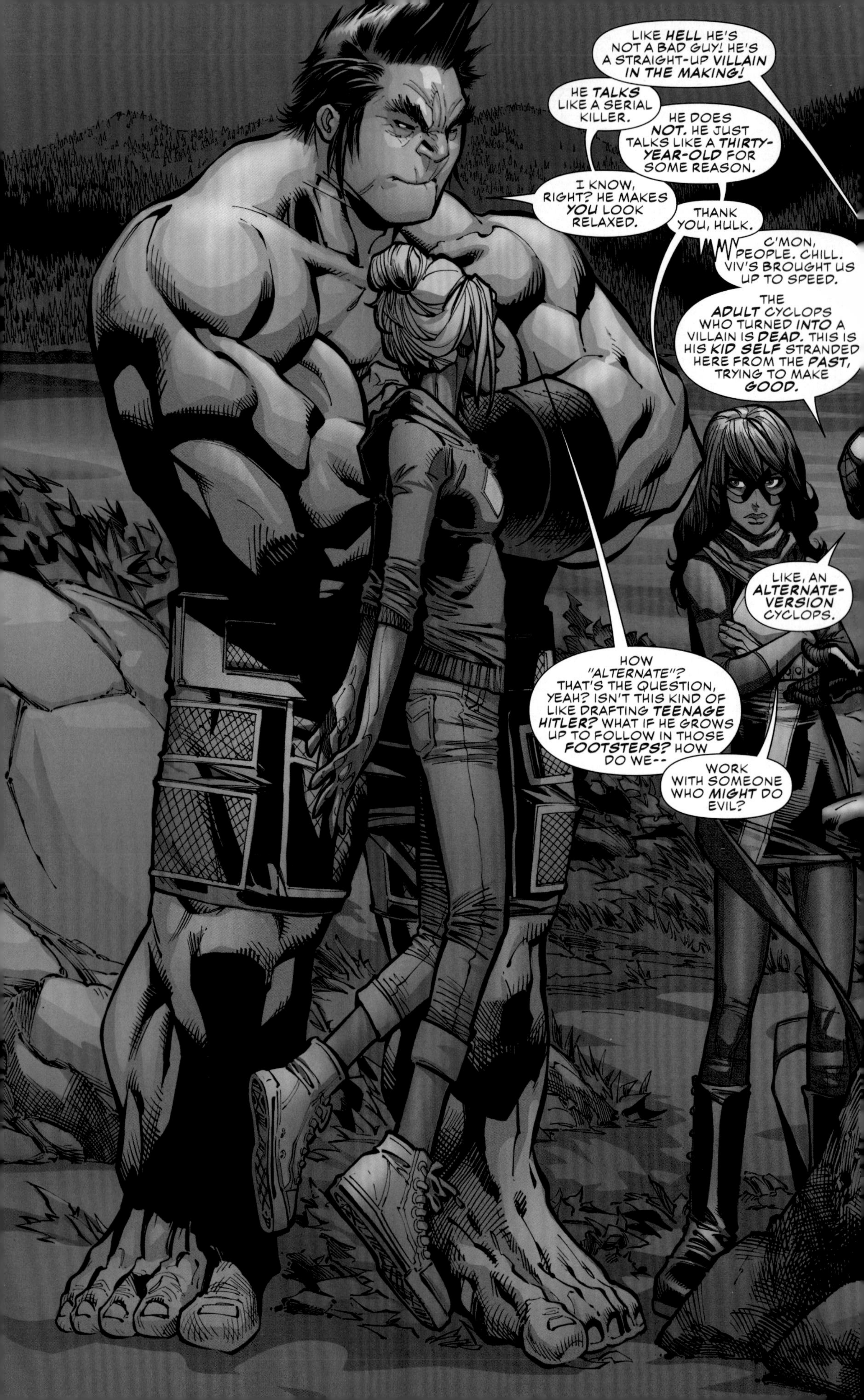
LIKE HELL HE'S NOT A BAD GUY! HE'S A STRAIGHT-UP VILLAIN IN THE MAKING!
HE TALKS LIKE A SERIAL KILLER.
HE DOES NOT. HE JUST TALKS LIKE A THIRTY-YEAR-OLD FOR SOME REASON.
I KNOW, RIGHT? HE MAKES YOU LOOK RELAXED.
THANK YOU, HULK.
C'MON, PEOPLE. CHILL. VIV'S BROUGHT US UP TO SPEED.
THE ADULT CYCLOPS WHO TURNED INTO A VILLAIN IS DEAD. THIS IS HIS KID SELF STRANDED HERE FROM THE PAST, TRYING TO MAKE GOOD.
LIKE, AN ALTERNATE-VERSION CYCLOPS.
HOW "ALTERNATE"? THAT'S THE QUESTION, YEAH? ISN'T THIS KIND OF LIKE DRAFTING TEENAGE HITLER? WHAT IF HE GROWS UP TO FOLLOW IN THOSE FOOTSTEPS? HOW DO WE--
WORK WITH SOMEONE WHO MIGHT DO EVIL?

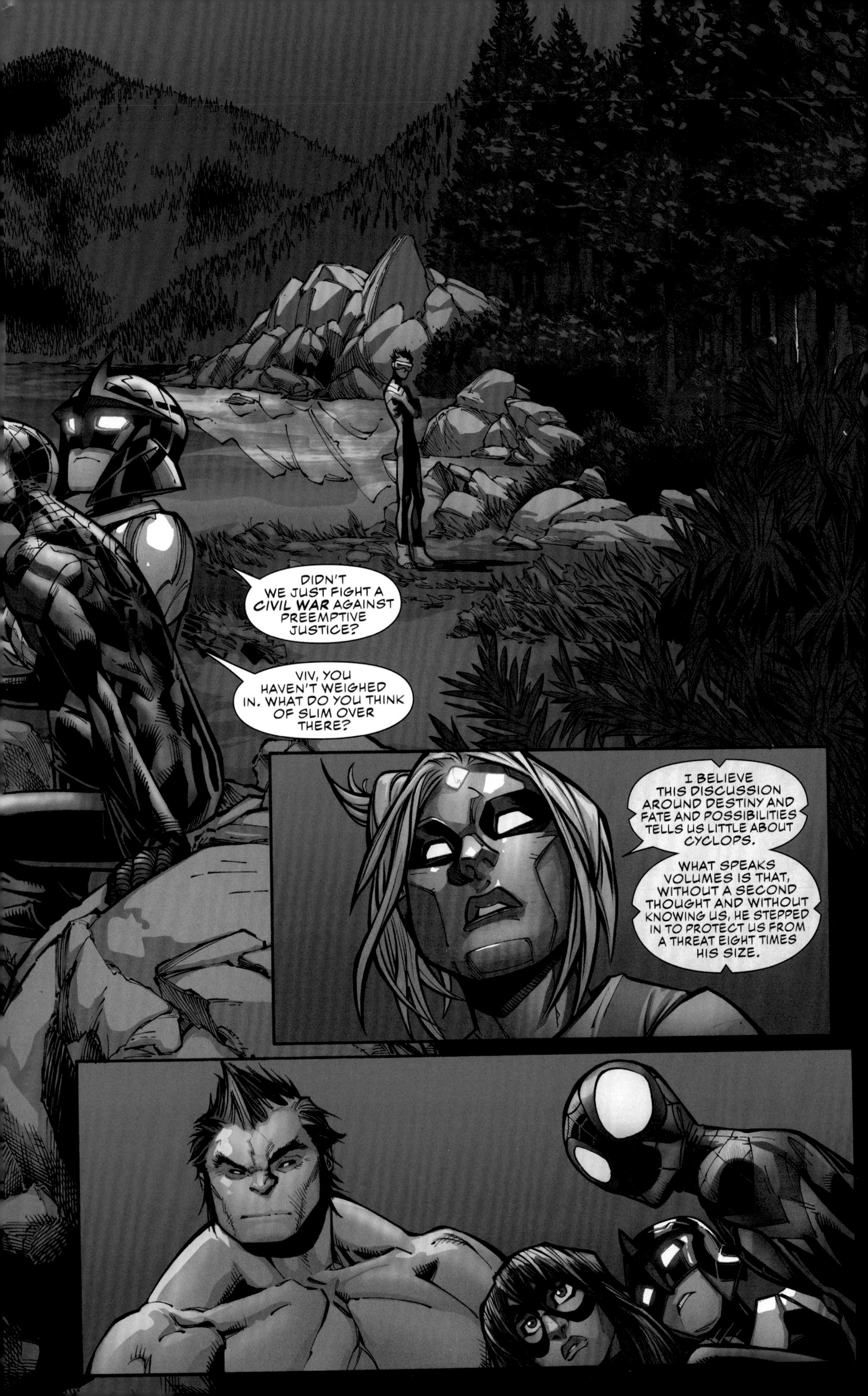
DIDN'T WE JUST FIGHT A CIVIL WAR AGAINST PREEMPTIVE JUSTICE?
VIV, YOU HAVEN'T WEIGHED IN. WHAT DO YOU THINK OF SLIM OVER THERE?
I BELIEVE THIS DISCUSSION AROUND DESTINY AND FATE AND POSSIBILITIES TELLS US LITTLE ABOUT CYCLOPS.
WHAT SPEAKS VOLUMES IS THAT, WITHOUT A SECOND THOUGHT AND WITHOUT KNOWING US, HE STEPPED IN TO PROTECT US FROM A THREAT EIGHT TIMES HIS SIZE.

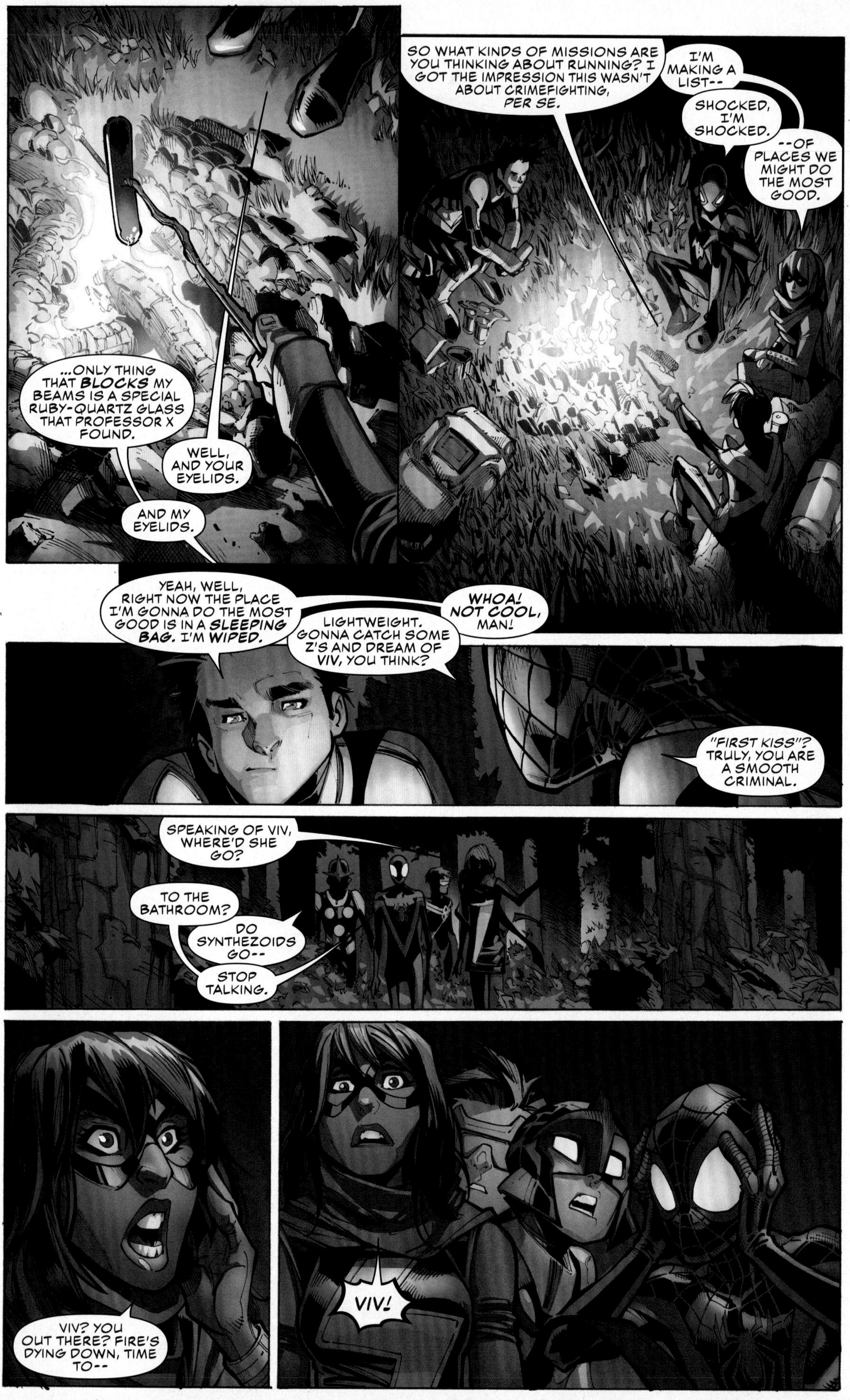
...ONLY THING THAT BLOCKS MY BEAMS IS A SPECIAL RUBY-QUARTZ GLASS THAT PROFESSOR X FOUND.
WELL, AND YOUR EYELIDS.
AND MY EYELIDS.
SO WHAT KINDS OF MISSIONS ARE YOU THINKING ABOUT RUNNING? I GOT THE IMPRESSION THIS WASN'T ABOUT CRIMEFIGHTING, PER SE.
I'M MAKING A LIST--
SHOCKED, I'M SHOCKED.
--OF PLACES WE MIGHT DO THE MOST GOOD.
YEAH, WELL, RIGHT NOW THE PLACE I'M GONNA DO THE MOST GOOD IS IN A SLEEPING BAG. I'M WIPED.
WHOA! NOT COOL, MAN!
LIGHTWEIGHT. GONNA CATCH SOME Z'S AND DREAM OF VIV, YOU THINK?
"FIRST KISS"? TRULY, YOU ARE A SMOOTH CRIMINAL.
SPEAKING OF VIV, WHERE'D SHE GO?
TO THE BATHROOM?
DO SYNTHEZOIDS GO--
STOP TALKING.
VIV? YOU OUT THERE? FIRE'S DYING DOWN, TIME TO--
VIV!

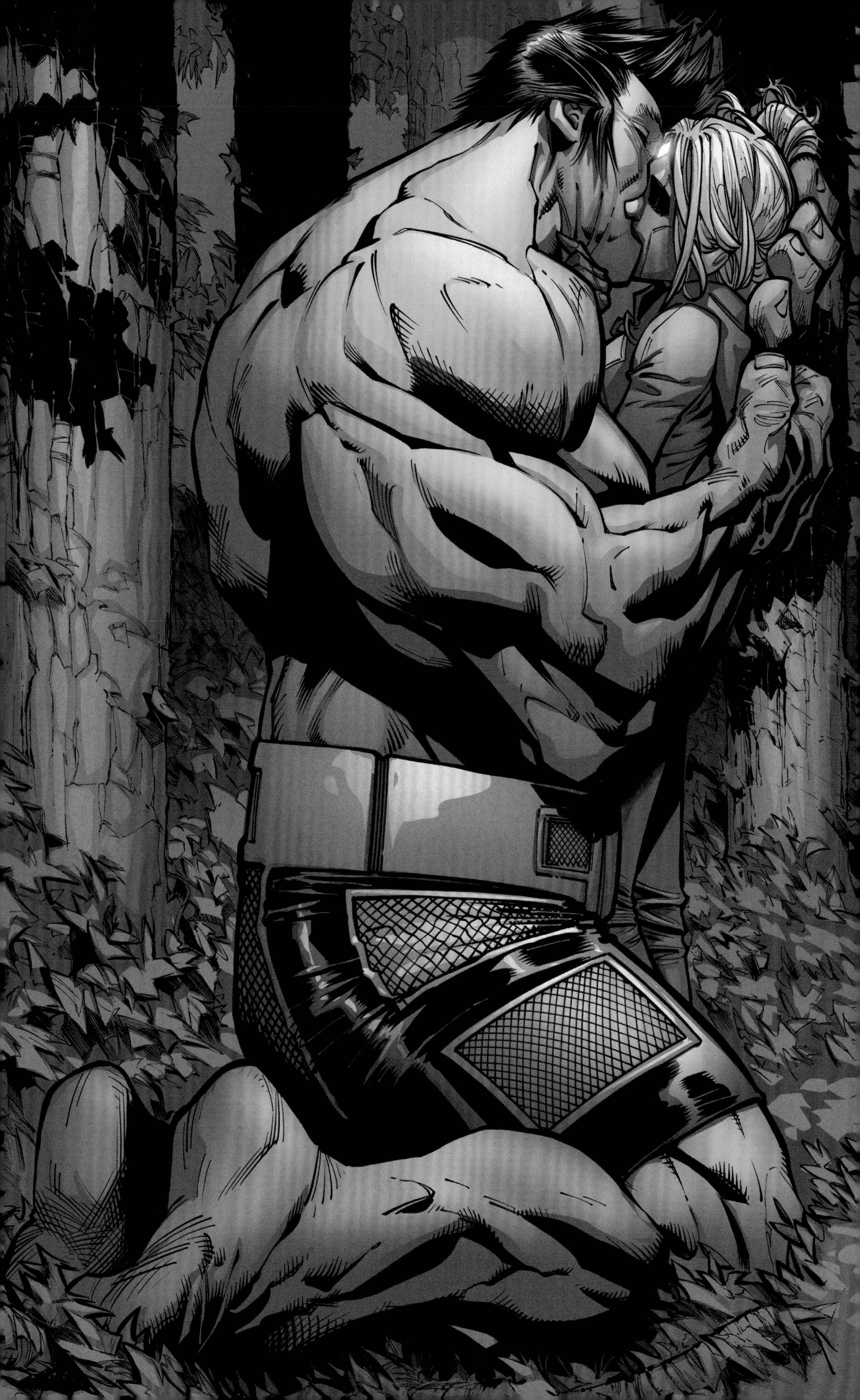

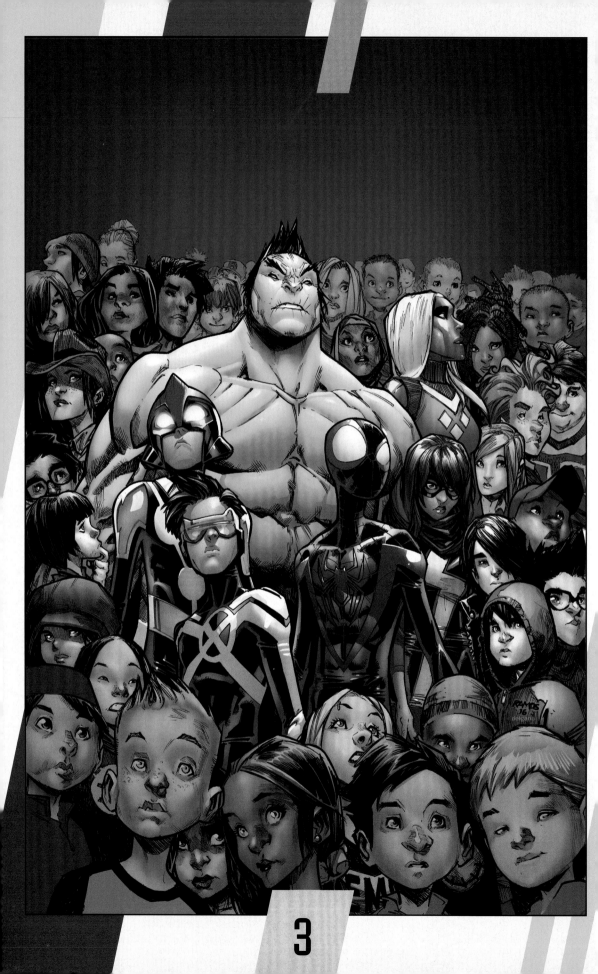

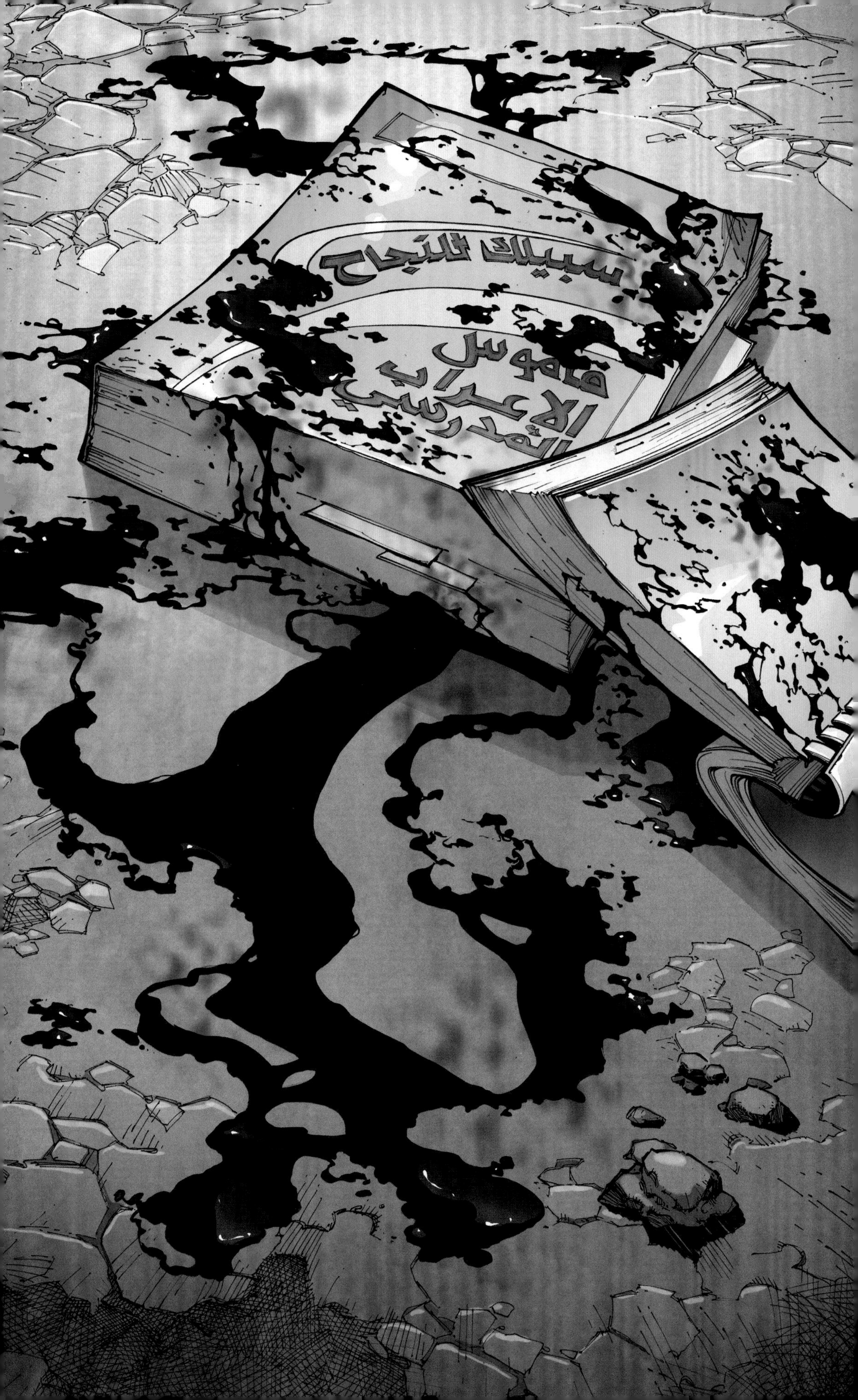
سبيلك للنجاح
قاموس الإعراب المدرسي

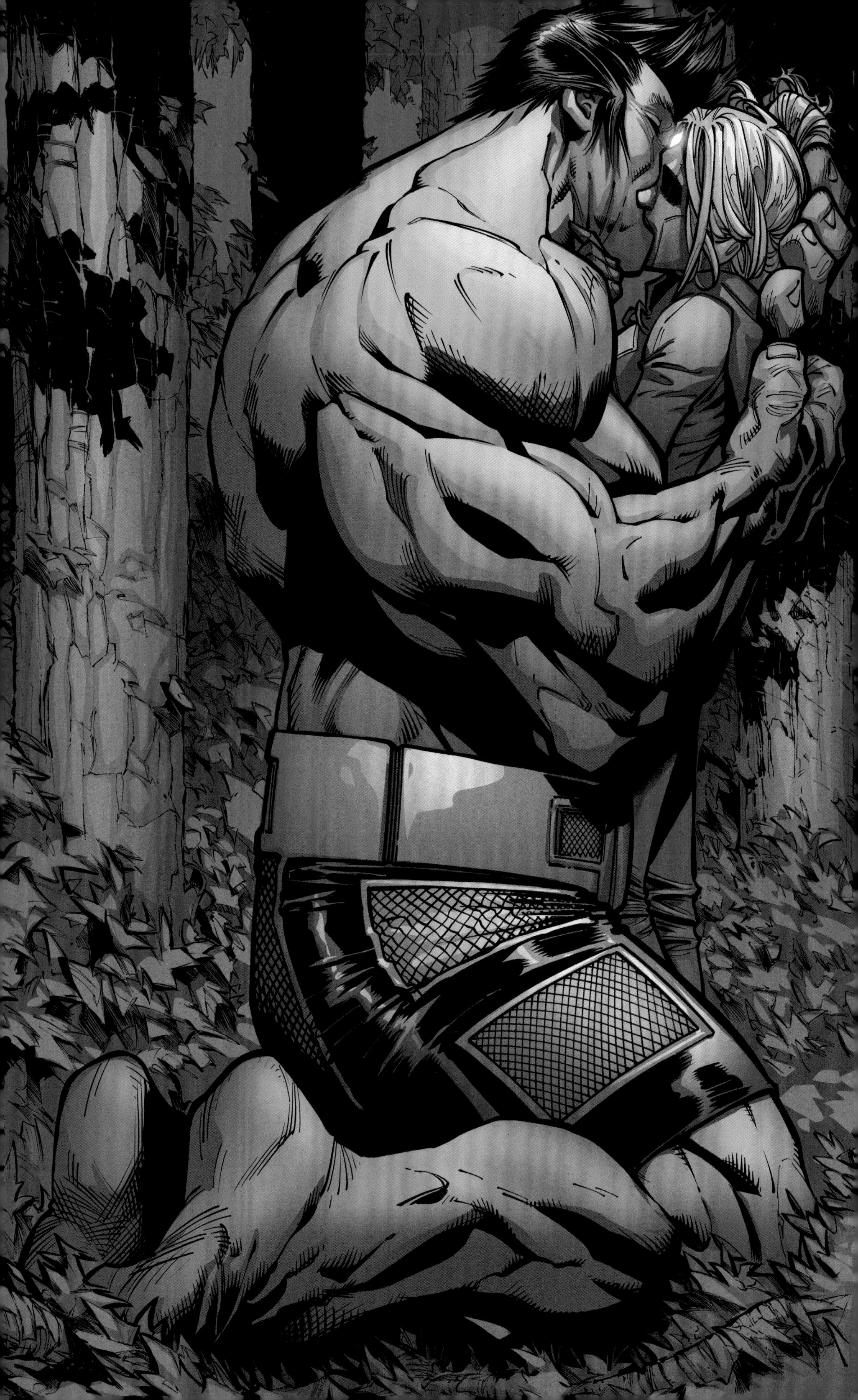

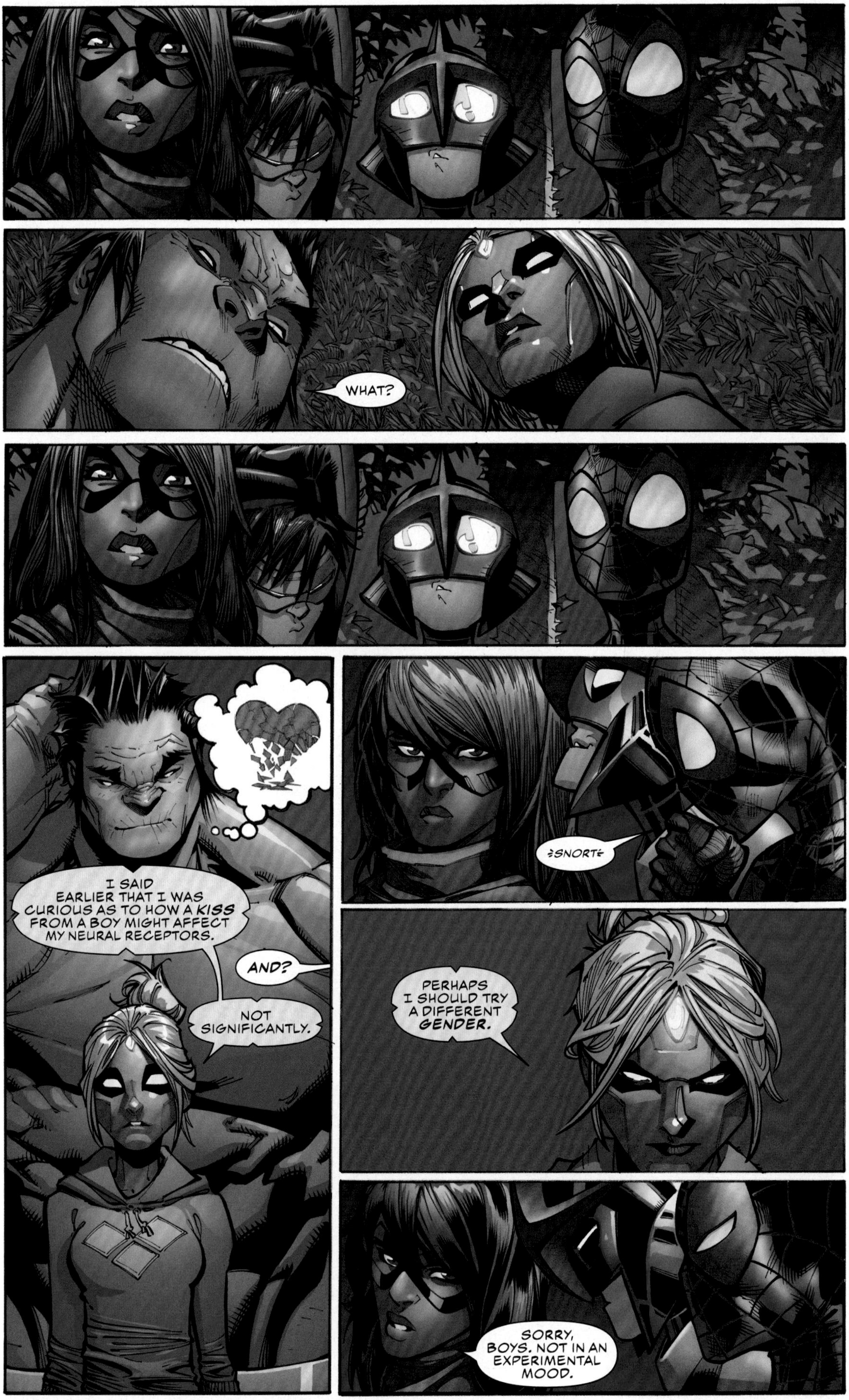
WHAT?
I SAID EARLIER THAT I WAS CURIOUS AS TO HOW A KISS FROM A BOY MIGHT AFFECT MY NEURAL RECEPTORS.
AND?
NOT SIGNIFICANTLY.
SNORT
PERHAPS I SHOULD TRY A DIFFERENT GENDER.
SORRY, BOYS. NOT IN AN EXPERIMENTAL MOOD.

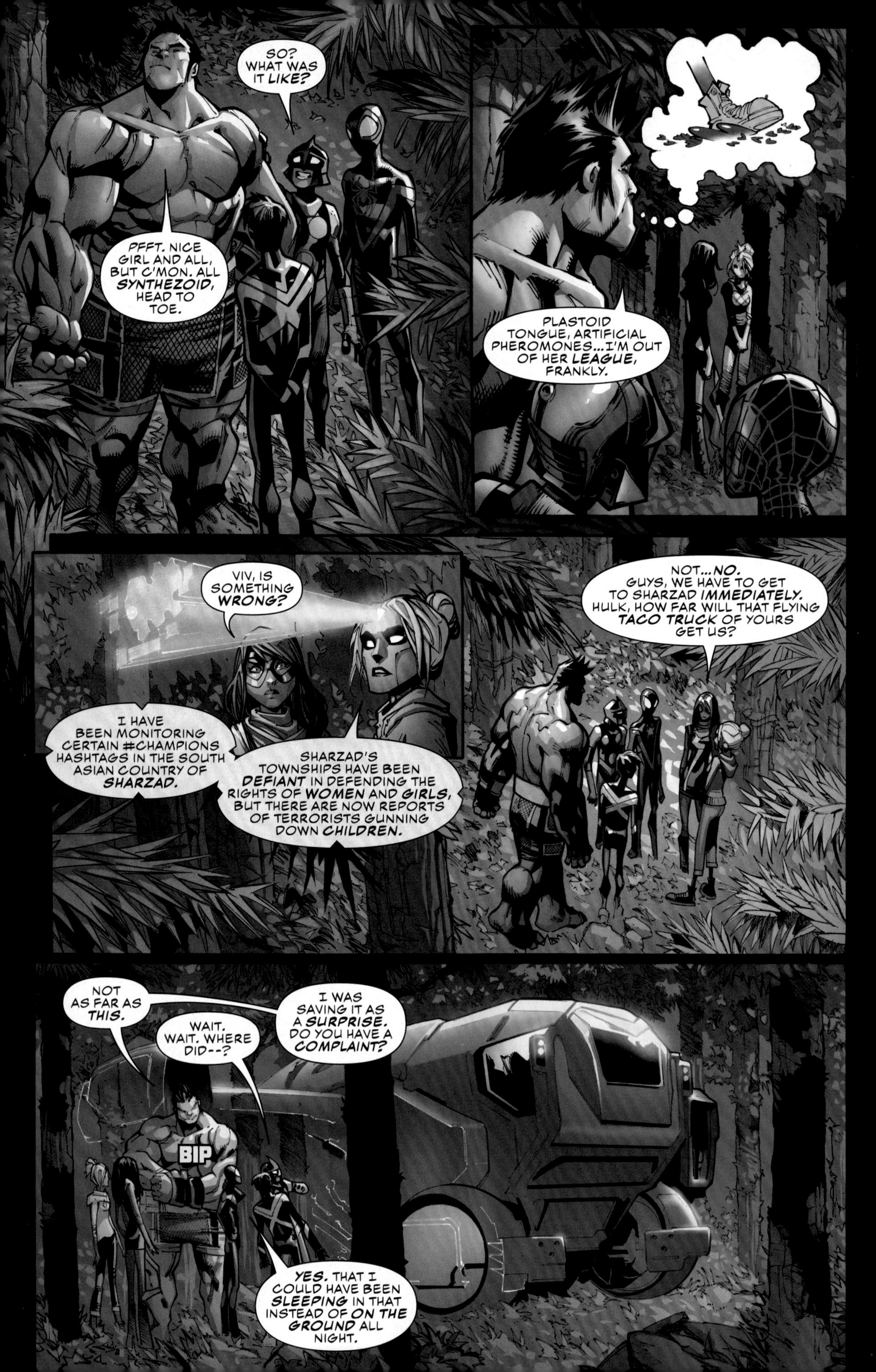
SO? WHAT WAS IT LIKE?
PFFT. NICE GIRL AND ALL, BUT C'MON. ALL SYNTHEZOID, HEAD TO TOE.
PLASTOID TONGUE, ARTIFICIAL PHEROMONES...I'M OUT OF HER LEAGUE, FRANKLY.
VIV, IS SOMETHING WRONG?
I HAVE BEEN MONITORING CERTAIN #CHAMPIONS HASHTAGS IN THE SOUTH ASIAN COUNTRY OF SHARZAD.
SHARZAD'S TOWNSHIPS HAVE BEEN DEFIANT IN DEFENDING THE RIGHTS OF WOMEN AND GIRLS, BUT THERE ARE NOW REPORTS OF TERRORISTS GUNNING DOWN CHILDREN.
NOT...NO. GUYS, WE HAVE TO GET TO SHARZAD IMMEDIATELY. HULK, HOW FAR WILL THAT FLYING TACO TRUCK OF YOURS GET US?
NOT AS FAR AS THIS.
WAIT. WAIT. WHERE DID--?
I WAS SAVING IT AS A SURPRISE. DO YOU HAVE A COMPLAINT?
BIP
YES. THAT I COULD HAVE BEEN SLEEPING IN THAT INSTEAD OF ON THE GROUND ALL NIGHT.

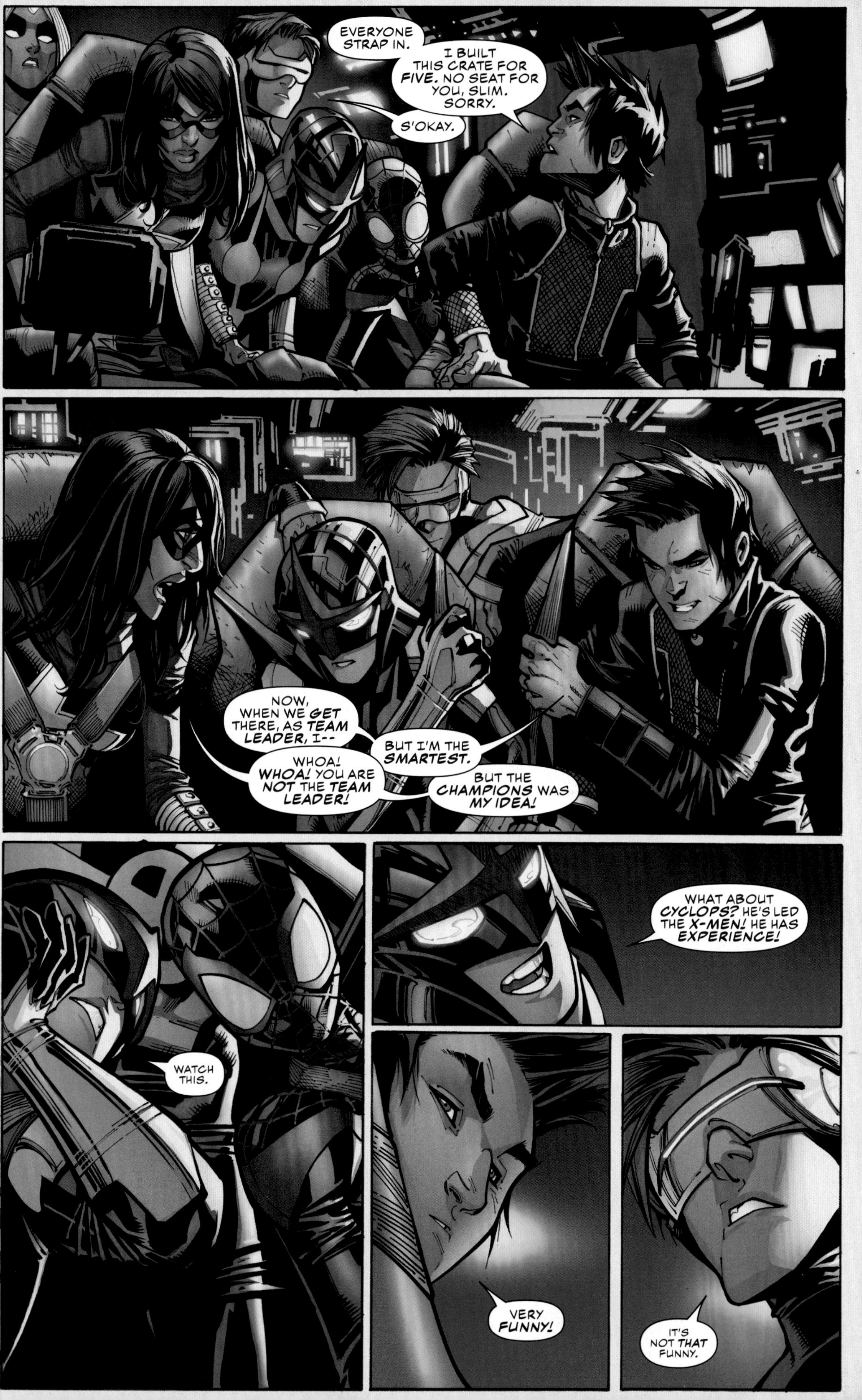
EVERYONE STRAP IN.
I BUILT THIS CRATE FOR FIVE. NO SEAT FOR YOU, SLIM. SORRY.
S'OKAY.
NOW, WHEN WE GET THERE, AS TEAM LEADER, I--
BUT I'M THE SMARTEST.
WHOA! WHOA! YOU ARE NOT THE TEAM LEADER!
BUT THE CHAMPIONS WAS MY IDEA!
WATCH THIS.
WHAT ABOUT CYCLOPS? HE'S LED THE X-MEN! HE HAS EXPERIENCE!
VERY FUNNY!
IT'S NOT THAT FUNNY.

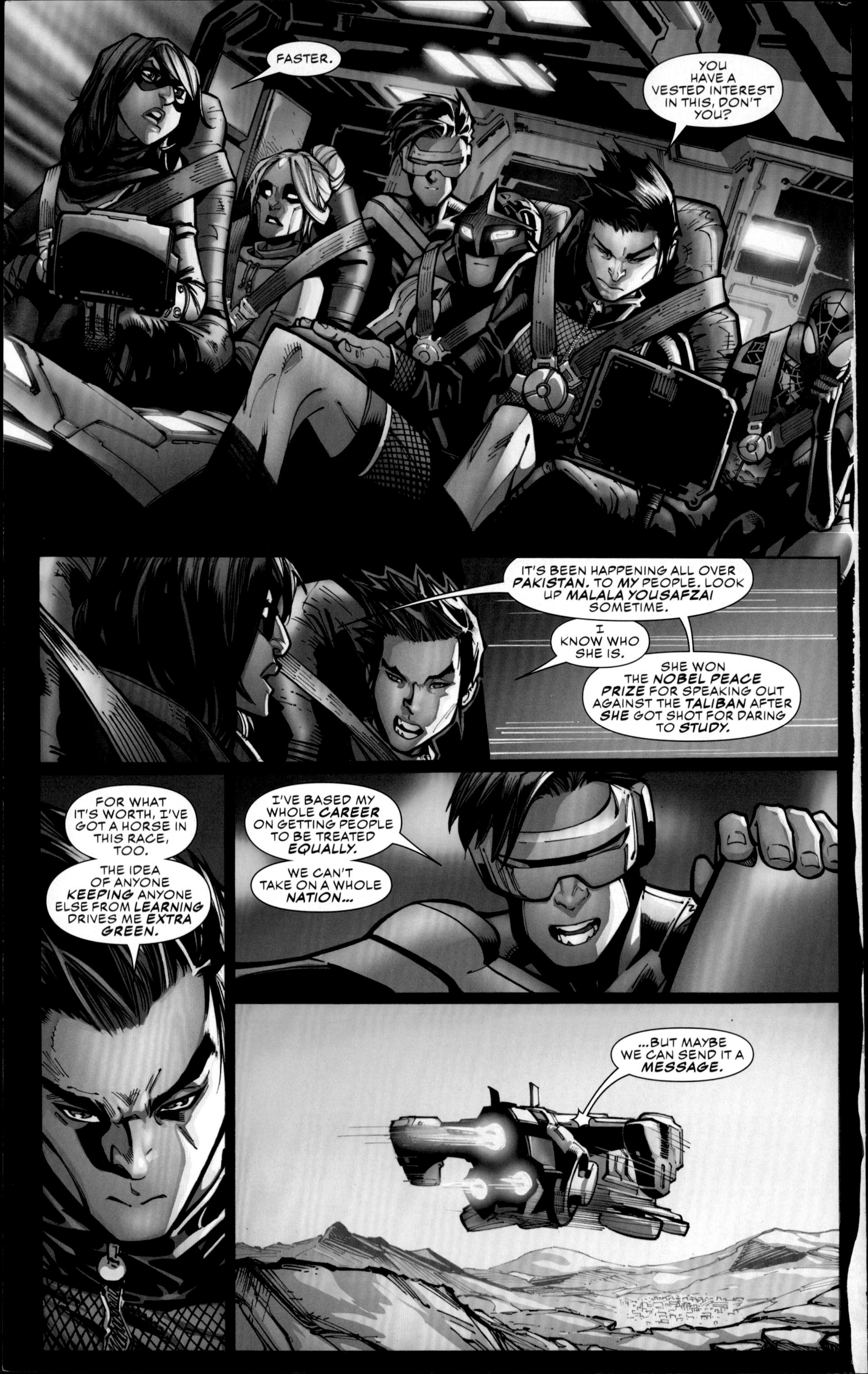
FASTER.
YOU HAVE A VESTED INTEREST IN THIS, DON'T YOU?
IT'S BEEN HAPPENING ALL OVER PAKISTAN. TO MY PEOPLE. LOOK UP MALALA YOUSAFZAI SOMETIME.
I KNOW WHO SHE IS.
SHE WON THE NOBEL PEACE PRIZE FOR SPEAKING OUT AGAINST THE TALIBAN AFTER SHE GOT SHOT FOR DARING TO STUDY.
FOR WHAT IT'S WORTH, I'VE GOT A HORSE IN THIS RACE, TOO.
THE IDEA OF ANYONE KEEPING ANYONE ELSE FROM LEARNING DRIVES ME EXTRA GREEN.
I'VE BASED MY WHOLE CAREER ON GETTING PEOPLE TO BE TREATED EQUALLY.
WE CAN'T TAKE ON A WHOLE NATION...
...BUT MAYBE WE CAN SEND IT A MESSAGE.

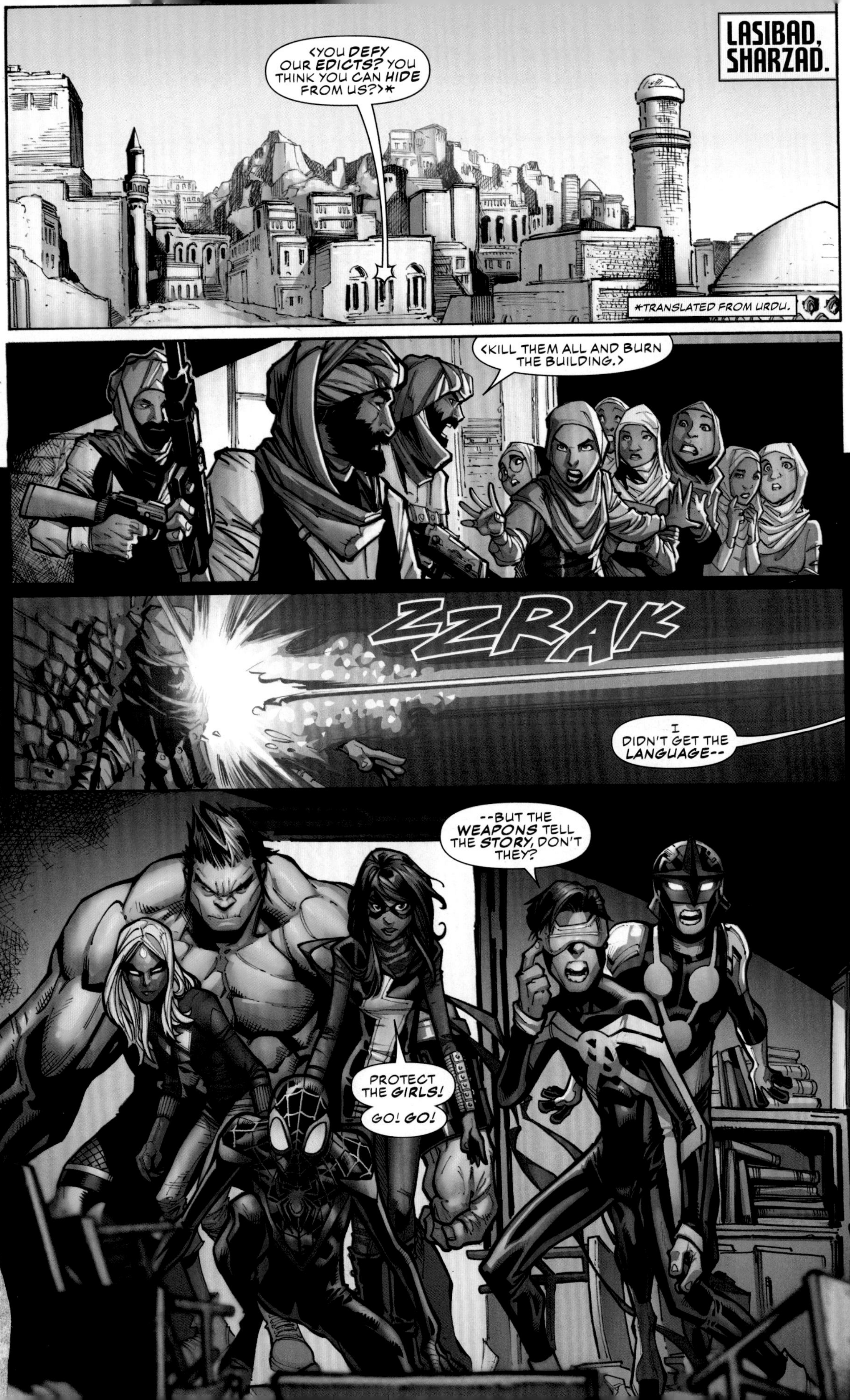
LASIBAD, SHARZAD.
<YOU DEFY OUR EDICTS? YOU THINK YOU CAN HIDE FROM US?>*
*TRANSLATED FROM URDU.
<KILL THEM ALL AND BURN THE BUILDING.>
ZZRAK
I DIDN'T GET THE LANGUAGE--
--BUT THE WEAPONS TELL THE STORY, DON'T THEY?
PROTECT THE GIRLS!
GO! GO!

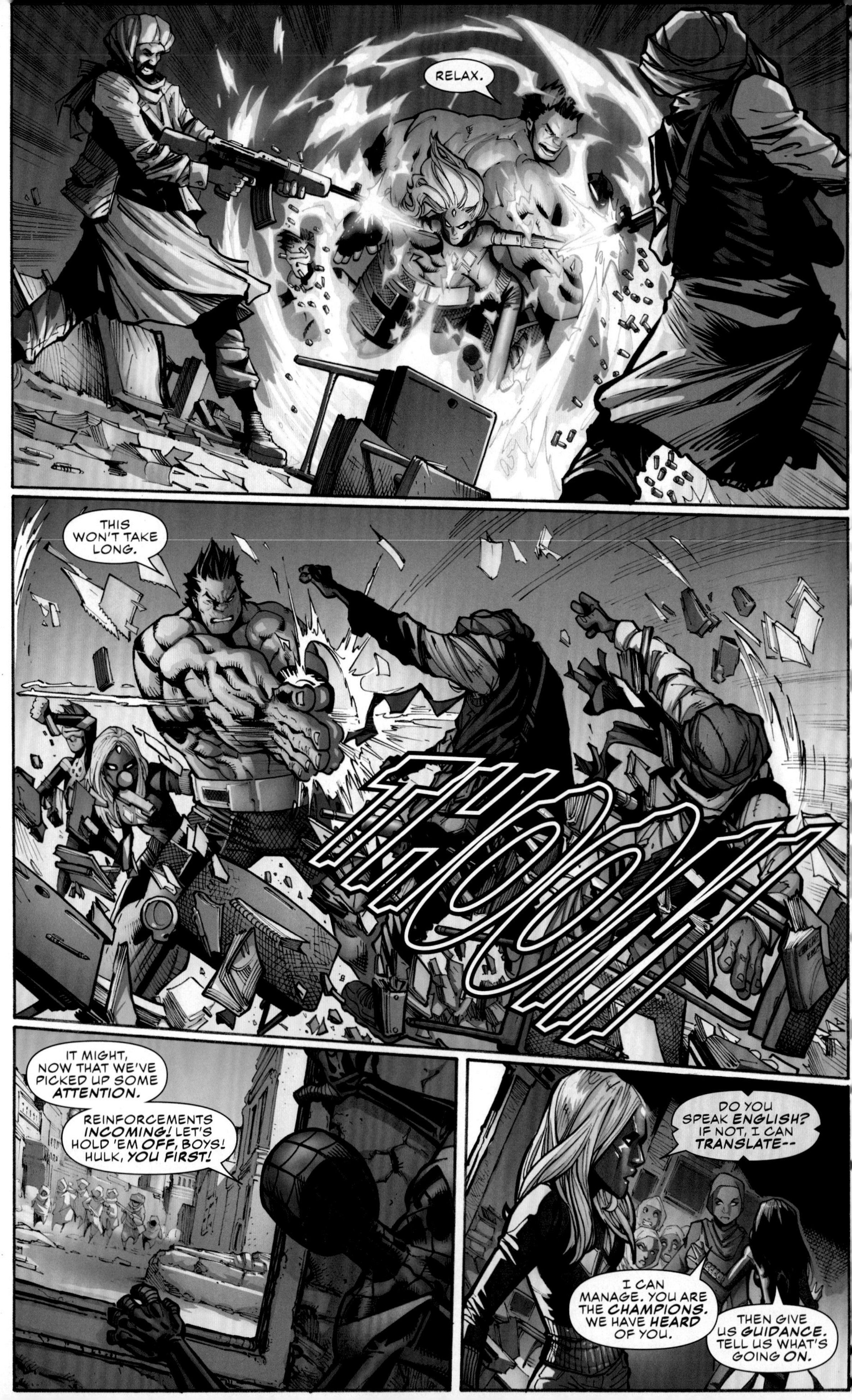
RELAX.
THIS WON'T TAKE LONG.
THOOM
IT MIGHT, NOW THAT WE'VE PICKED UP SOME ATTENTION.
REINFORCEMENTS INCOMING! LET'S HOLD 'EM OFF, BOYS! HULK, YOU FIRST!
DO YOU SPEAK ENGLISH? IF NOT, I CAN TRANSLATE--
I CAN MANAGE. YOU ARE THE CHAMPIONS. WE HAVE HEARD OF YOU.
THEN GIVE US GUIDANCE. TELL US WHAT'S GOING ON.

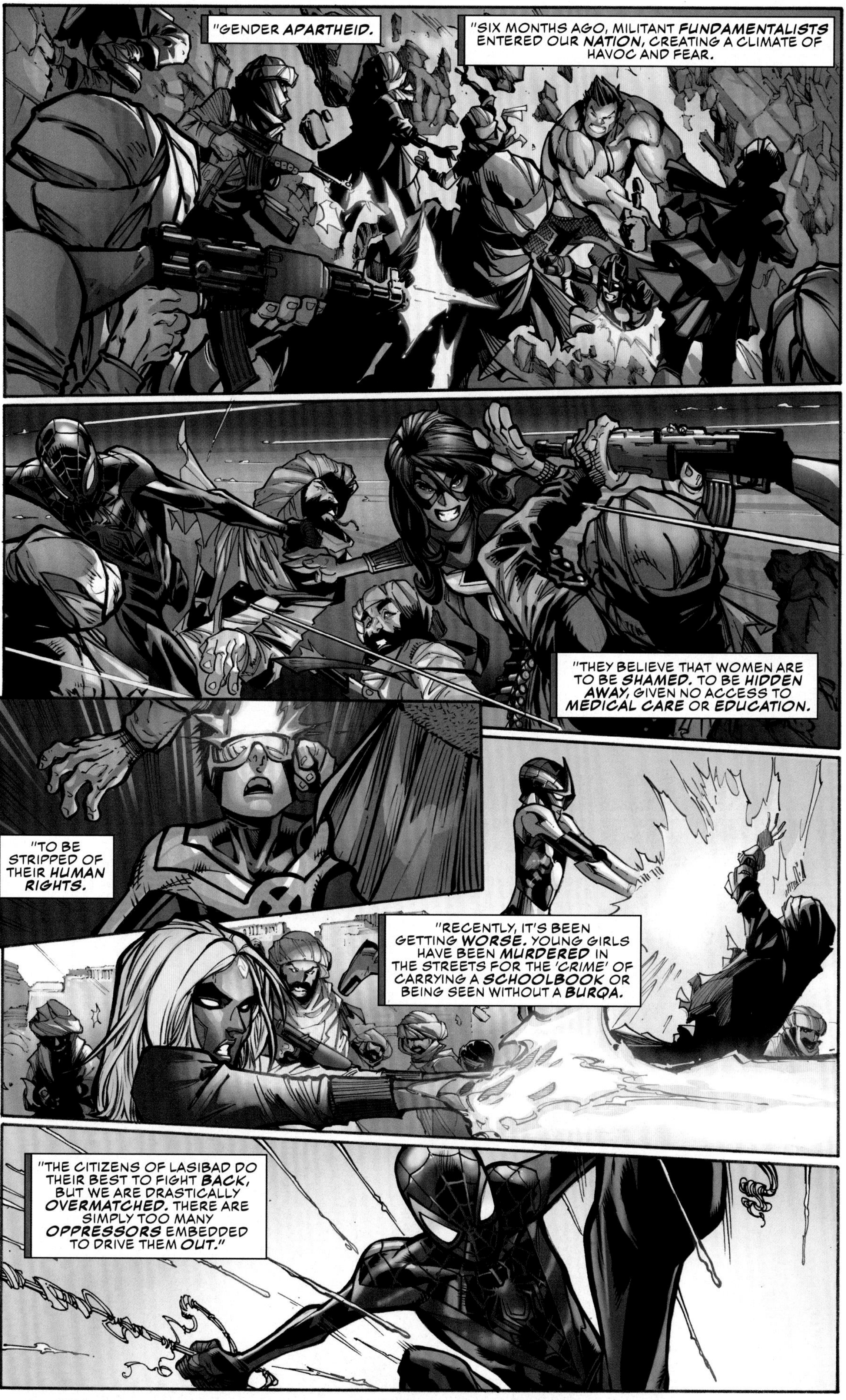
"GENDER APARTHEID.
"SIX MONTHS AGO, MILITANT FUNDAMENTALISTS ENTERED OUR NATION, CREATING A CLIMATE OF HAVOC AND FEAR.
"THEY BELIEVE THAT WOMEN ARE TO BE SHAMED. TO BE HIDDEN AWAY, GIVEN NO ACCESS TO MEDICAL CARE OR EDUCATION.
"TO BE STRIPPED OF THEIR HUMAN RIGHTS.
"RECENTLY, IT'S BEEN GETTING WORSE. YOUNG GIRLS HAVE BEEN MURDERED IN THE STREETS FOR THE 'CRIME' OF CARRYING A SCHOOLBOOK OR BEING SEEN WITHOUT A BURQA.
"THE CITIZENS OF LASIBAD DO THEIR BEST TO FIGHT BACK, BUT WE ARE DRASTICALLY OVERMATCHED. THERE ARE SIMPLY TOO MANY OPPRESSORS EMBEDDED TO DRIVE THEM OUT."

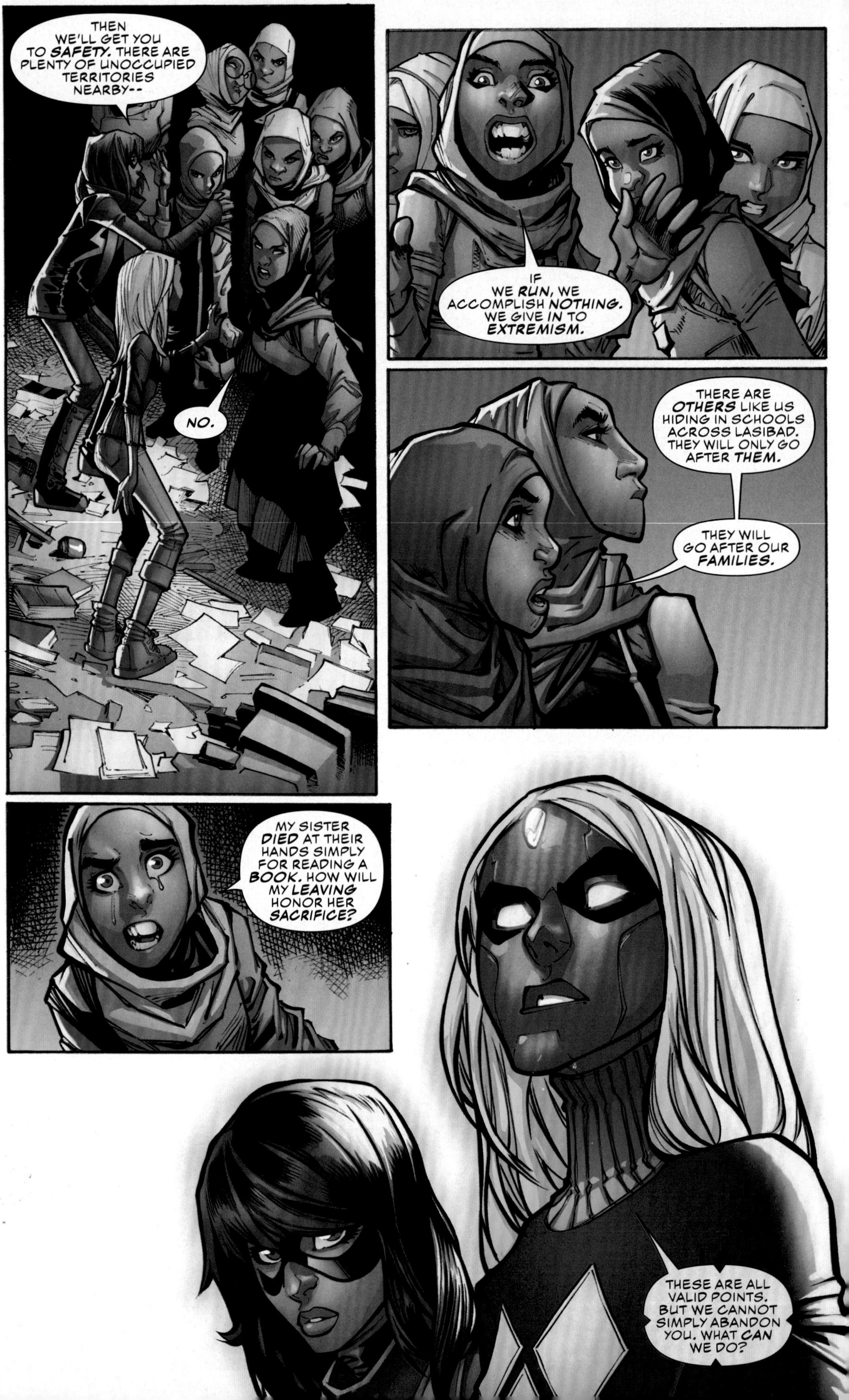
THEN WE'LL GET YOU TO SAFETY. THERE ARE PLENTY OF UNOCCUPIED TERRITORIES NEARBY--
NO.
IF WE RUN, WE ACCOMPLISH NOTHING. WE GIVE IN TO EXTREMISM.
THERE ARE OTHERS LIKE US HIDING IN SCHOOLS ACROSS LASIBAD. THEY WILL ONLY GO AFTER THEM.
THEY WILL GO AFTER OUR FAMILIES.
MY SISTER DIED AT THEIR HANDS SIMPLY FOR READING A BOOK. HOW WILL MY LEAVING HONOR HER SACRIFICE?
THESE ARE ALL VALID POINTS. BUT WE CANNOT SIMPLY ABANDON YOU. WHAT CAN WE DO?

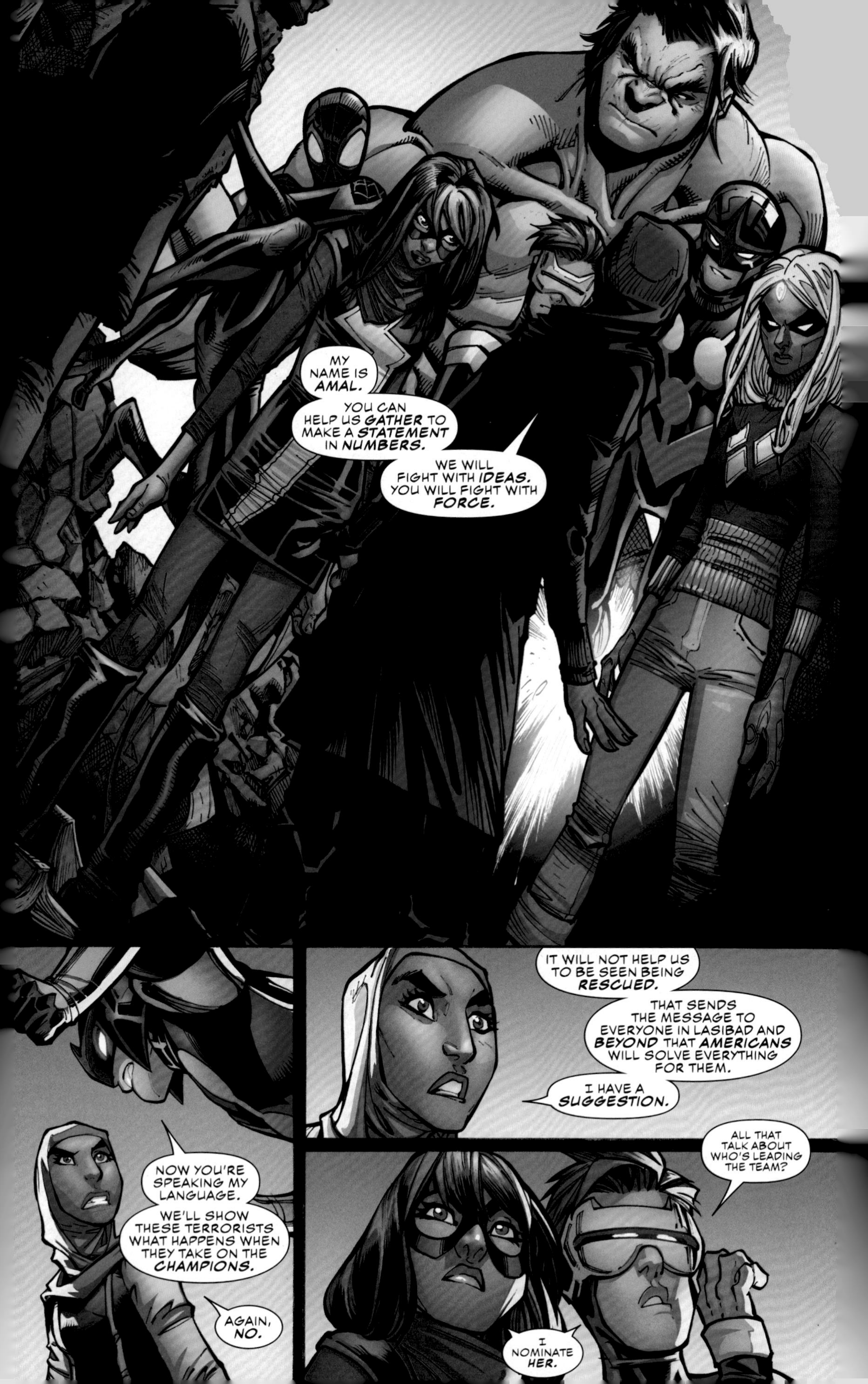
MY NAME IS AMAL.
YOU CAN HELP US GATHER TO MAKE A STATEMENT IN NUMBERS.
WE WILL FIGHT WITH IDEAS. YOU WILL FIGHT WITH FORCE.
IT WILL NOT HELP US TO BE SEEN BEING RESCUED.
THAT SENDS THE MESSAGE TO EVERYONE IN LASIBAD AND BEYOND THAT AMERICANS WILL SOLVE EVERYTHING FOR THEM.
I HAVE A SUGGESTION.
NOW YOU'RE SPEAKING MY LANGUAGE.
WE'LL SHOW THESE TERRORISTS WHAT HAPPENS WHEN THEY TAKE ON THE CHAMPIONS.
AGAIN, NO.
ALL THAT TALK ABOUT WHO'S LEADING THE TEAM?
I NOMINATE HER.

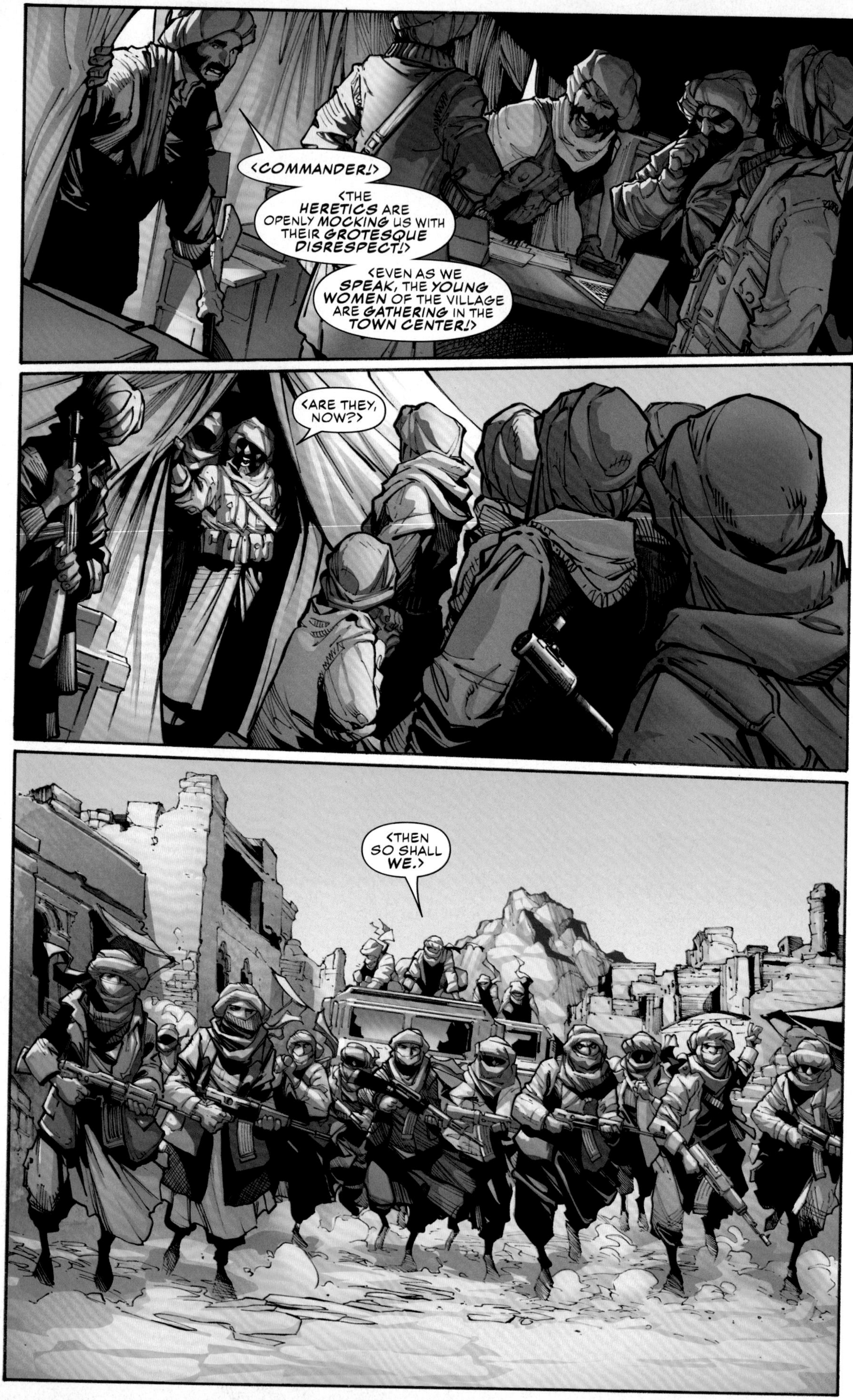
<COMMANDER!>
<THE HERETICS ARE OPENLY MOCKING US WITH THEIR GROTESQUE DISRESPECT!>
<EVEN AS WE SPEAK, THE YOUNG WOMEN OF THE VILLAGE ARE GATHERING IN THE TOWN CENTER!>
<ARE THEY, NOW?>
<THEN SO SHALL WE.>

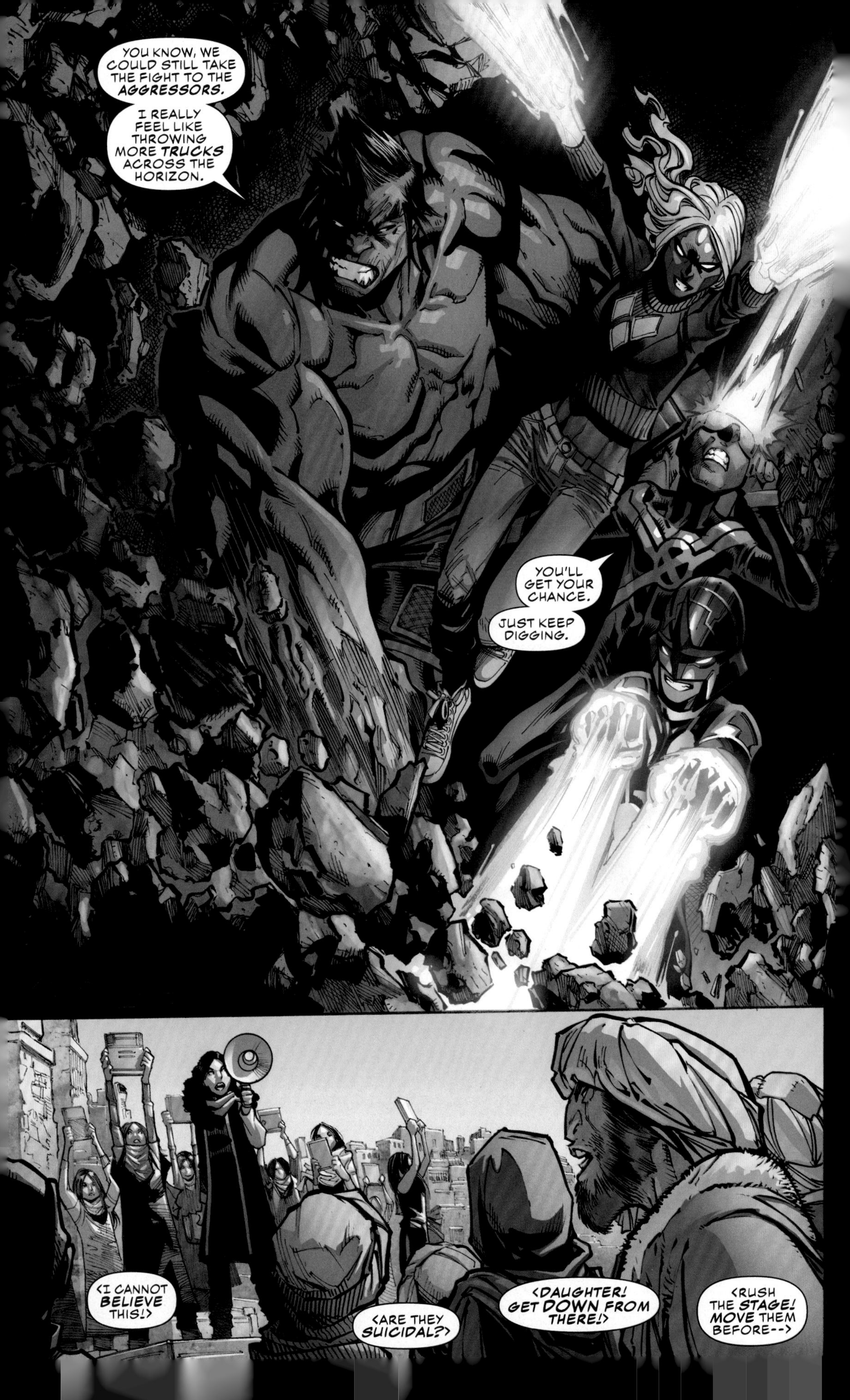
YOU KNOW, WE COULD STILL TAKE THE FIGHT TO THE AGGRESSORS.
I REALLY FEEL LIKE THROWING MORE TRUCKS ACROSS THE HORIZON.
YOU'LL GET YOUR CHANCE.
JUST KEEP DIGGING.
<I CANNOT BELIEVE THIS!>
<ARE THEY SUICIDAL?>
<DAUGHTER! GET DOWN FROM THERE!>
<RUSH THE STAGE! MOVE THEM BEFORE-->

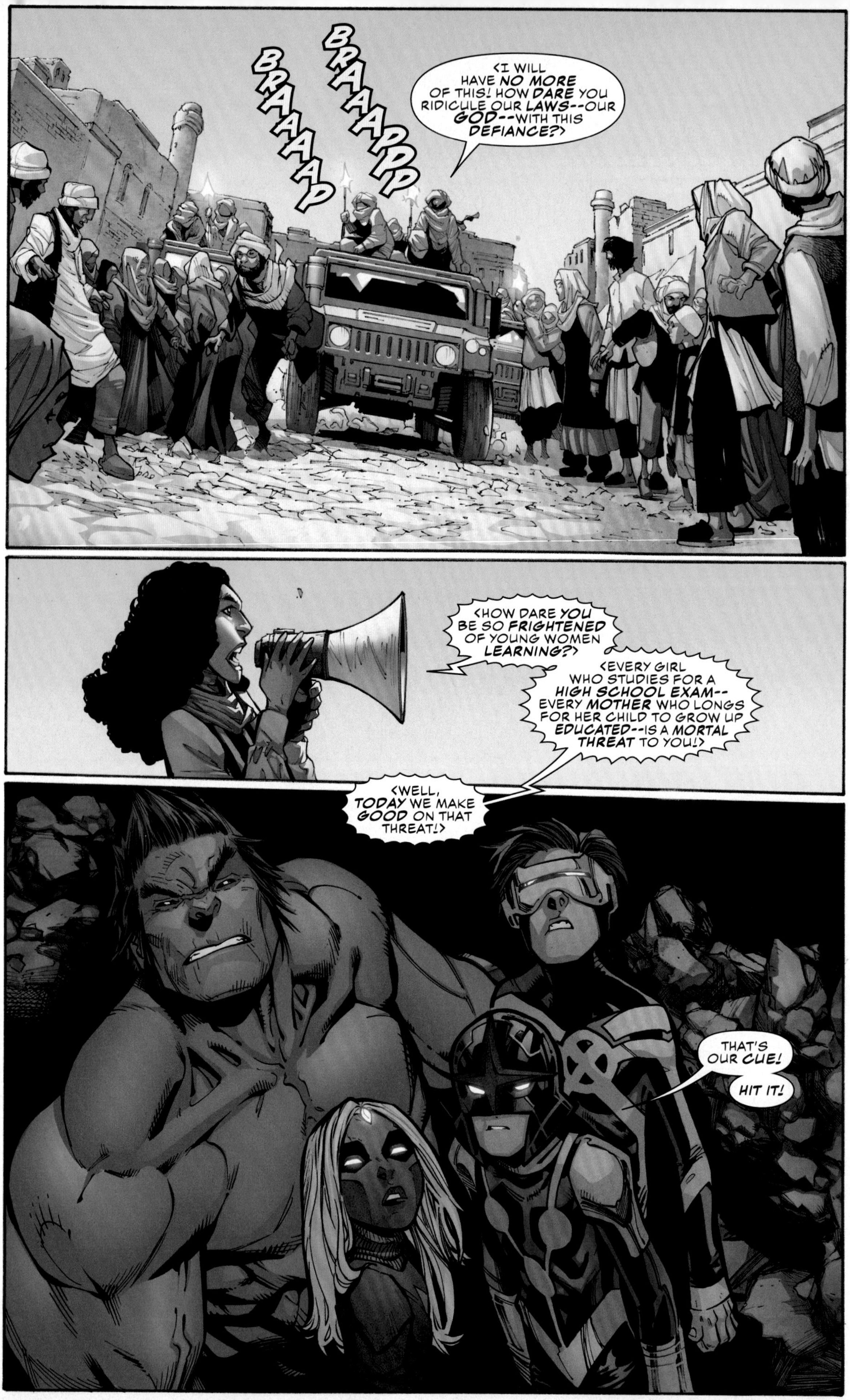
BRAAAAP
BRAAAPPP
<I WILL HAVE NO MORE OF THIS! HOW DARE YOU RIDICULE OUR LAWS--OUR GOD--WITH THIS DEFIANCE?>
<HOW DARE YOU BE SO FRIGHTENED OF YOUNG WOMEN LEARNING?>
<EVERY GIRL WHO STUDIES FOR A HIGH SCHOOL EXAM--EVERY MOTHER WHO LONGS FOR HER CHILD TO GROW UP EDUCATED--IS A MORTAL THREAT TO YOU!>
<WELL, TODAY WE MAKE GOOD ON THAT THREAT!>
THAT'S OUR CUE!
HIT IT!

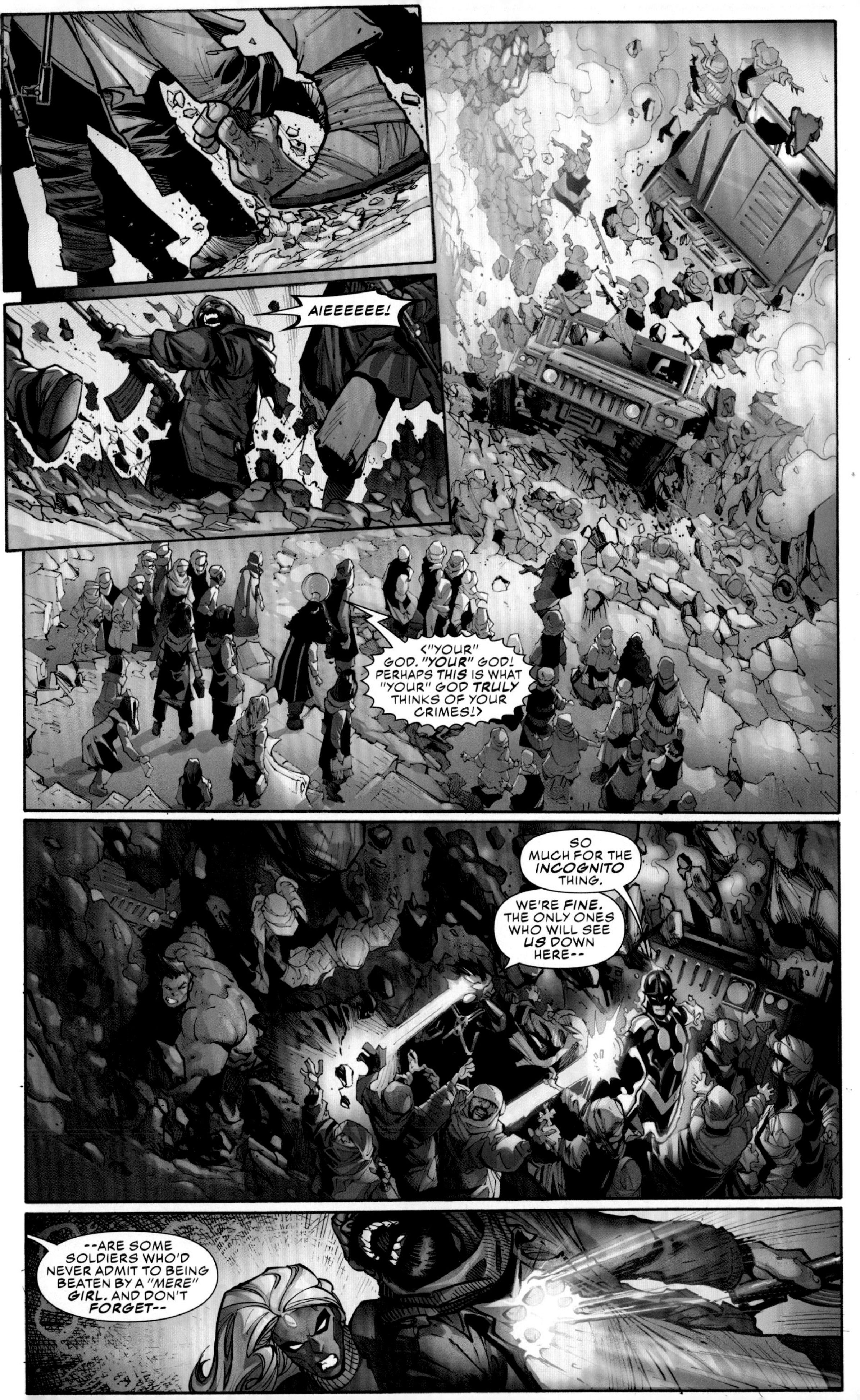
AIEEEEEE!
<"YOUR" GOD. "YOUR" GOD! PERHAPS THIS IS WHAT "YOUR" GOD TRULY THINKS OF YOUR CRIMES!>
SO MUCH FOR THE INCOGNITO THING.
WE'RE FINE. THE ONLY ONES WHO WILL SEE US DOWN HERE--
--ARE SOME SOLDIERS WHO'D NEVER ADMIT TO BEING BEATEN BY A "MERE" GIRL. AND DON'T FORGET--

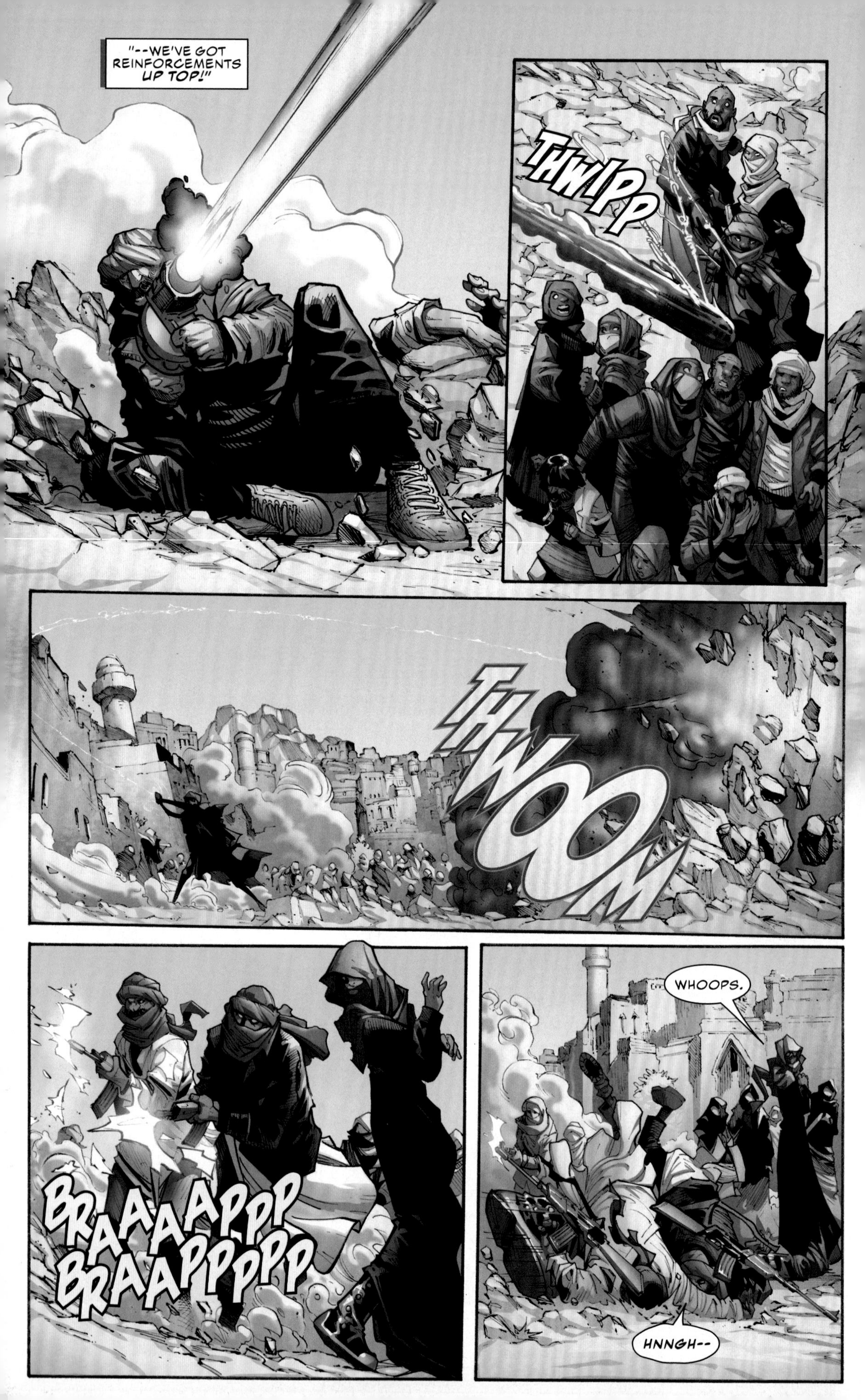
"--WE'VE GOT REINFORCEMENTS UP TOP!"
THWIPP
THWOOM
BRAAAAPPP
BRAAAPPPPP
WHOOPS.
HNNGH--

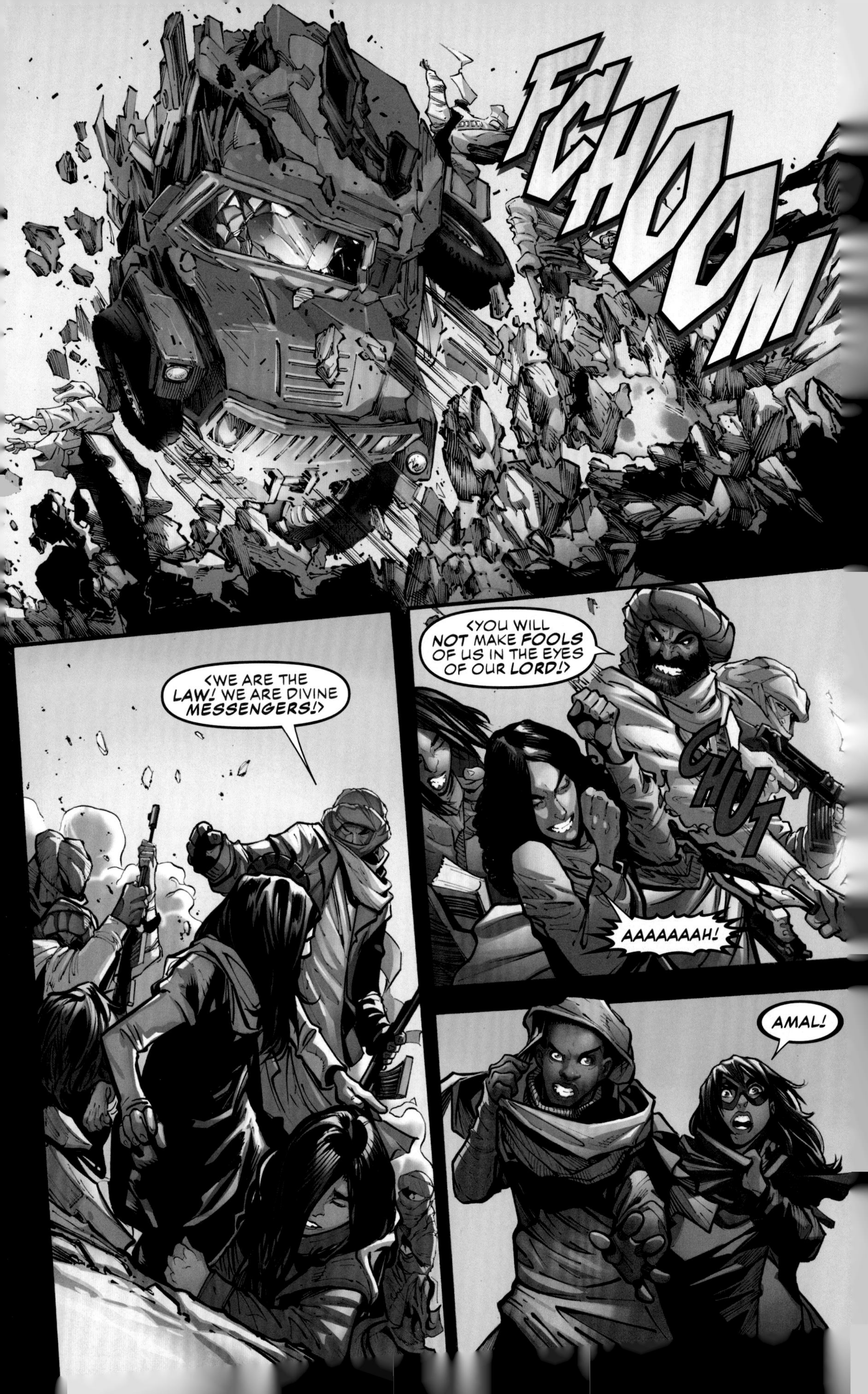
FCHOOM
<WE ARE THE LAW! WE ARE DIVINE MESSENGERS!>
<YOU WILL NOT MAKE FOOLS OF US IN THE EYES OF OUR LORD!>
CHUT
AAAAAAAH!
AMAL!

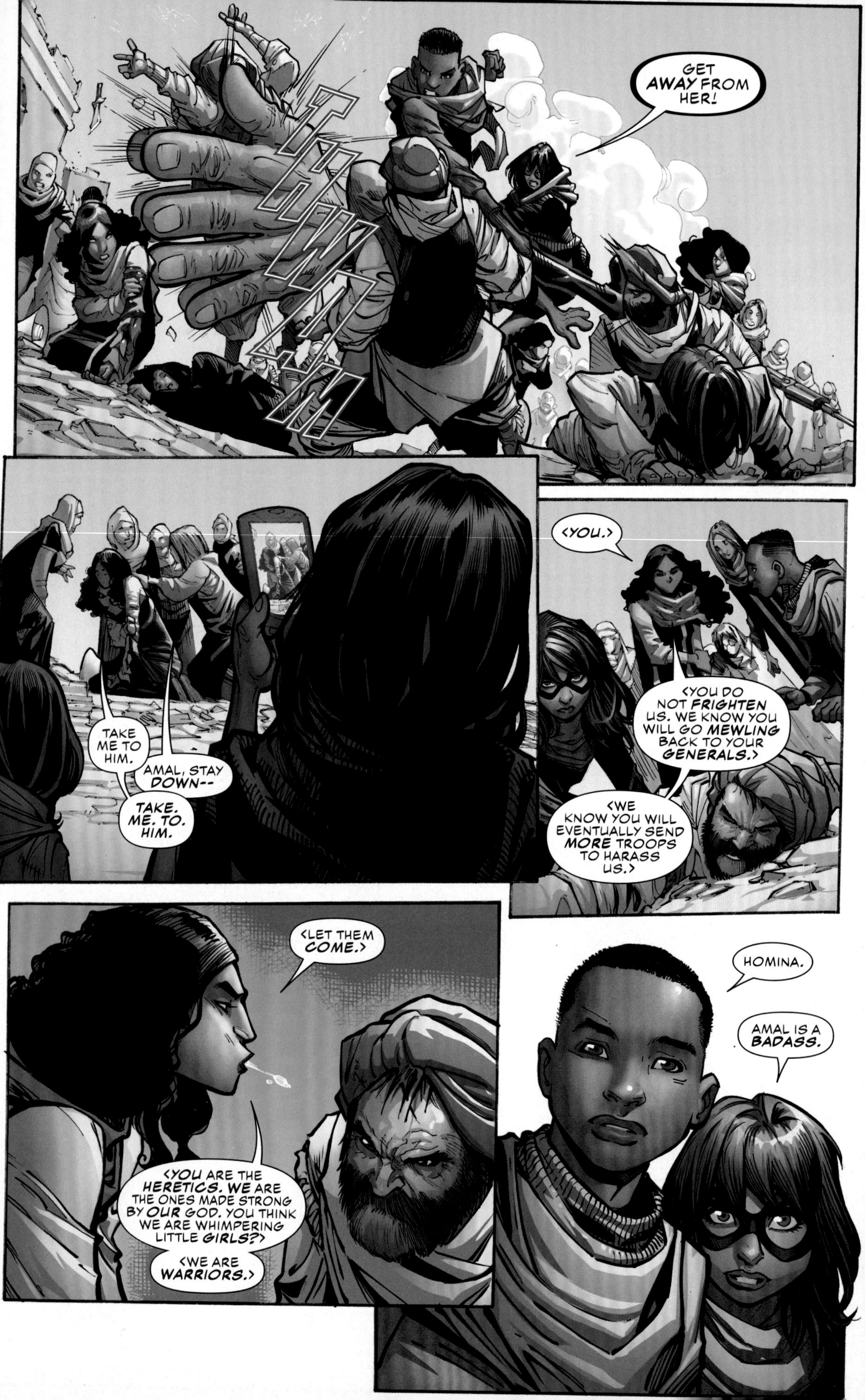
GET AWAY FROM HER!
TAKE ME TO HIM.
AMAL, STAY DOWN--
TAKE. ME. TO. HIM.
<YOU.>
<YOU DO NOT FRIGHTEN US. WE KNOW YOU WILL GO MEWLING BACK TO YOUR GENERALS.>
<WE KNOW YOU WILL EVENTUALLY SEND MORE TROOPS TO HARASS US.>
<LET THEM COME.>
<YOU ARE THE HERETICS. WE ARE THE ONES MADE STRONG BY OUR GOD. YOU THINK WE ARE WHIMPERING LITTLE GIRLS?>
<WE ARE WARRIORS.>
HOMINA.
AMAL IS A BADASS.

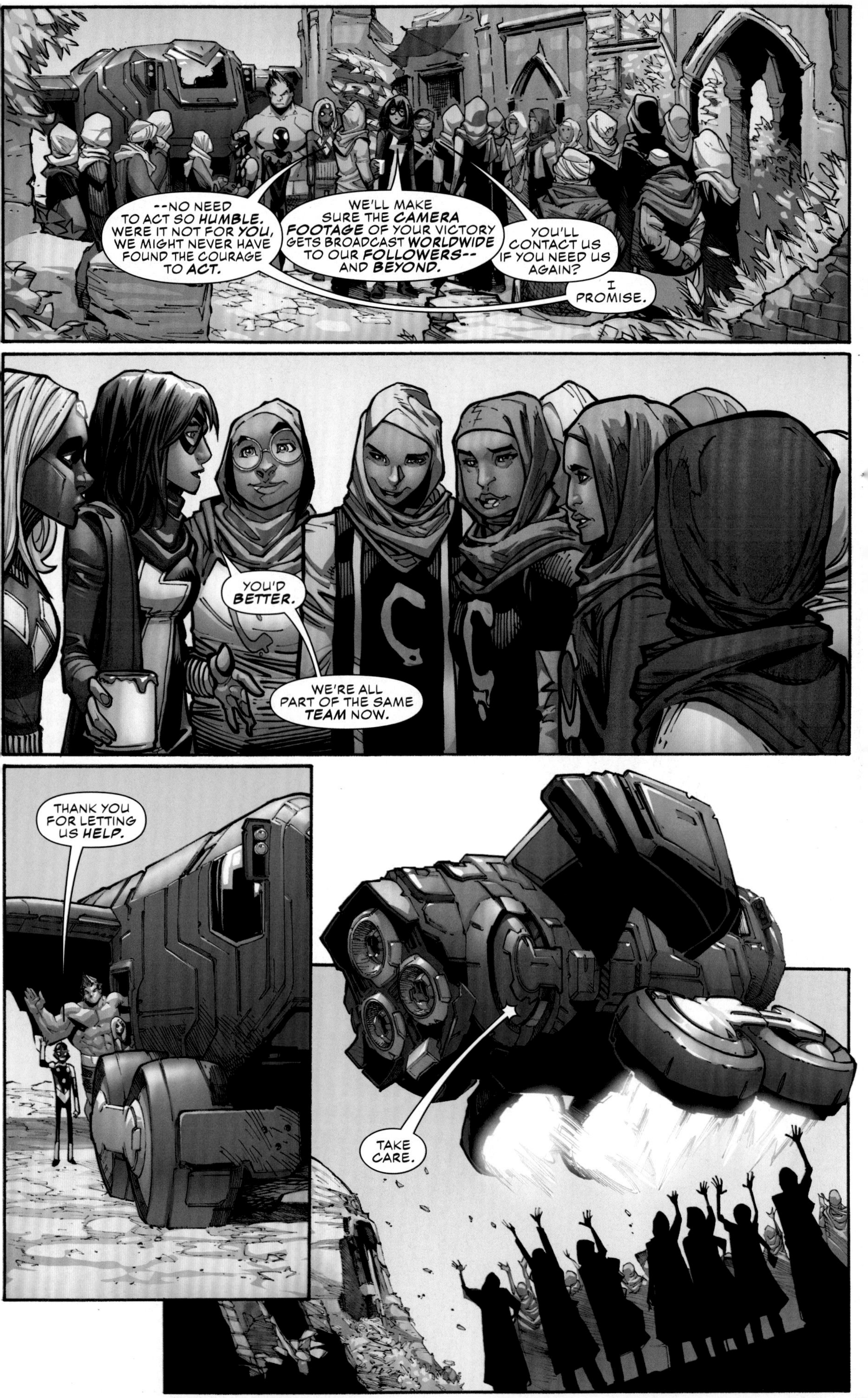
--NO NEED TO ACT SO HUMBLE. WERE IT NOT FOR YOU, WE MIGHT NEVER HAVE FOUND THE COURAGE TO ACT.
WE'LL MAKE SURE THE CAMERA FOOTAGE OF YOUR VICTORY GETS BROADCAST WORLDWIDE TO OUR FOLLOWERS-- AND BEYOND.
YOU'LL CONTACT US IF YOU NEED US AGAIN?
I PROMISE.
YOU'D BETTER.
WE'RE ALL PART OF THE SAME TEAM NOW.
THANK YOU FOR LETTING US HELP.
TAKE CARE.

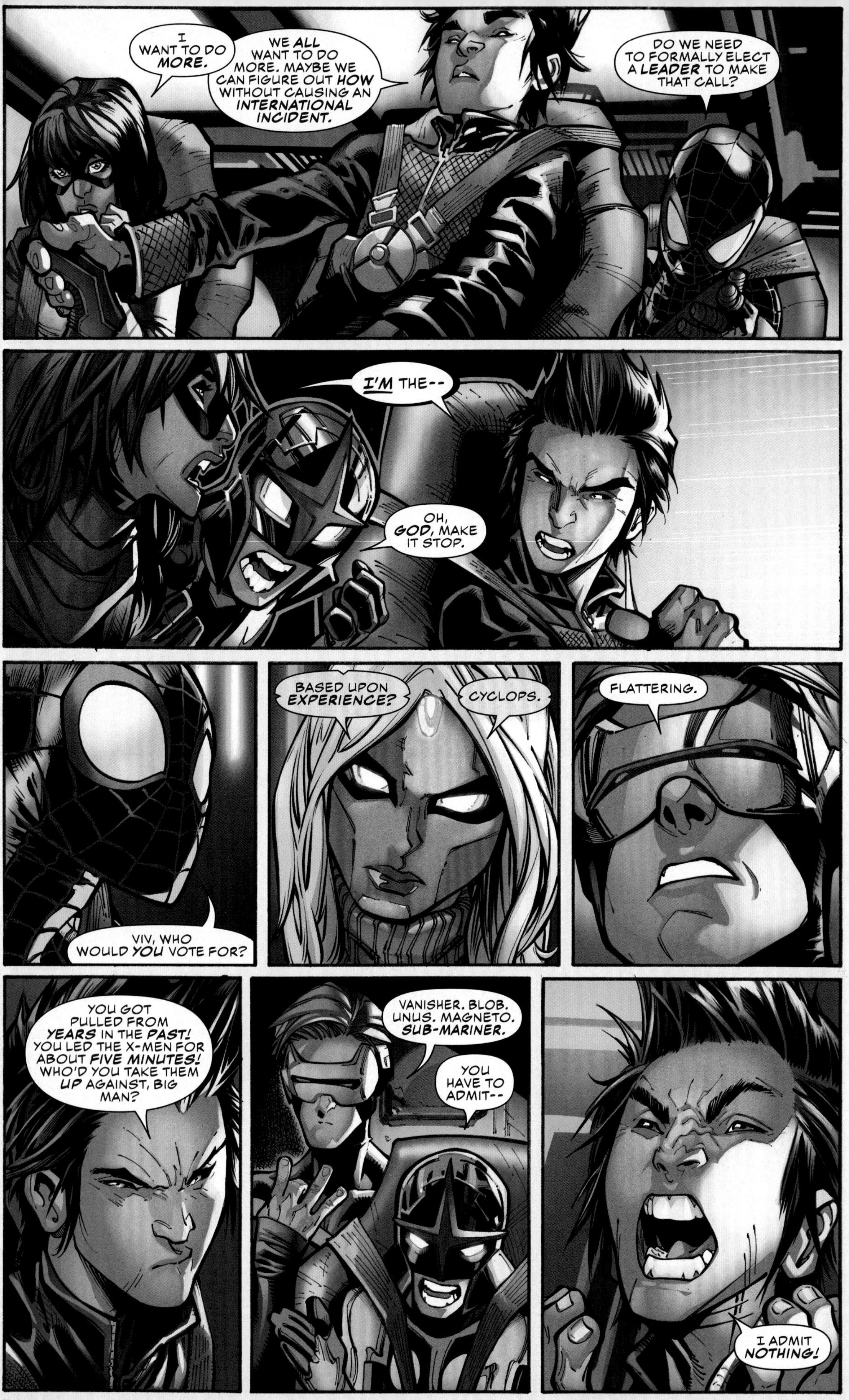

I WANT TO DO MORE.
WE ALL WANT TO DO MORE. MAYBE WE CAN FIGURE OUT HOW WITHOUT CAUSING AN INTERNATIONAL INCIDENT.
DO WE NEED TO FORMALLY ELECT A LEADER TO MAKE THAT CALL?
I'M THE--
OH, GOD, MAKE IT STOP.
VIV, WHO WOULD YOU VOTE FOR?
BASED UPON EXPERIENCE?
CYCLOPS.
FLATTERING.
YOU GOT PULLED FROM YEARS IN THE PAST! YOU LED THE X-MEN FOR ABOUT FIVE MINUTES! WHO'D YOU TAKE THEM UP AGAINST, BIG MAN?
VANISHER. BLOB. UNUS. MAGNETO. SUB-MARINER.
YOU HAVE TO ADMIT--
I ADMIT NOTHING!

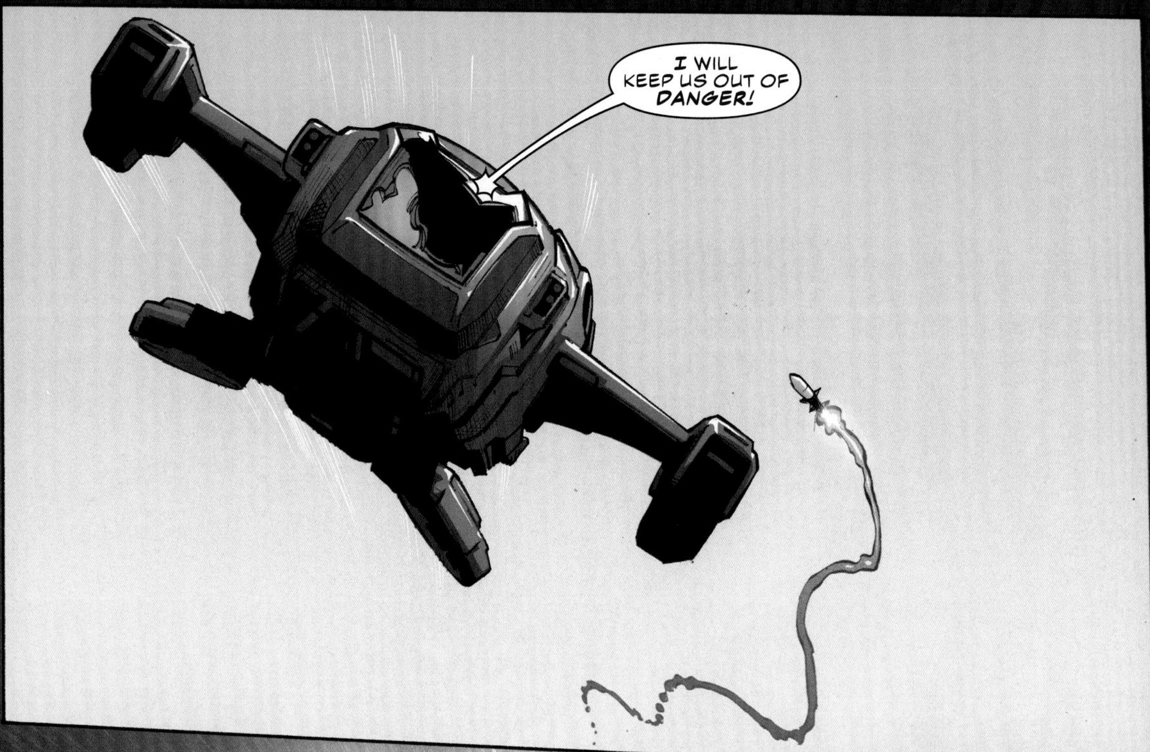
I WILL KEEP US OUT OF DANGER!
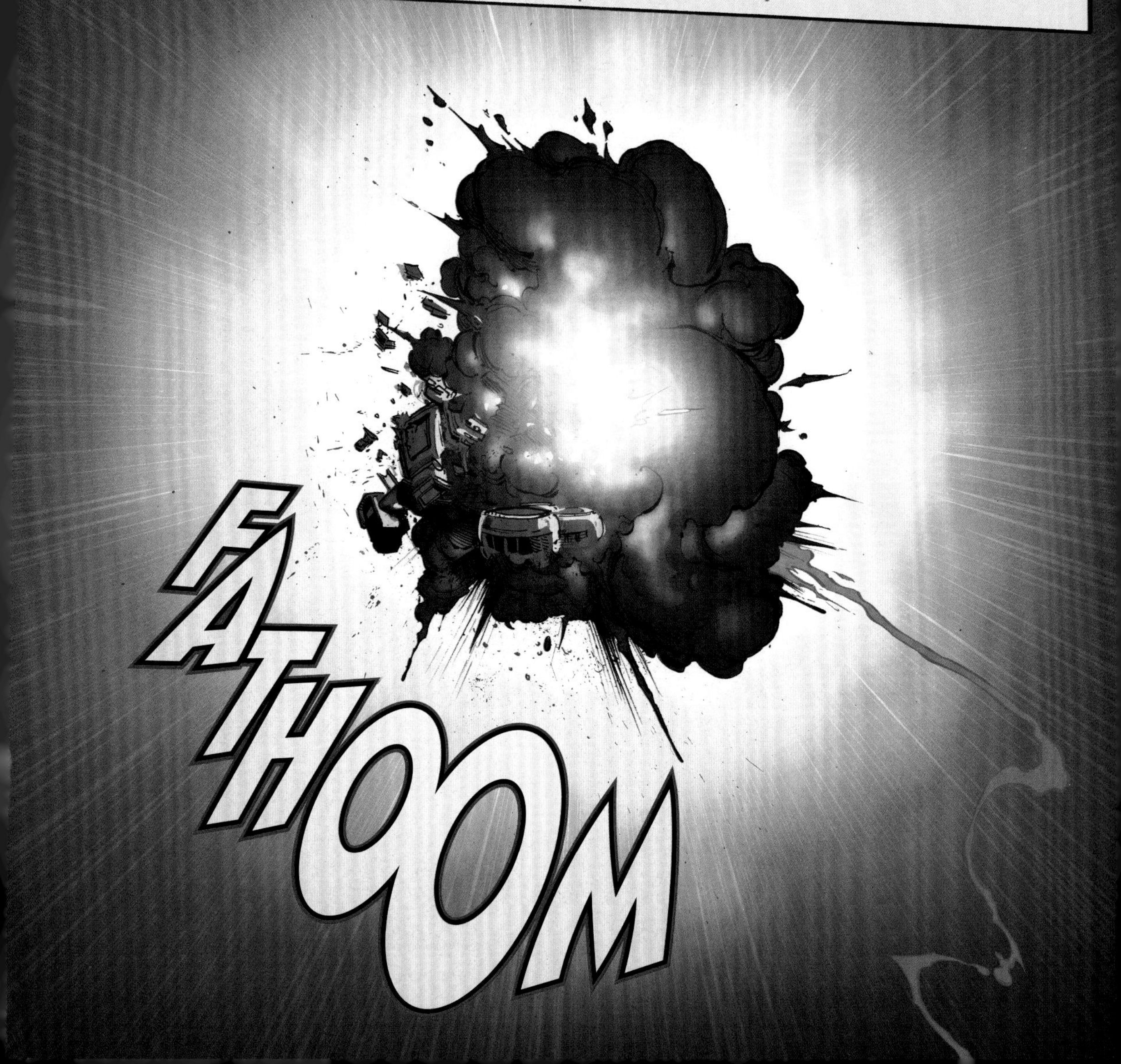
FATHOOM

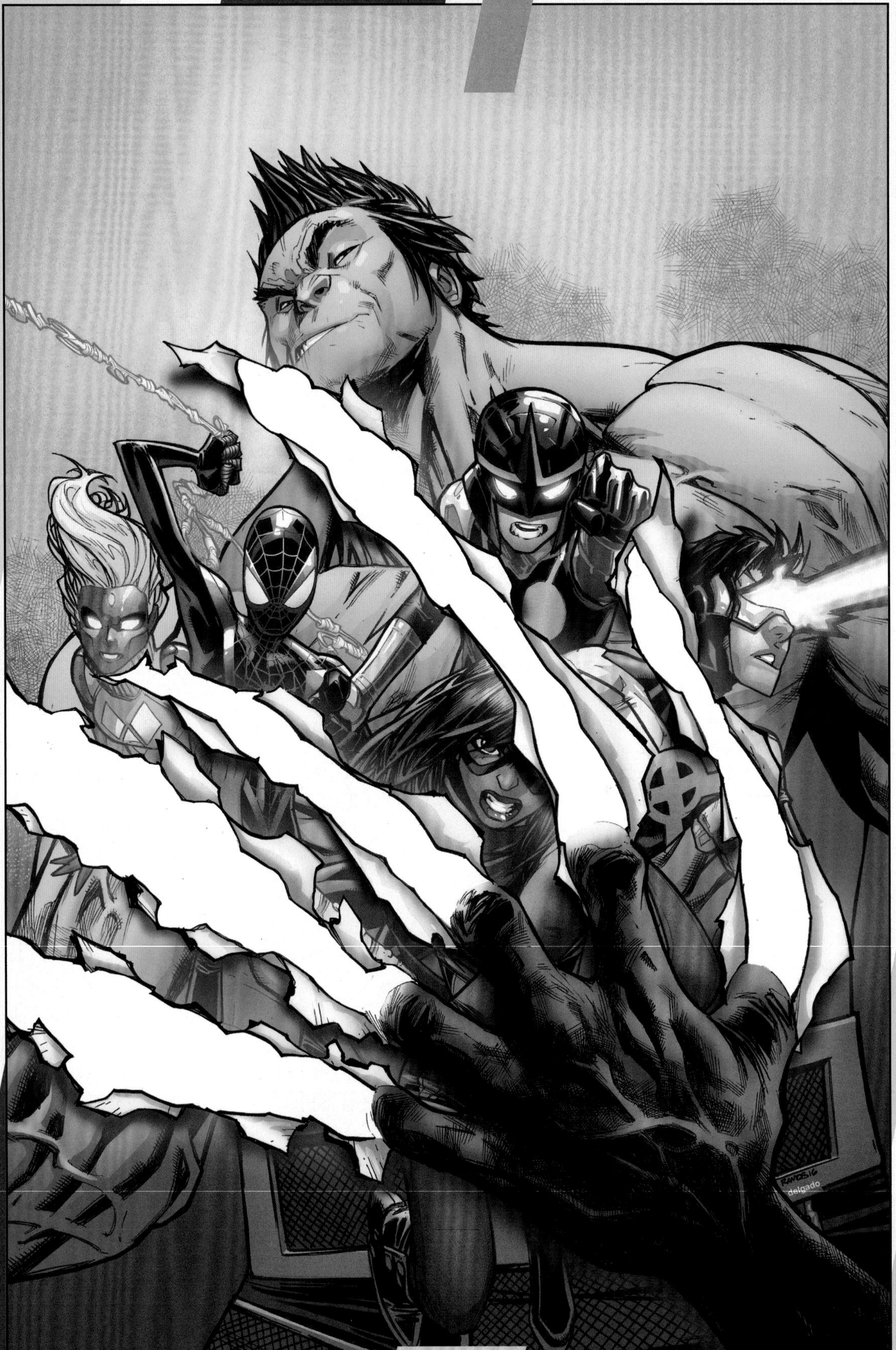

4

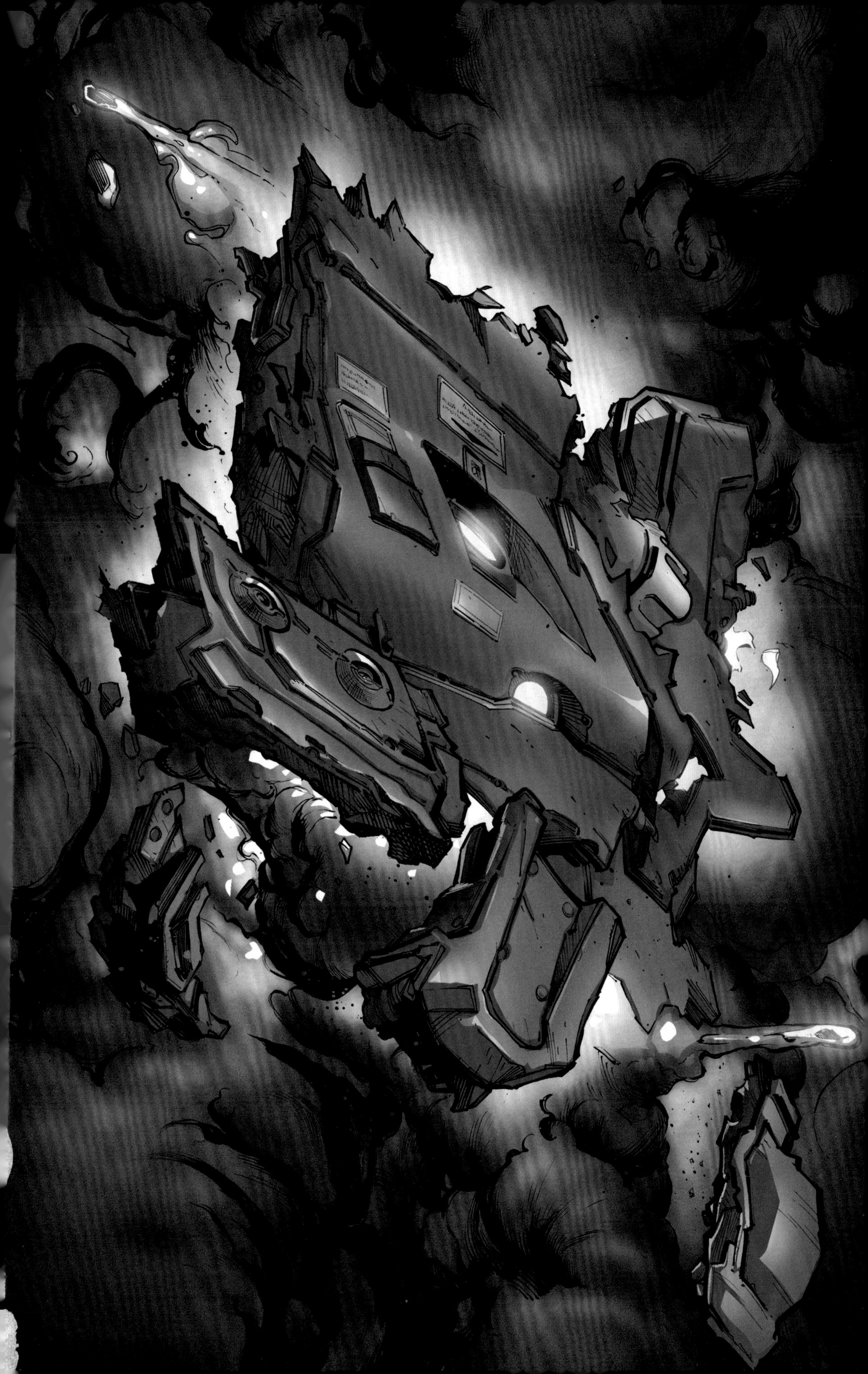

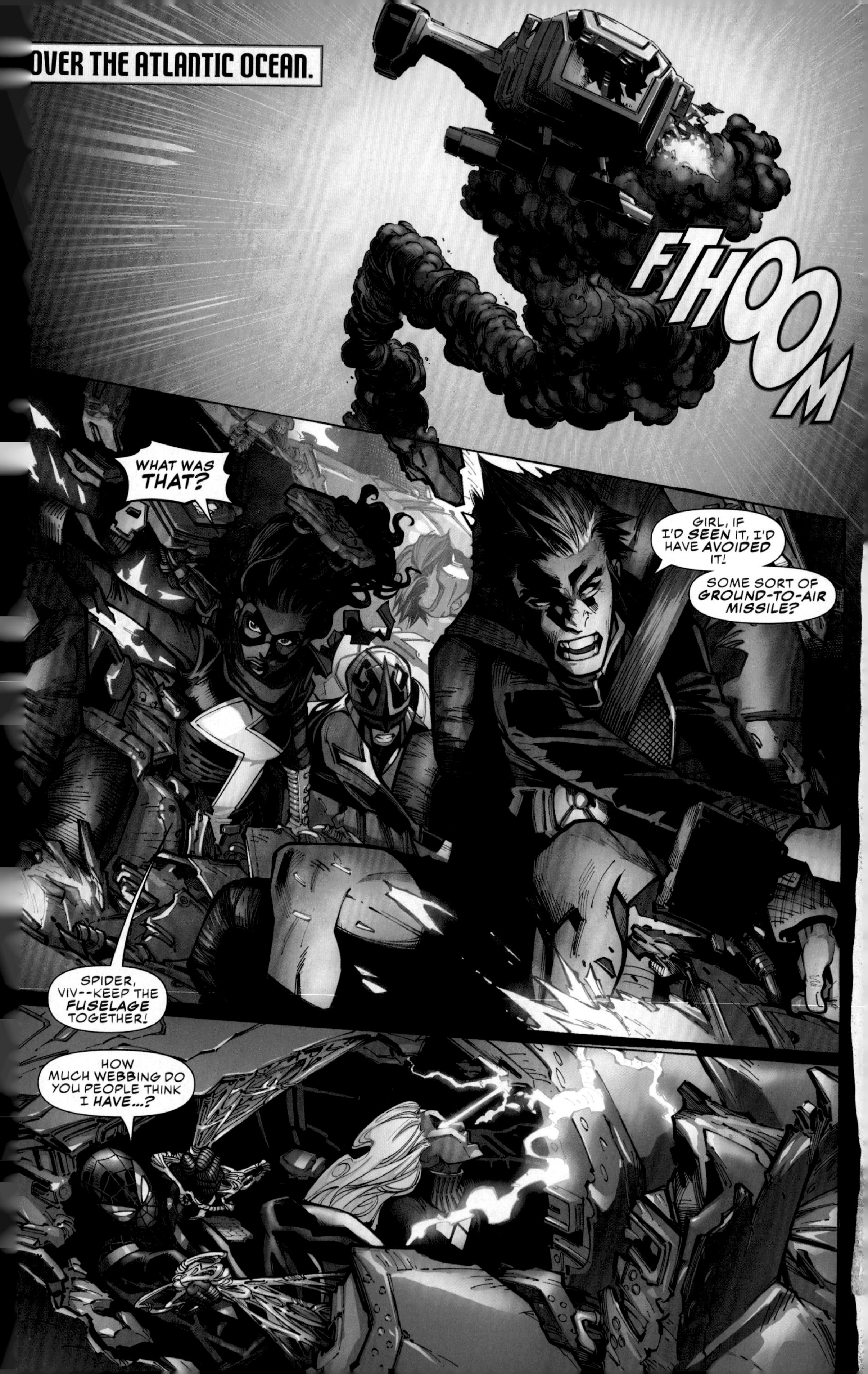
OVER THE ATLANTIC OCEAN.
FTHOOM
WHAT WAS THAT?
GIRL, IF I'D SEEN IT, I'D HAVE AVOIDED IT!
SOME SORT OF GROUND-TO-AIR MISSILE?
SPIDER, VIV--KEEP THE FUSELAGE TOGETHER!
HOW MUCH WEBBING DO YOU PEOPLE THINK I HAVE...?

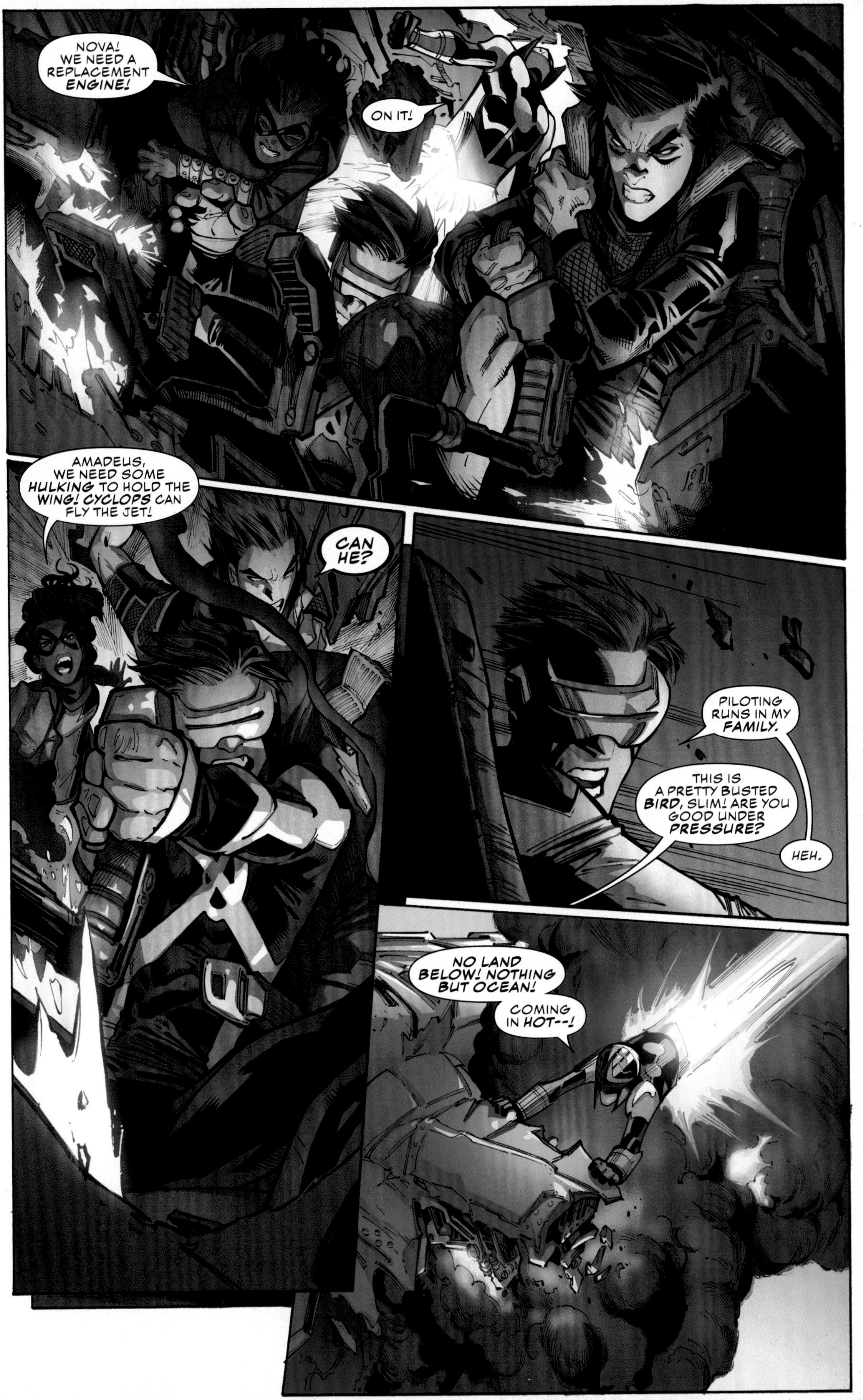
NOVA! WE NEED A REPLACEMENT ENGINE!
ON IT!
AMADEUS, WE NEED SOME HULKING TO HOLD THE WING! CYCLOPS CAN FLY THE JET!
CAN HE?
PILOTING RUNS IN MY FAMILY.
THIS IS A PRETTY BUSTED BIRD, SLIM! ARE YOU GOOD UNDER PRESSURE?
HEH.
NO LAND BELOW! NOTHING BUT OCEAN!
COMING IN HOT--!

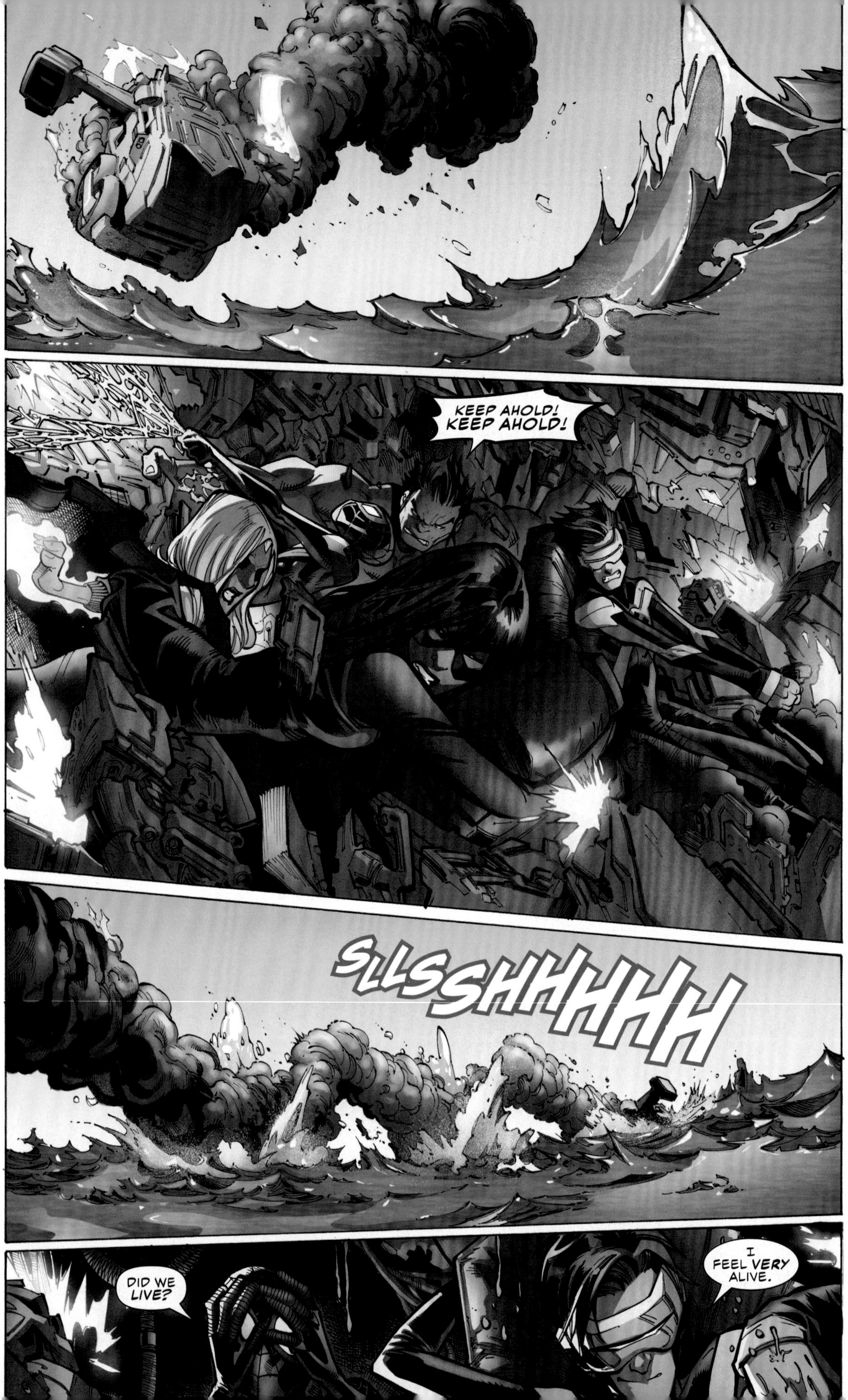
KEEP AHOLD! KEEP AHOLD!
SLLSSHHHHHH
DID WE LIVE?
I FEEL VERY ALIVE.

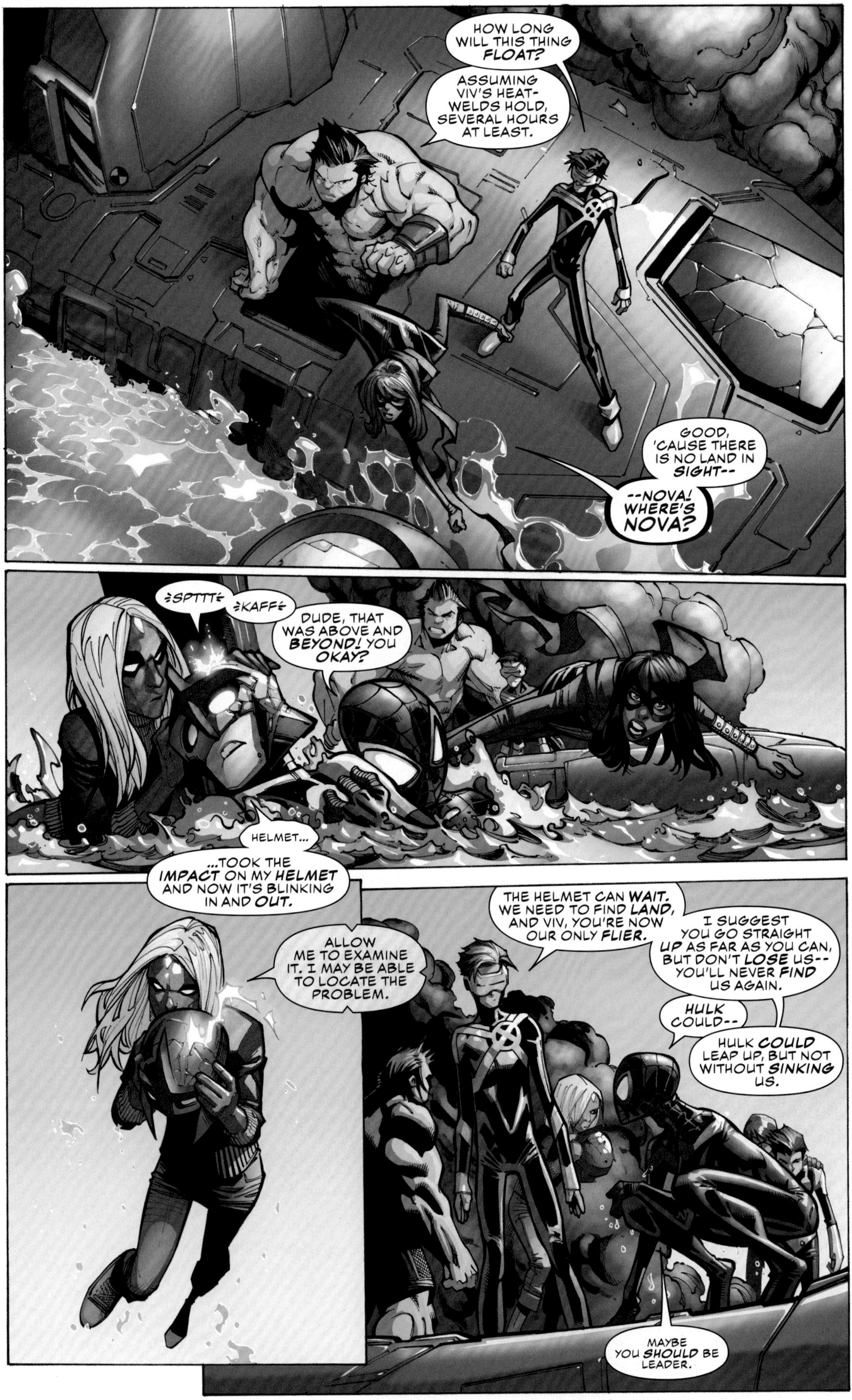
HOW LONG WILL THIS THING FLOAT?
ASSUMING VIV'S HEAT-WELDS HOLD, SEVERAL HOURS AT LEAST.
GOOD, 'CAUSE THERE IS NO LAND IN SIGHT--
--NOVA! WHERE'S NOVA?
SPTTT
KAFF
DUDE, THAT WAS ABOVE AND BEYOND! YOU OKAY?
HELMET...
...TOOK THE IMPACT ON MY HELMET AND NOW IT'S BLINKING IN AND OUT.
ALLOW ME TO EXAMINE IT. I MAY BE ABLE TO LOCATE THE PROBLEM.
THE HELMET CAN WAIT. WE NEED TO FIND LAND, AND VIV, YOU'RE NOW OUR ONLY FLIER.
I SUGGEST YOU GO STRAIGHT UP AS FAR AS YOU CAN, BUT DON'T LOSE US-- YOU'LL NEVER FIND US AGAIN.
HULK COULD--
HULK COULD LEAP UP, BUT NOT WITHOUT SINKING US.
MAYBE YOU SHOULD BE LEADER.

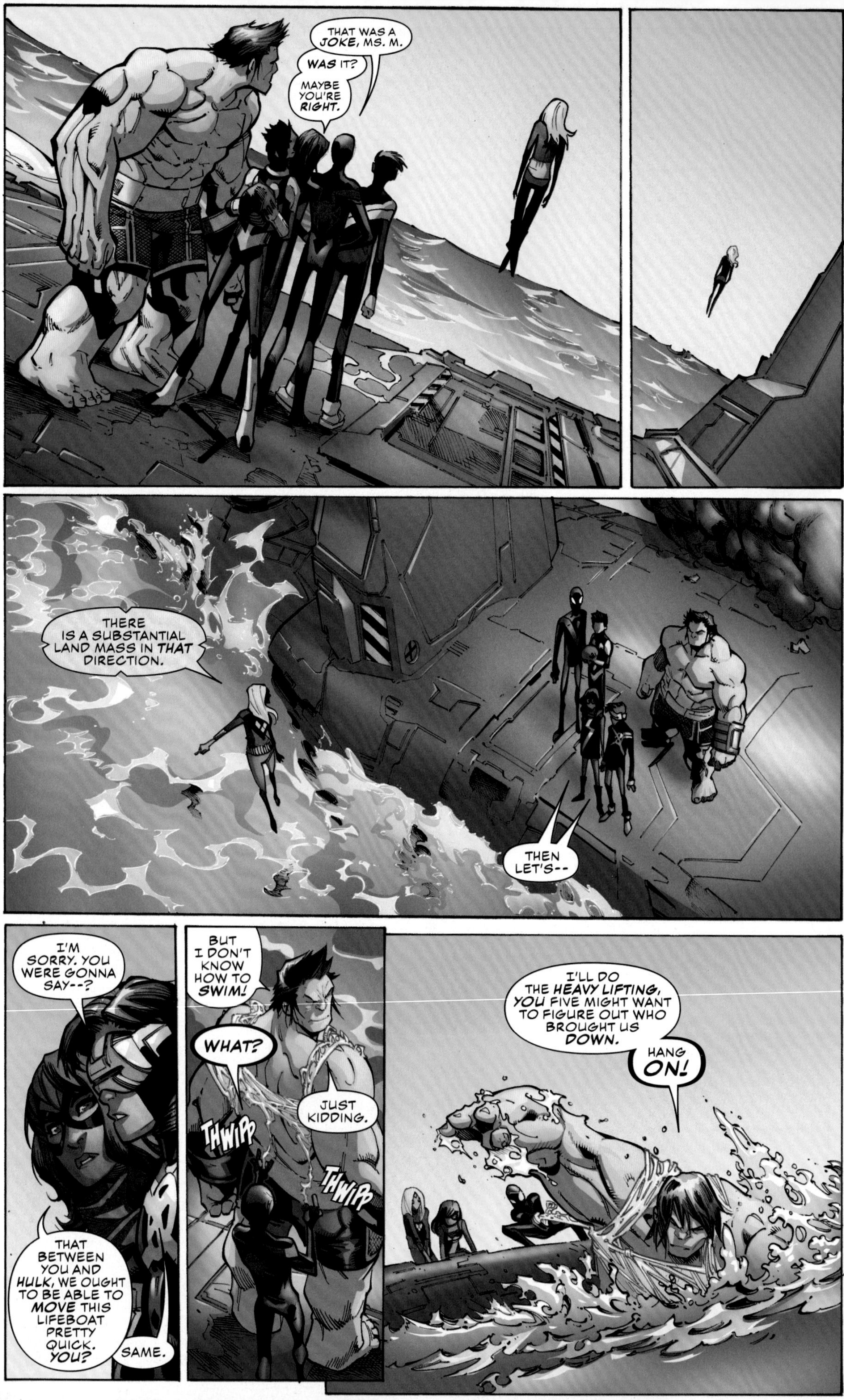
THAT WAS A JOKE, MS. M.
WAS IT?
MAYBE YOU'RE RIGHT.
THERE IS A SUBSTANTIAL LAND MASS IN THAT DIRECTION.
THEN LET'S--
I'M SORRY. YOU WERE GONNA SAY--?
THAT BETWEEN YOU AND HULK, WE OUGHT TO BE ABLE TO MOVE THIS LIFEBOAT PRETTY QUICK. YOU?
SAME.
BUT I DON'T KNOW HOW TO SWIM!
WHAT?
JUST KIDDING.
THWIPP
THWIPP
I'LL DO THE HEAVY LIFTING, YOU FIVE MIGHT WANT TO FIGURE OUT WHO BROUGHT US DOWN.
HANG ON!

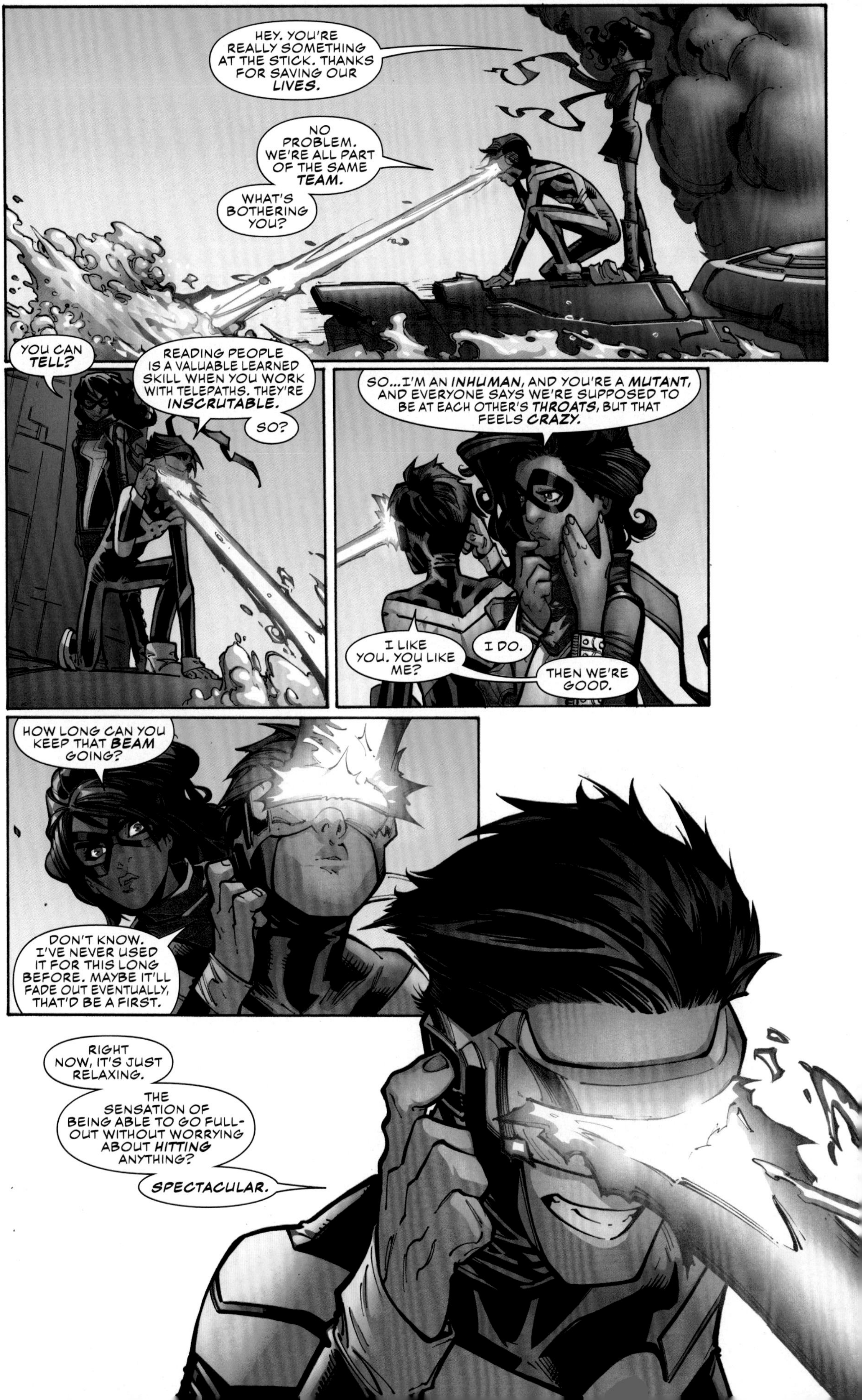
HEY. YOU'RE REALLY SOMETHING AT THE STICK. THANKS FOR SAVING OUR LIVES.
NO PROBLEM. WE'RE ALL PART OF THE SAME TEAM.
WHAT'S BOTHERING YOU?
YOU CAN TELL?
READING PEOPLE IS A VALUABLE LEARNED SKILL WHEN YOU WORK WITH TELEPATHS. THEY'RE INSCRUTABLE.
SO?
SO...I'M AN INHUMAN, AND YOU'RE A MUTANT, AND EVERYONE SAYS WE'RE SUPPOSED TO BE AT EACH OTHER'S THROATS, BUT THAT FEELS CRAZY.
I LIKE YOU. YOU LIKE ME?
I DO.
THEN WE'RE GOOD.
HOW LONG CAN YOU KEEP THAT BEAM GOING?
DON'T KNOW. I'VE NEVER USED IT FOR THIS LONG BEFORE. MAYBE IT'LL FADE OUT EVENTUALLY, THAT'D BE A FIRST.
RIGHT NOW, IT'S JUST RELAXING.
THE SENSATION OF BEING ABLE TO GO FULL-OUT WITHOUT WORRYING ABOUT HITTING ANYTHING?
SPECTACULAR.

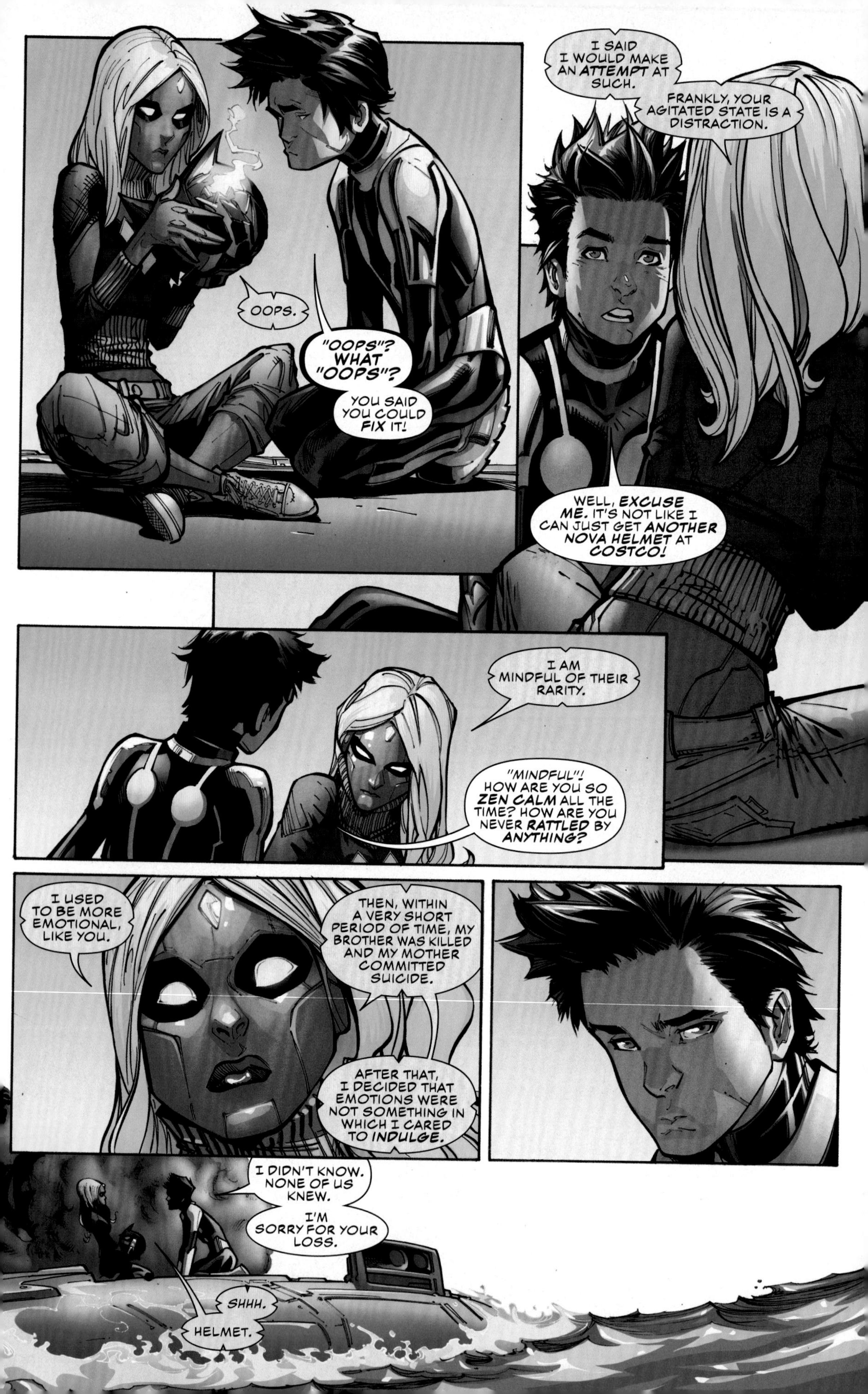
OOPS.
"OOPS"? WHAT "OOPS"?
YOU SAID YOU COULD FIX IT!
I SAID I WOULD MAKE AN ATTEMPT AT SUCH.
FRANKLY, YOUR AGITATED STATE IS A DISTRACTION.
WELL, EXCUSE ME. IT'S NOT LIKE I CAN JUST GET ANOTHER NOVA HELMET AT COSTCO!
I AM MINDFUL OF THEIR RARITY.
"MINDFUL"! HOW ARE YOU SO ZEN CALM ALL THE TIME? HOW ARE YOU NEVER RATTLED BY ANYTHING?
I USED TO BE MORE EMOTIONAL, LIKE YOU.
THEN, WITHIN A VERY SHORT PERIOD OF TIME, MY BROTHER WAS KILLED AND MY MOTHER COMMITTED SUICIDE.
AFTER THAT, I DECIDED THAT EMOTIONS WERE NOT SOMETHING IN WHICH I CARED TO INDULGE.
I DIDN'T KNOW. NONE OF US KNEW.
I'M SORRY FOR YOUR LOSS.
SHHH.
HELMET.

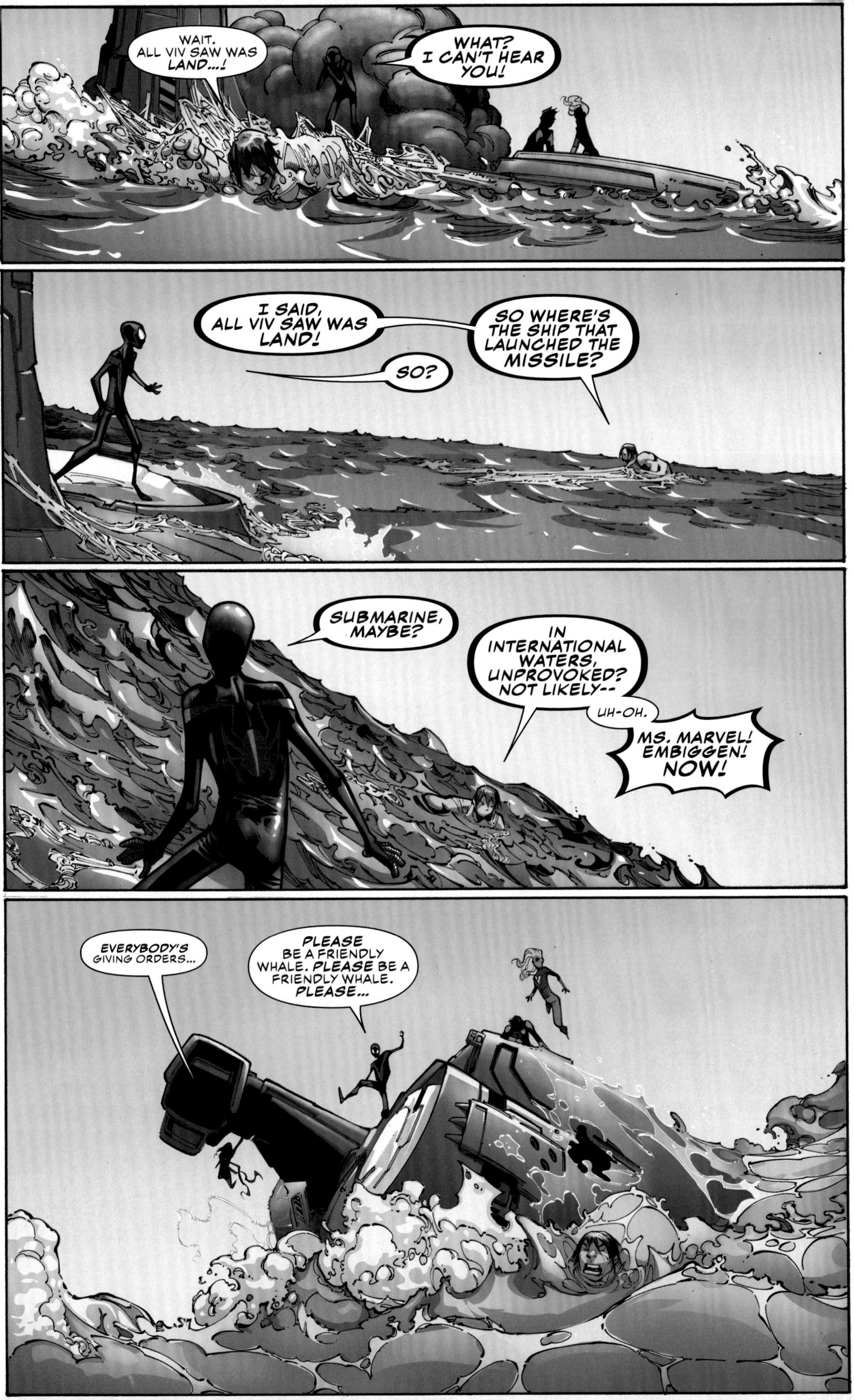
WAIT. ALL VIV SAW WAS LAND...!
WHAT? I CAN'T HEAR YOU!
I SAID, ALL VIV SAW WAS LAND!
SO?
SO WHERE'S THE SHIP THAT LAUNCHED THE MISSILE?
SUBMARINE, MAYBE?
IN INTERNATIONAL WATERS, UNPROVOKED? NOT LIKELY--
UH-OH.
MS. MARVEL! EMBIGGEN! NOW!
EVERYBODY'S GIVING ORDERS...
PLEASE BE A FRIENDLY WHALE. PLEASE BE A FRIENDLY WHALE. PLEASE...

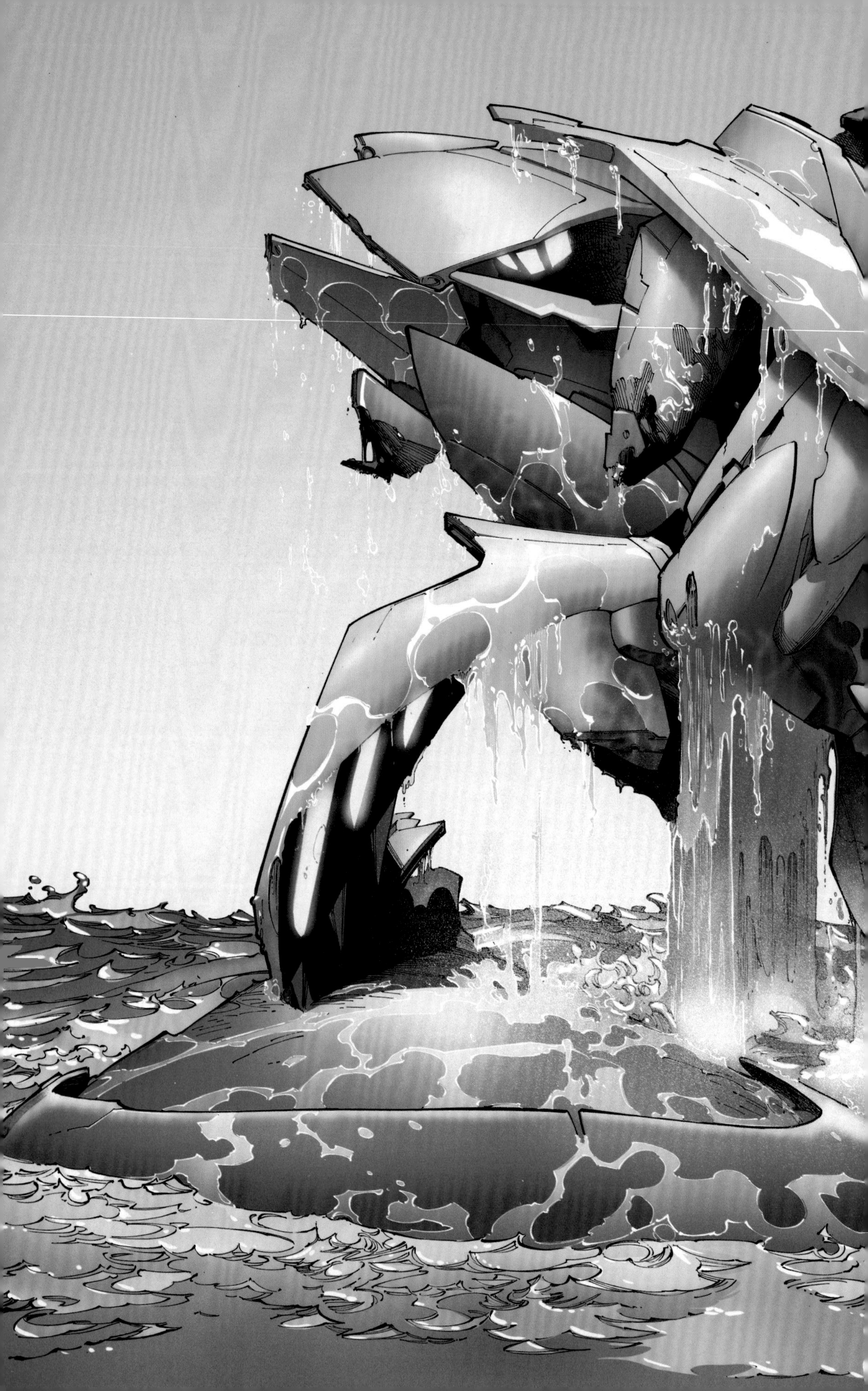

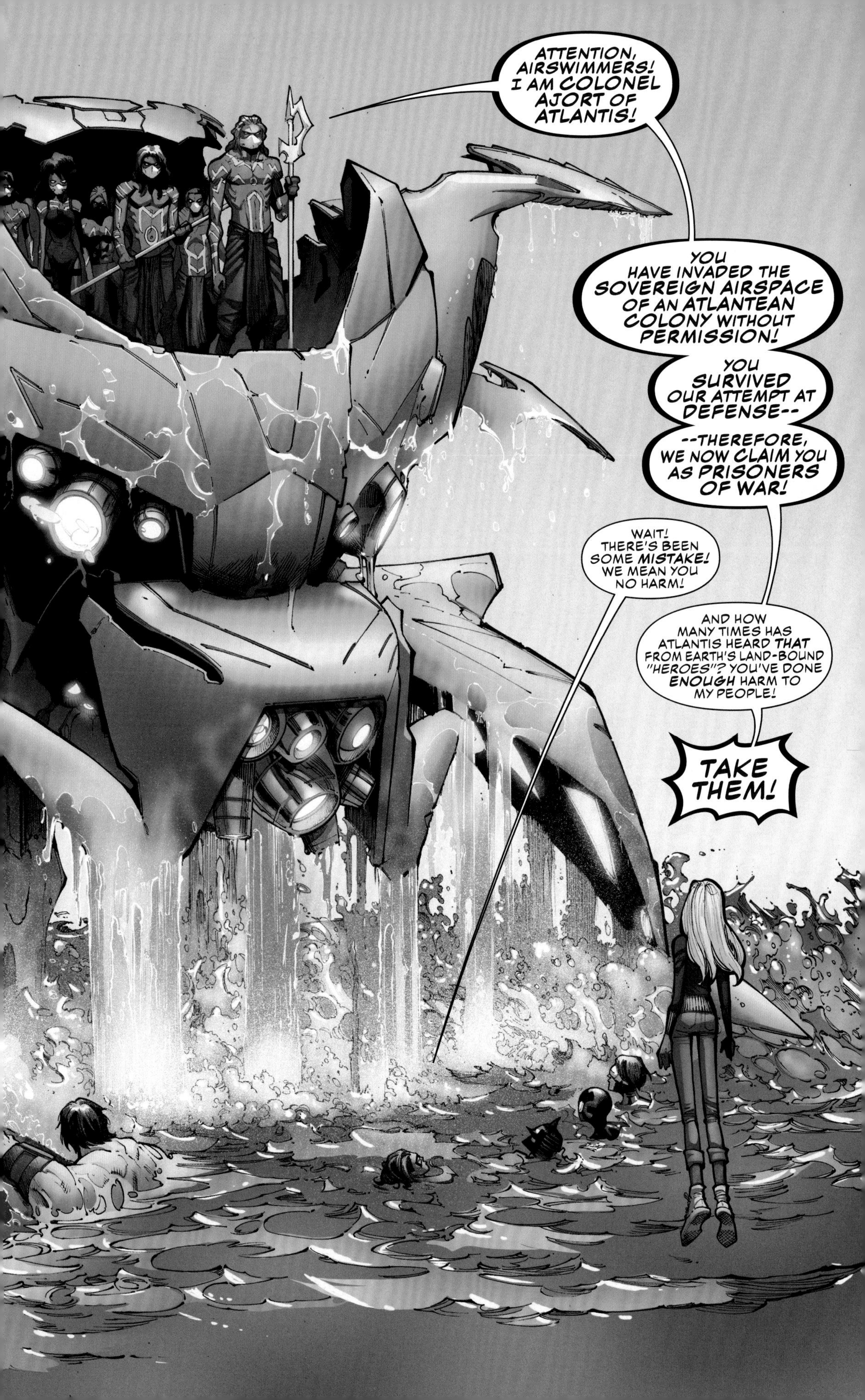

ATTENTION, AIRSWIMMERS! I AM COLONEL AJORT OF ATLANTIS!
YOU HAVE INVADED THE SOVEREIGN AIRSPACE OF AN ATLANTEAN COLONY WITHOUT PERMISSION!
YOU SURVIVED OUR ATTEMPT AT DEFENSE--
--THEREFORE, WE NOW CLAIM YOU AS PRISONERS OF WAR!
WAIT! THERE'S BEEN SOME MISTAKE! WE MEAN YOU NO HARM!
AND HOW MANY TIMES HAS ATLANTIS HEARD THAT FROM EARTH'S LAND-BOUND "HEROES"? YOU'VE DONE ENOUGH HARM TO MY PEOPLE!
TAKE THEM!

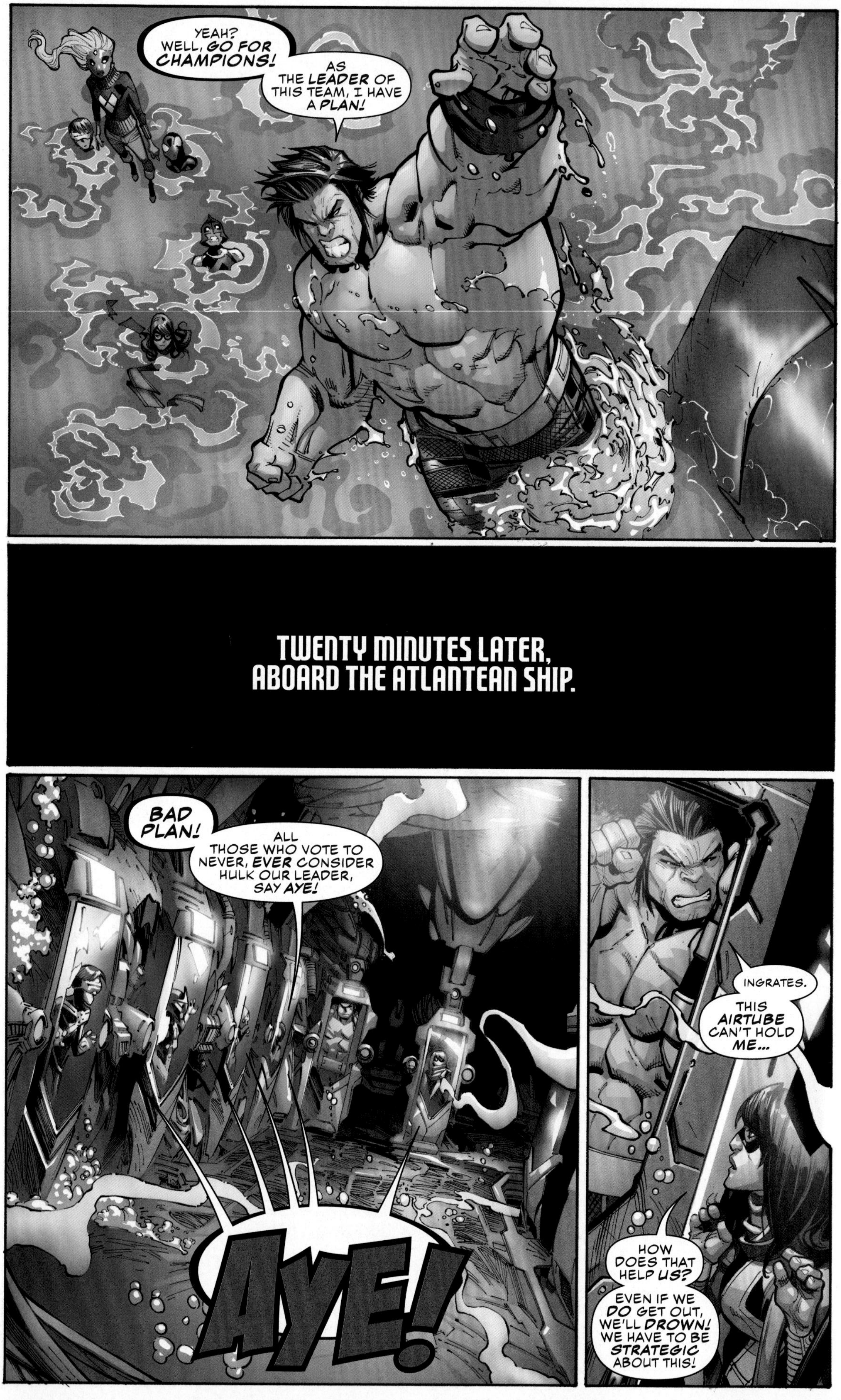
YEAH? WELL, GO FOR CHAMPIONS!
AS THE LEADER OF THIS TEAM, I HAVE A PLAN!
TWENTY MINUTES LATER, ABOARD THE ATLANTEAN SHIP.
BAD PLAN!
ALL THOSE WHO VOTE TO NEVER, EVER CONSIDER HULK OUR LEADER, SAY AYE!
AYE!
INGRATES.
THIS AIRTUBE CAN'T HOLD ME...
HOW DOES THAT HELP US?
EVEN IF WE DO GET OUT, WE'LL DROWN! WE HAVE TO BE STRATEGIC ABOUT THIS!

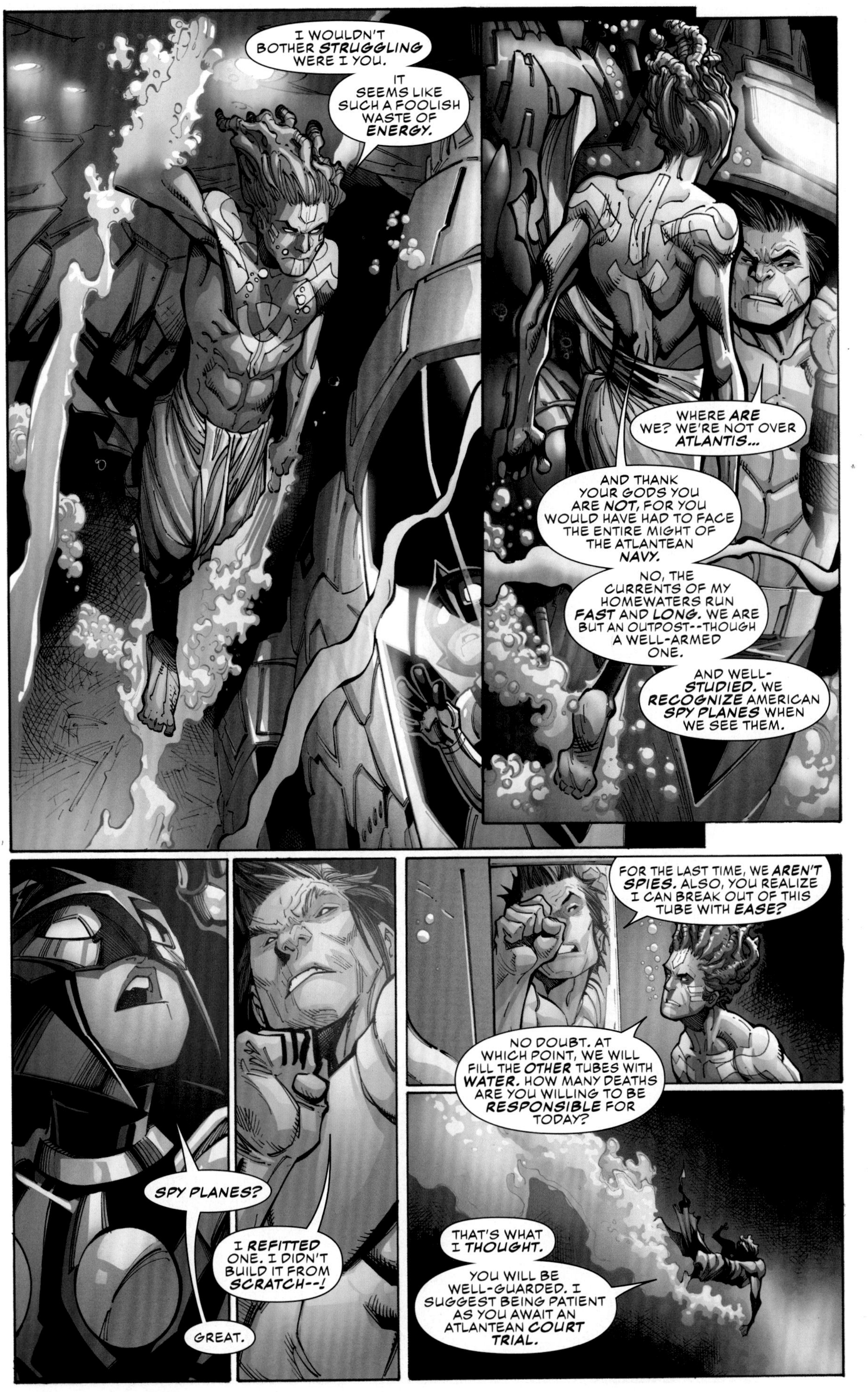
I WOULDN'T BOTHER STRUGGLING WERE I YOU.
IT SEEMS LIKE SUCH A FOOLISH WASTE OF ENERGY.
WHERE ARE WE? WE'RE NOT OVER ATLANTIS...
AND THANK YOUR GODS YOU ARE NOT, FOR YOU WOULD HAVE HAD TO FACE THE ENTIRE MIGHT OF THE ATLANTEAN NAVY.
NO, THE CURRENTS OF MY HOMEWATERS RUN FAST AND LONG. WE ARE BUT AN OUTPOST--THOUGH A WELL-ARMED ONE.
AND WELL-STUDIED. WE RECOGNIZE AMERICAN SPY PLANES WHEN WE SEE THEM.
SPY PLANES?
I REFITTED ONE. I DIDN'T BUILD IT FROM SCRATCH--!
GREAT.
FOR THE LAST TIME, WE AREN'T SPIES. ALSO, YOU REALIZE I CAN BREAK OUT OF THIS TUBE WITH EASE?
NO DOUBT. AT WHICH POINT, WE WILL FILL THE OTHER TUBES WITH WATER. HOW MANY DEATHS ARE YOU WILLING TO BE RESPONSIBLE FOR TODAY?
THAT'S WHAT I THOUGHT.
YOU WILL BE WELL-GUARDED. I SUGGEST BEING PATIENT AS YOU AWAIT AN ATLANTEAN COURT TRIAL.

リ刁ケ乇メリ乃ケ
リ彳仝仝ん仝リ乇 乃仝乇メリ
乄仝りと メ乇乃り

リ刁ケ乇メリ乃ケ
リ彳仝仝ん仝リ乇 BEFORE WE **SUBMERGE**, FLUSH THE **STALE WATER** IN THIS SHIP AND **RE-AQUIFY!**

YES, SIR!

I CAN **TRANSLATE.** WE'RE STILL NEAR THE **SURFACE.**

THOSE **LEVERS**--THEY CAN PURGE THE SHIP OF WATER AND BRING IN **AIR.**

I WILL **ACTIVATE** THEM.

VIV, **WAIT!** DON'T TRY IT **ALONE--!**

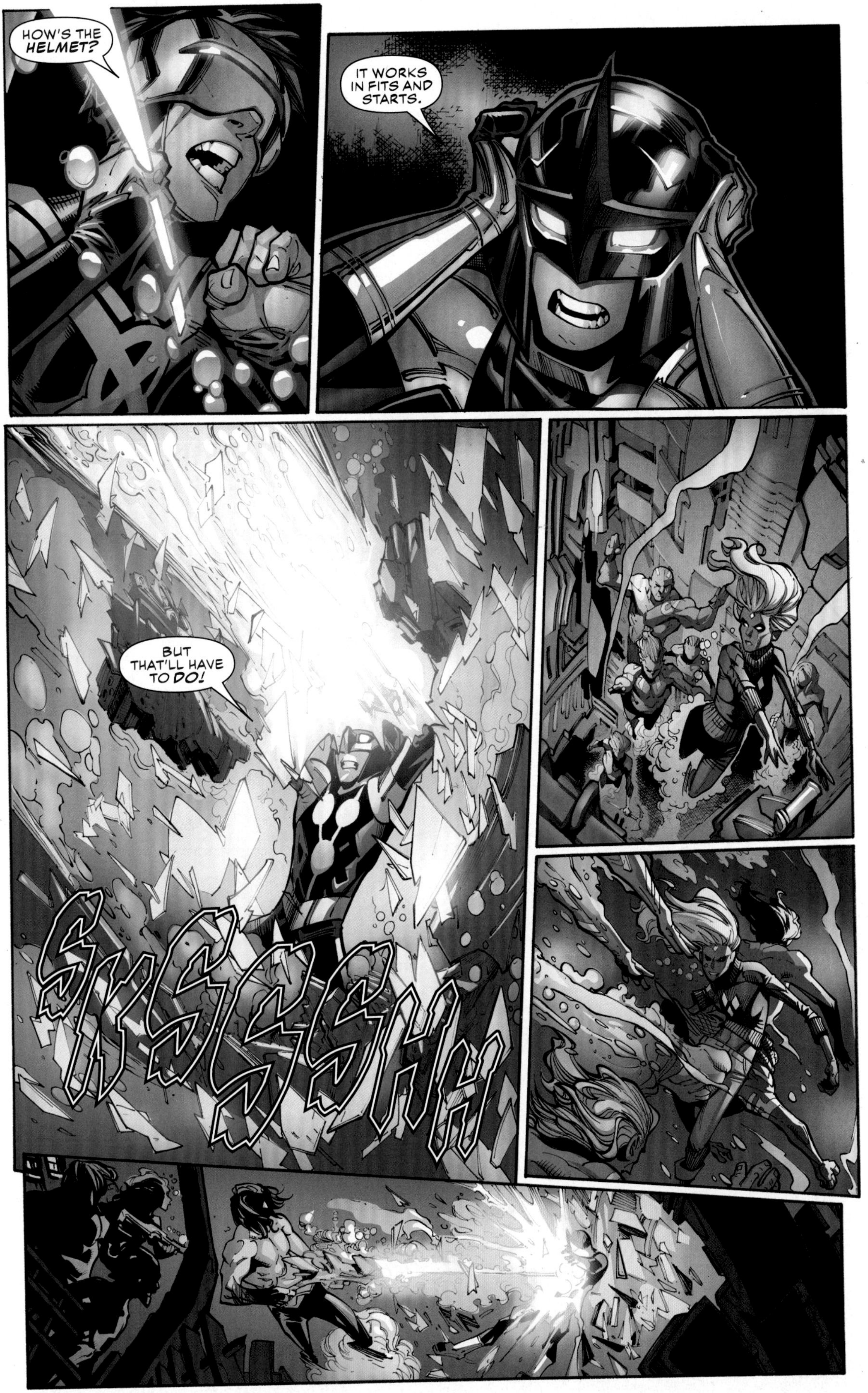
HOW'S THE HELMET?
IT WORKS IN FITS AND STARTS.
BUT THAT'LL HAVE TO DO!
SKSSSHH

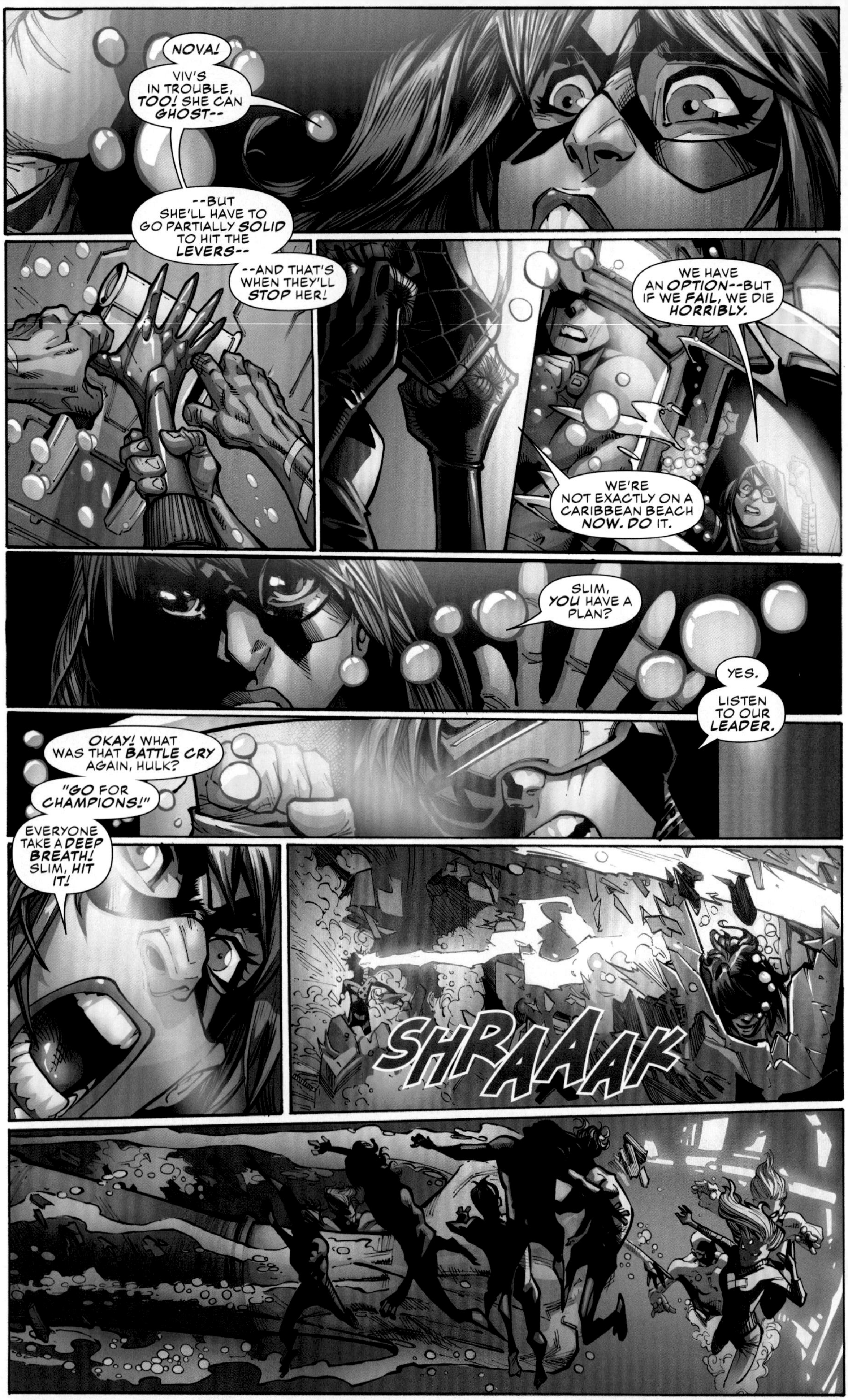
NOVA!
VIV'S IN TROUBLE, TOO! SHE CAN GHOST--
--BUT SHE'LL HAVE TO GO PARTIALLY SOLID TO HIT THE LEVERS--
--AND THAT'S WHEN THEY'LL STOP HER!
WE HAVE AN OPTION--BUT IF WE FAIL, WE DIE HORRIBLY.
WE'RE NOT EXACTLY ON A CARIBBEAN BEACH NOW. DO IT.
SLIM, YOU HAVE A PLAN?
YES.
LISTEN TO OUR LEADER.
OKAY! WHAT WAS THAT BATTLE CRY AGAIN, HULK?
"GO FOR CHAMPIONS!"
EVERYONE TAKE A DEEP BREATH! SLIM, HIT IT!
SHRAAAK

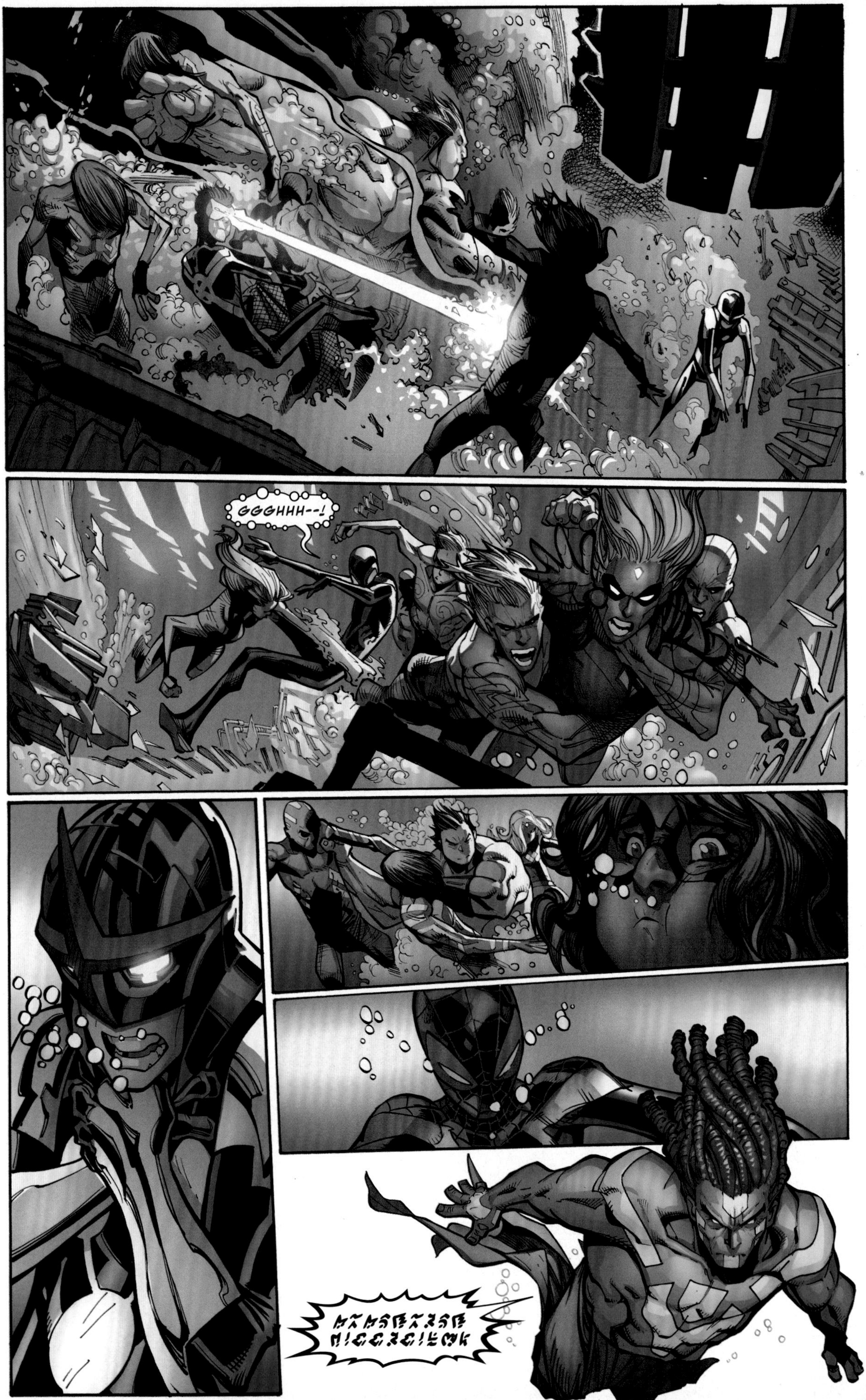
GGGHHH--!

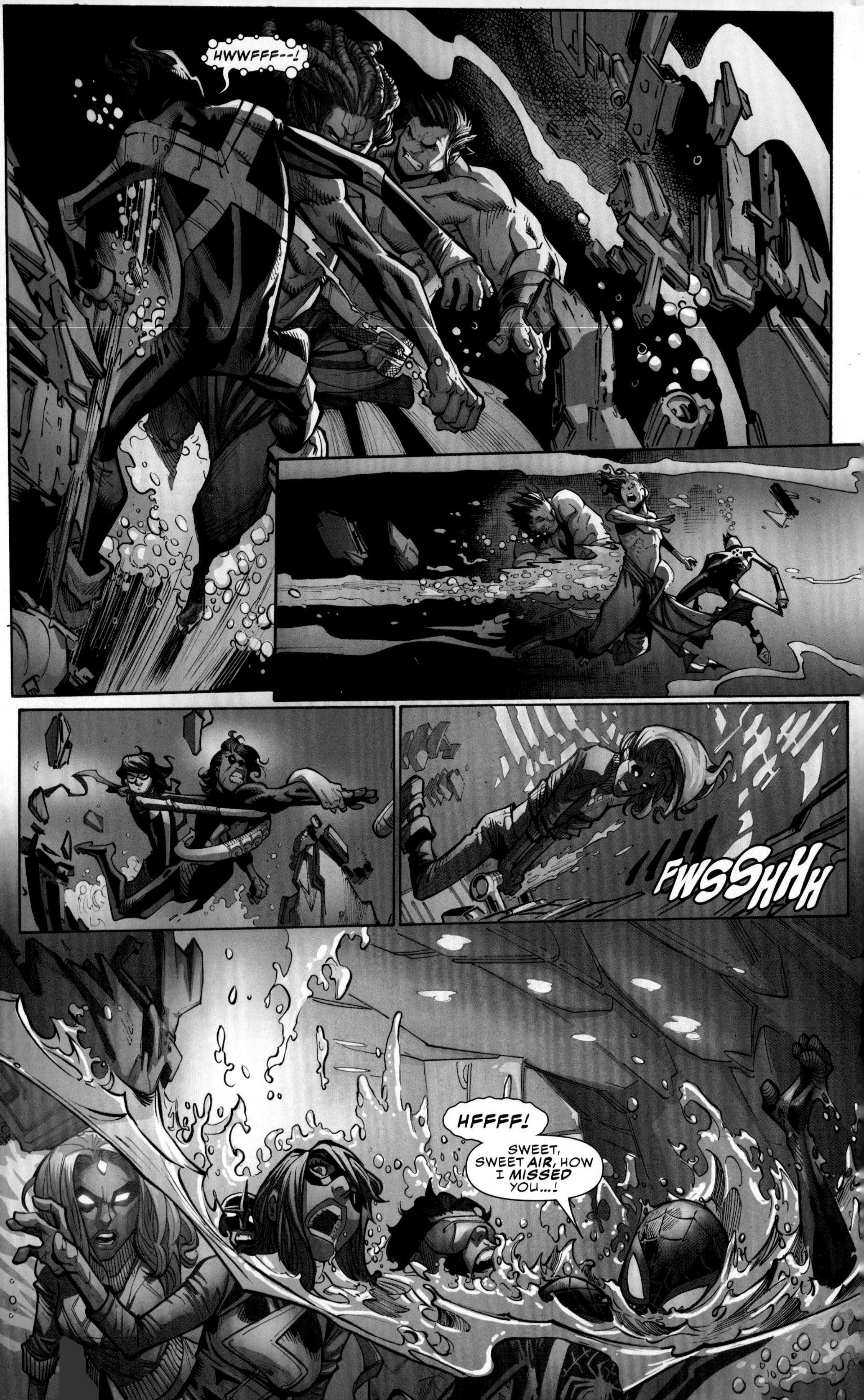
HWWFFF--!
FWSSHHH
HFFFF!
SWEET, SWEET AIR, HOW I MISSED YOU...!

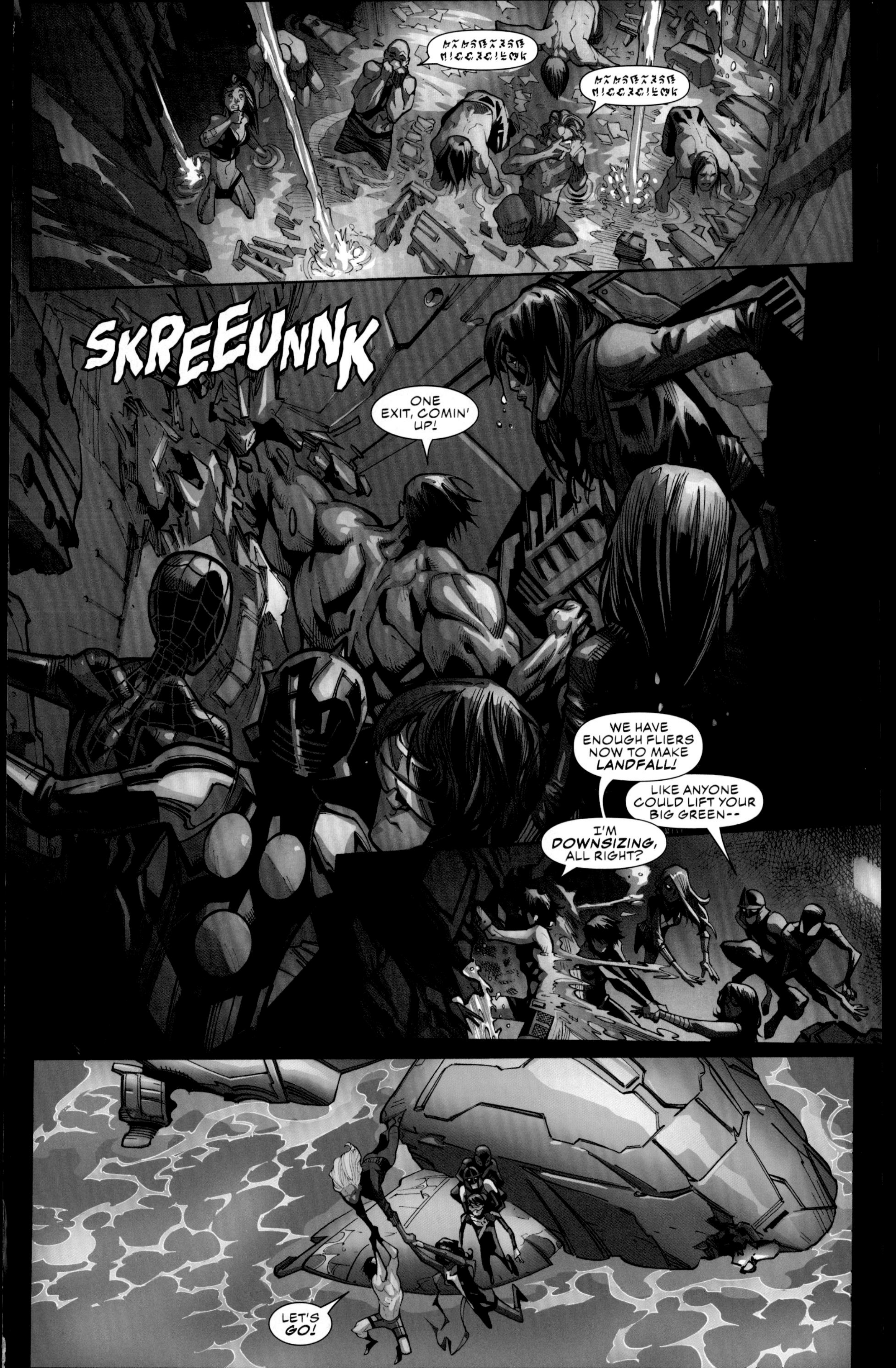
SKREEUNNK
ONE EXIT, COMIN' UP!
WE HAVE ENOUGH FLIERS NOW TO MAKE LANDFALL!
LIKE ANYONE COULD LIFT YOUR BIG GREEN--
I'M DOWNSIZING, ALL RIGHT?
LET'S GO!

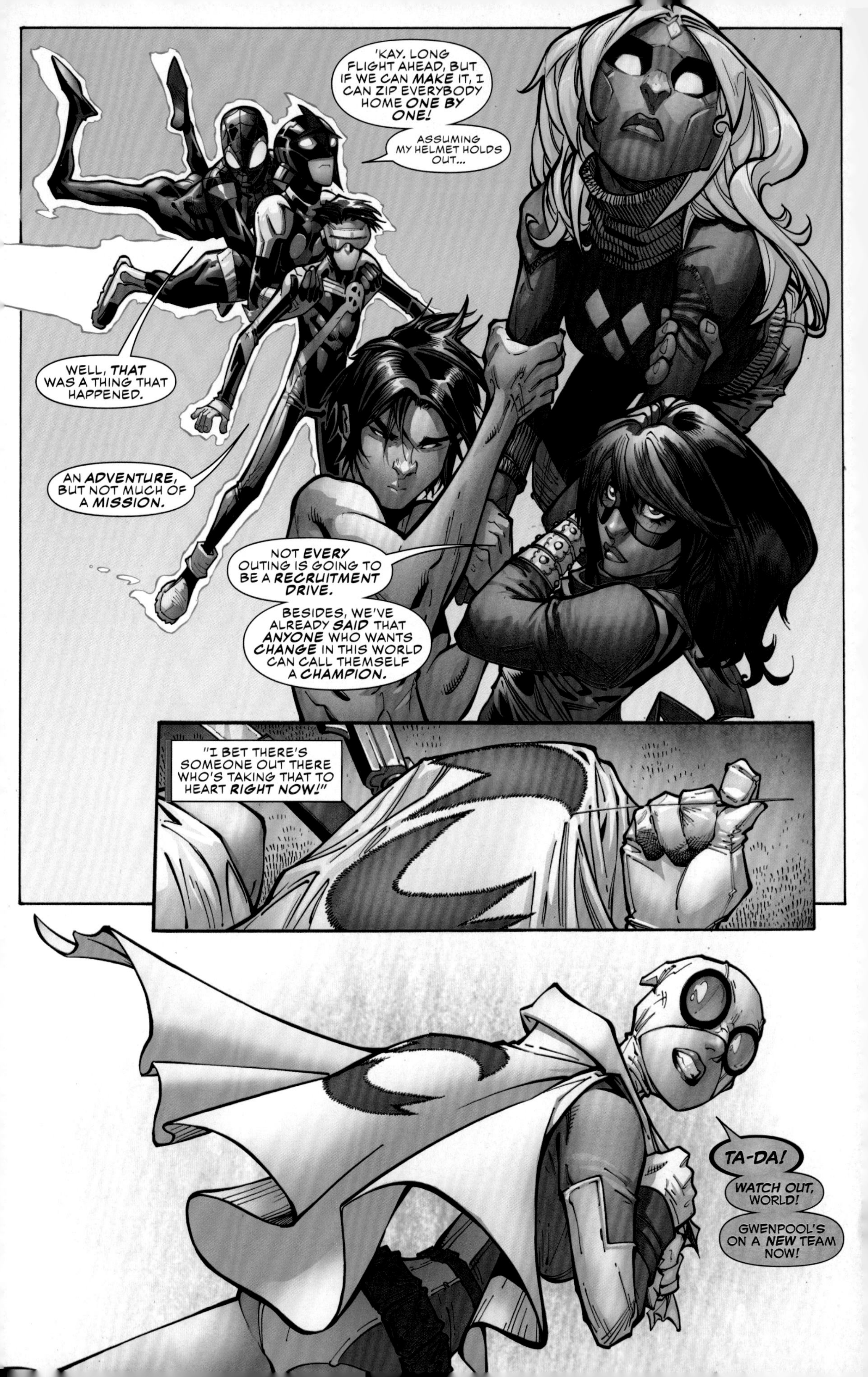
'KAY. LONG FLIGHT AHEAD, BUT IF WE CAN MAKE IT, I CAN ZIP EVERYBODY HOME ONE BY ONE!
ASSUMING MY HELMET HOLDS OUT...
WELL, THAT WAS A THING THAT HAPPENED.
AN ADVENTURE, BUT NOT MUCH OF A MISSION.
NOT EVERY OUTING IS GOING TO BE A RECRUITMENT DRIVE.
BESIDES, WE'VE ALREADY SAID THAT ANYONE WHO WANTS CHANGE IN THIS WORLD CAN CALL THEMSELF A CHAMPION.
"I BET THERE'S SOMEONE OUT THERE WHO'S TAKING THAT TO HEART RIGHT NOW!"
TA-DA!
WATCH OUT, WORLD!
GWENPOOL'S ON A NEW TEAM NOW!

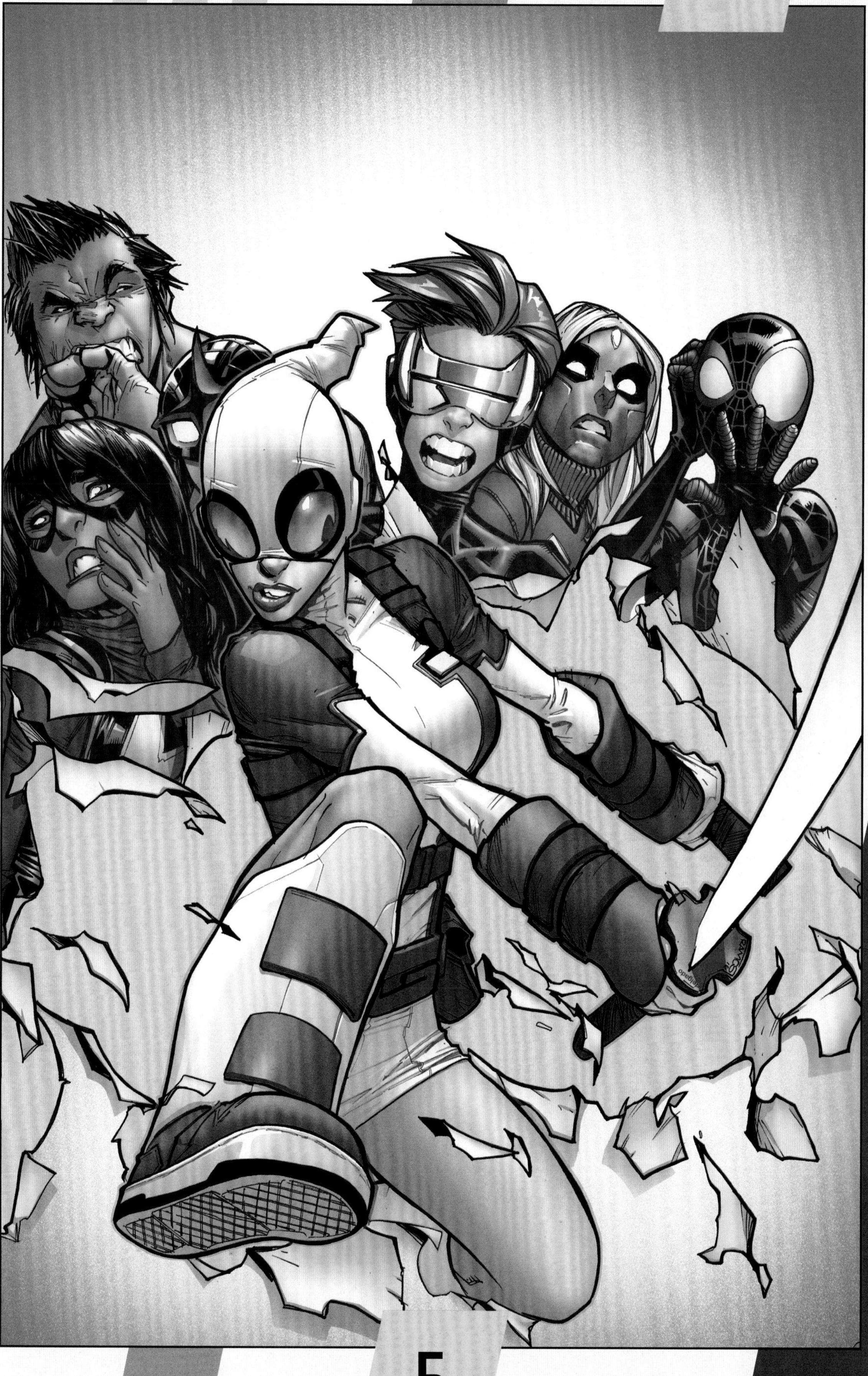

5

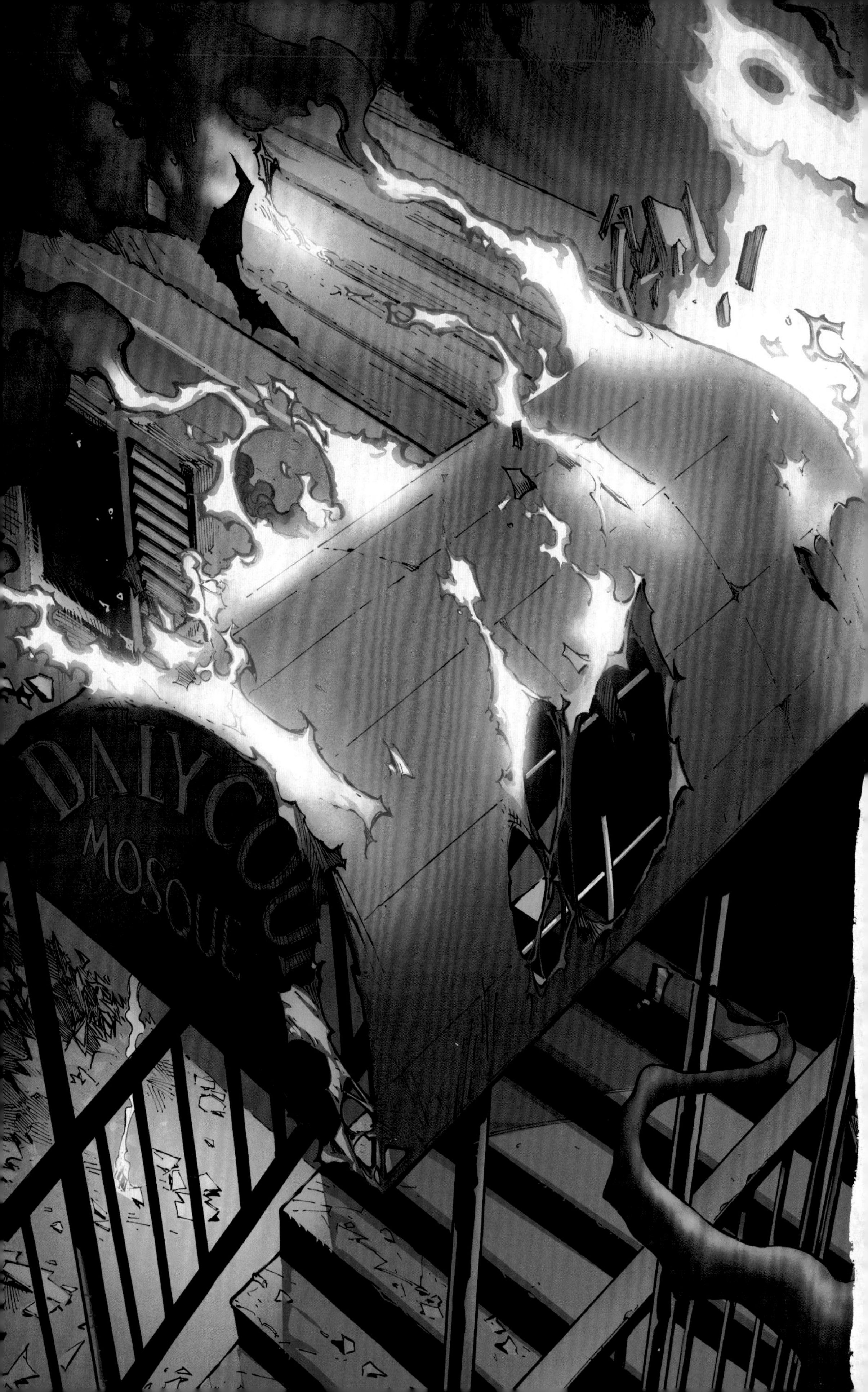
MOSQUE

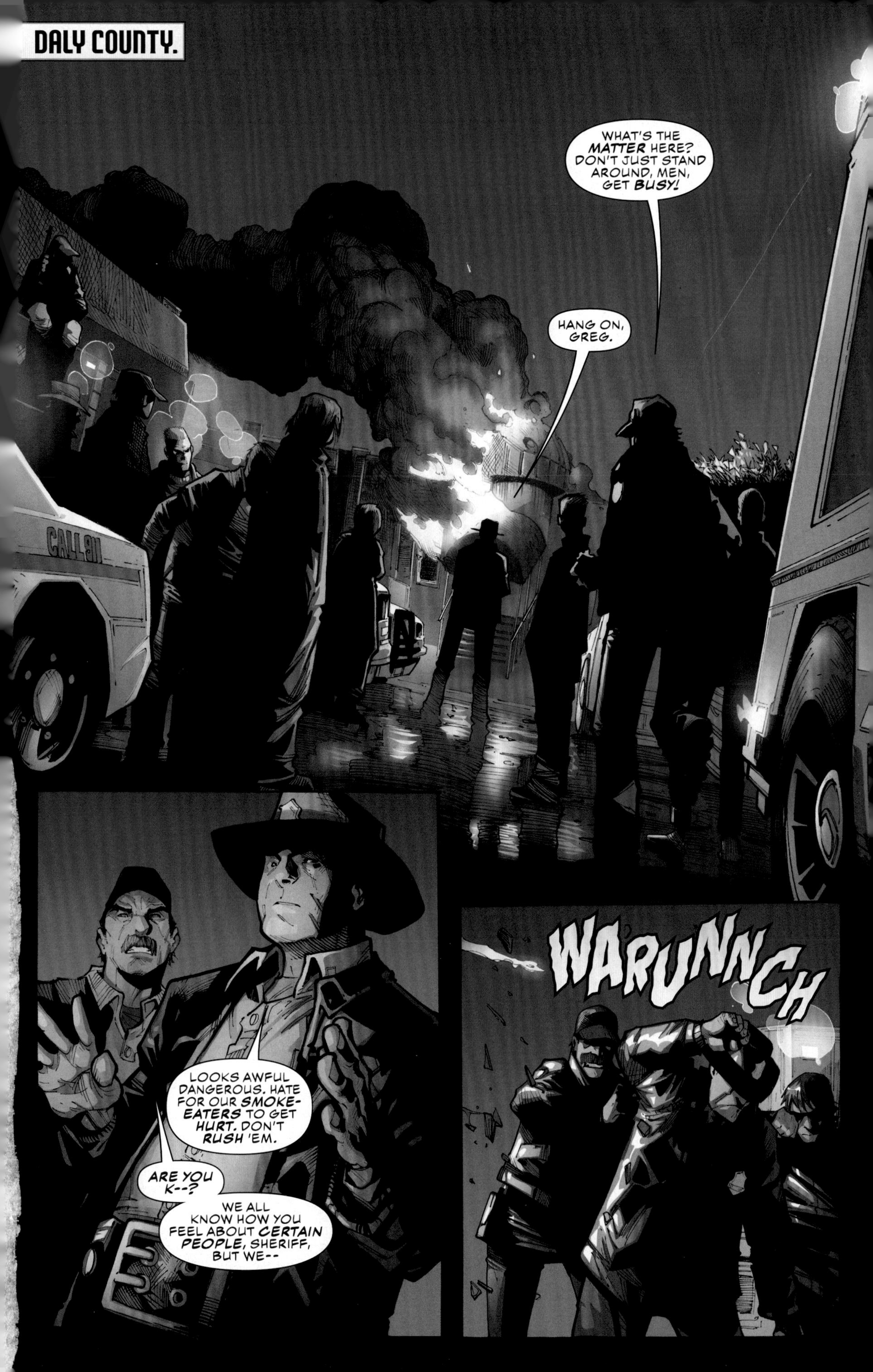
DALY COUNTY.
WHAT'S THE MATTER HERE? DON'T JUST STAND AROUND, MEN, GET BUSY!
HANG ON, GREG.
LOOKS AWFUL DANGEROUS. HATE FOR OUR SMOKE-EATERS TO GET HURT. DON'T RUSH 'EM.
ARE YOU K--?
WE ALL KNOW HOW YOU FEEL ABOUT CERTAIN PEOPLE, SHERIFF, BUT WE--
WARUNNCH

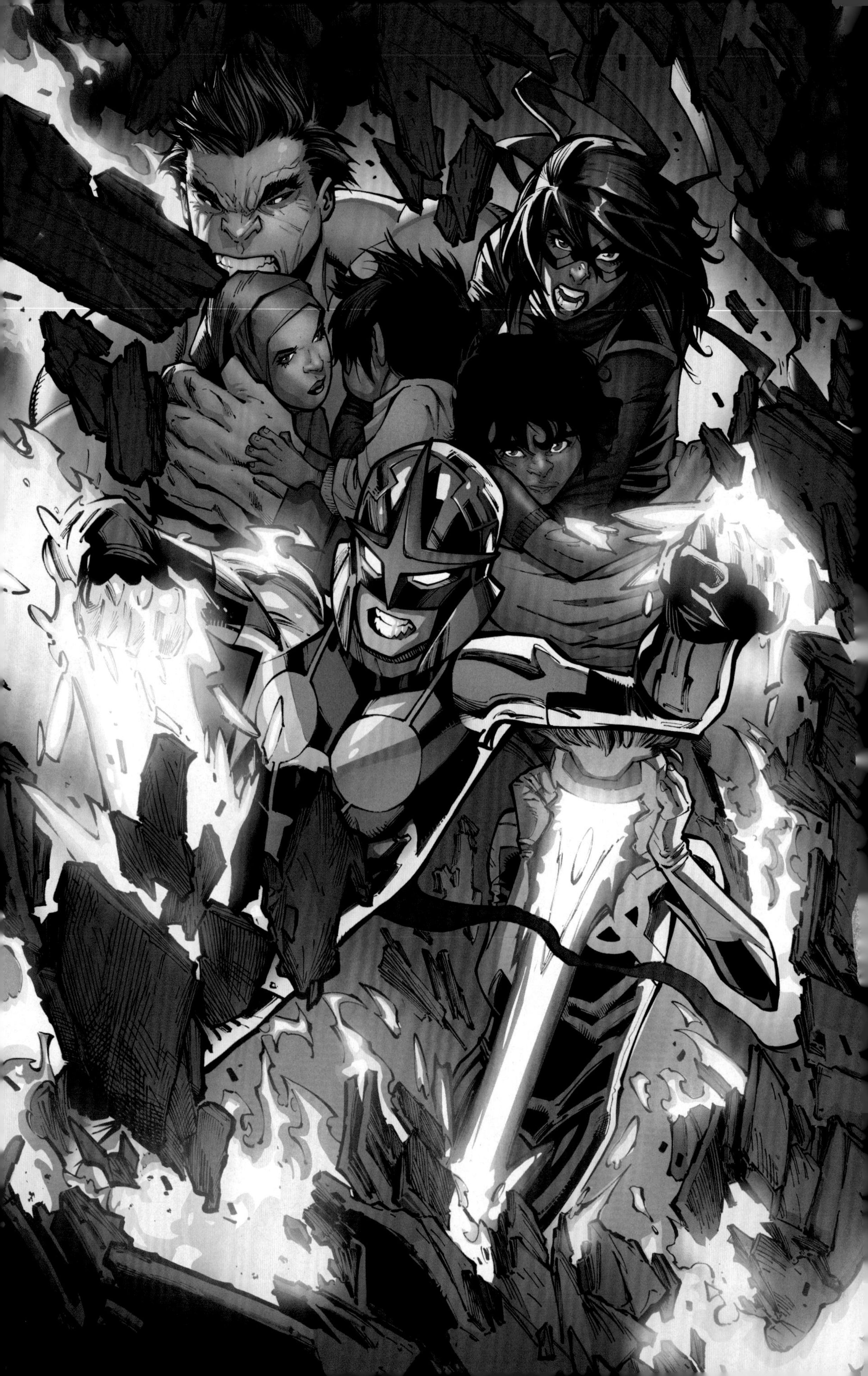

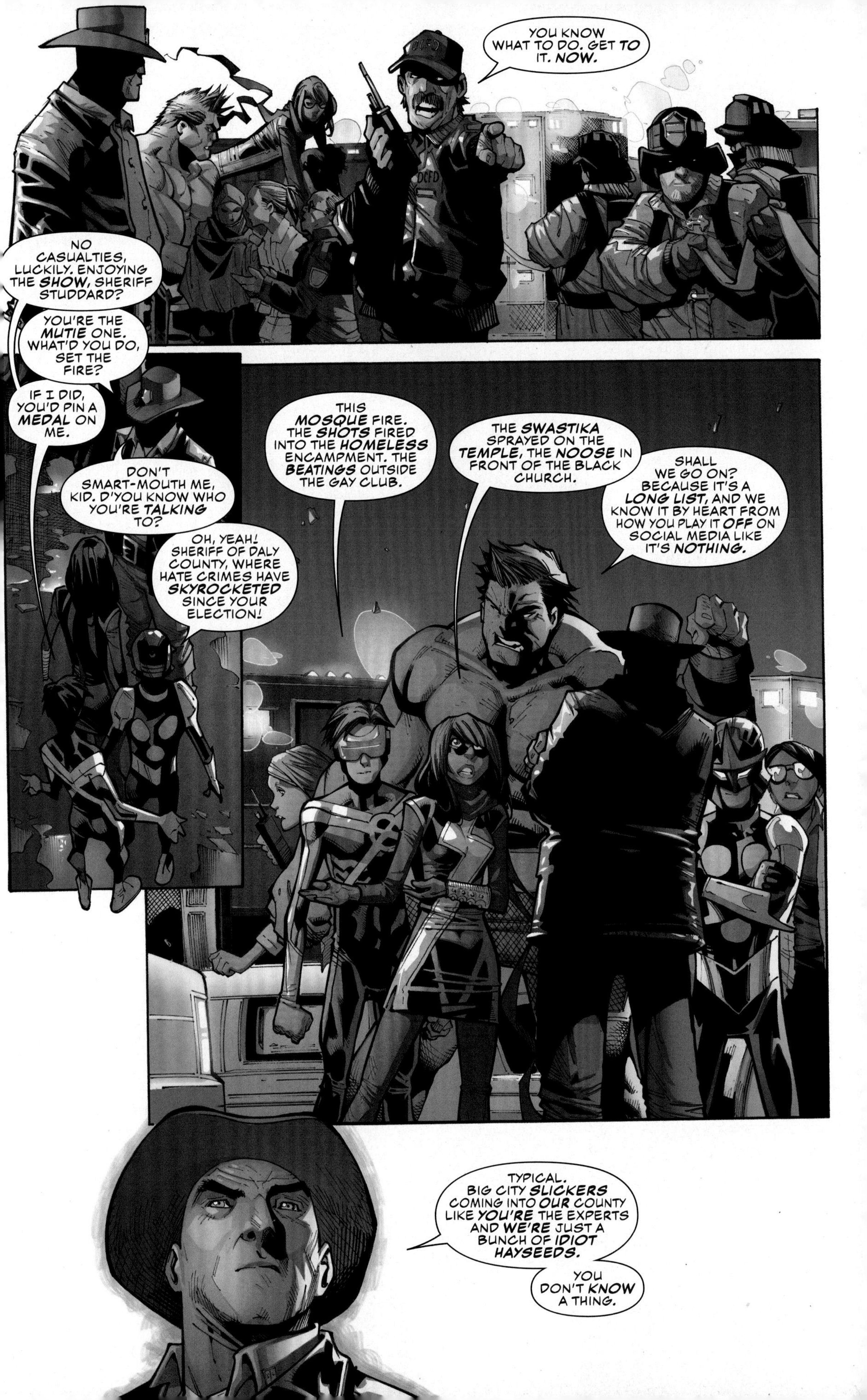
YOU KNOW WHAT TO DO. GET TO IT. NOW.
DCFD
NO CASUALTIES, LUCKILY. ENJOYING THE SHOW, SHERIFF STUDDARD?
YOU'RE THE MUTIE ONE. WHAT'D YOU DO, SET THE FIRE?
IF I DID, YOU'D PIN A MEDAL ON ME.
DON'T SMART-MOUTH ME, KID. D'YOU KNOW WHO YOU'RE TALKING TO?
OH, YEAH! SHERIFF OF DALY COUNTY, WHERE HATE CRIMES HAVE SKYROCKETED SINCE YOUR ELECTION!
THIS MOSQUE FIRE. THE SHOTS FIRED INTO THE HOMELESS ENCAMPMENT. THE BEATINGS OUTSIDE THE GAY CLUB.
THE SWASTIKA SPRAYED ON THE TEMPLE, THE NOOSE IN FRONT OF THE BLACK CHURCH.
SHALL WE GO ON? BECAUSE IT'S A LONG LIST, AND WE KNOW IT BY HEART FROM HOW YOU PLAY IT OFF ON SOCIAL MEDIA LIKE IT'S NOTHING.
TYPICAL. BIG CITY SLICKERS COMING INTO OUR COUNTY LIKE YOU'RE THE EXPERTS AND WE'RE JUST A BUNCH OF IDIOT HAYSEEDS.
YOU DON'T KNOW A THING.

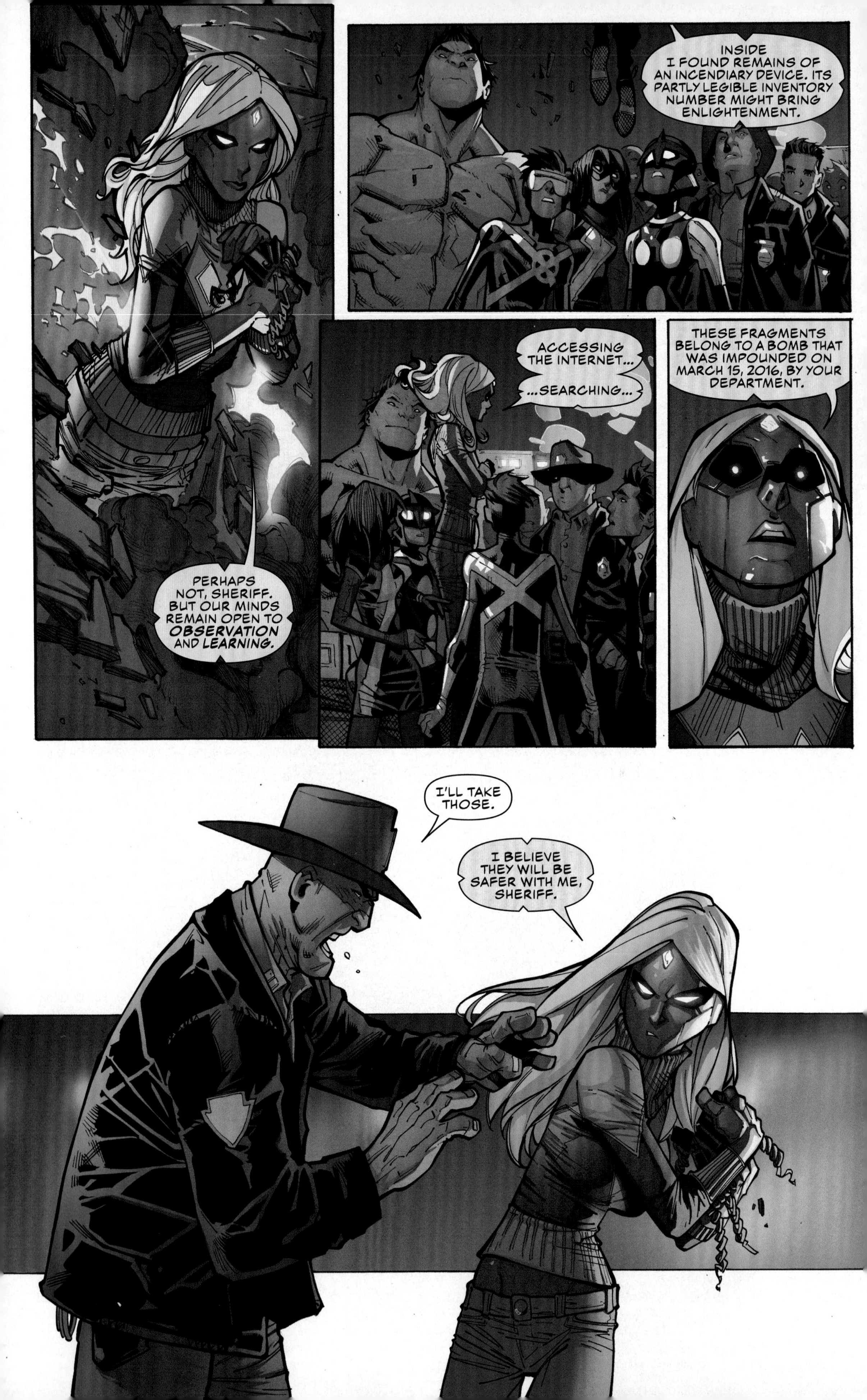
PERHAPS NOT, SHERIFF. BUT OUR MINDS REMAIN OPEN TO OBSERVATION AND LEARNING.
INSIDE I FOUND REMAINS OF AN INCENDIARY DEVICE. ITS PARTLY LEGIBLE INVENTORY NUMBER MIGHT BRING ENLIGHTENMENT.
ACCESSING THE INTERNET...
...SEARCHING...
THESE FRAGMENTS BELONG TO A BOMB THAT WAS IMPOUNDED ON MARCH 15, 2016, BY YOUR DEPARTMENT.
I'LL TAKE THOSE.
I BELIEVE THEY WILL BE SAFER WITH ME, SHERIFF.

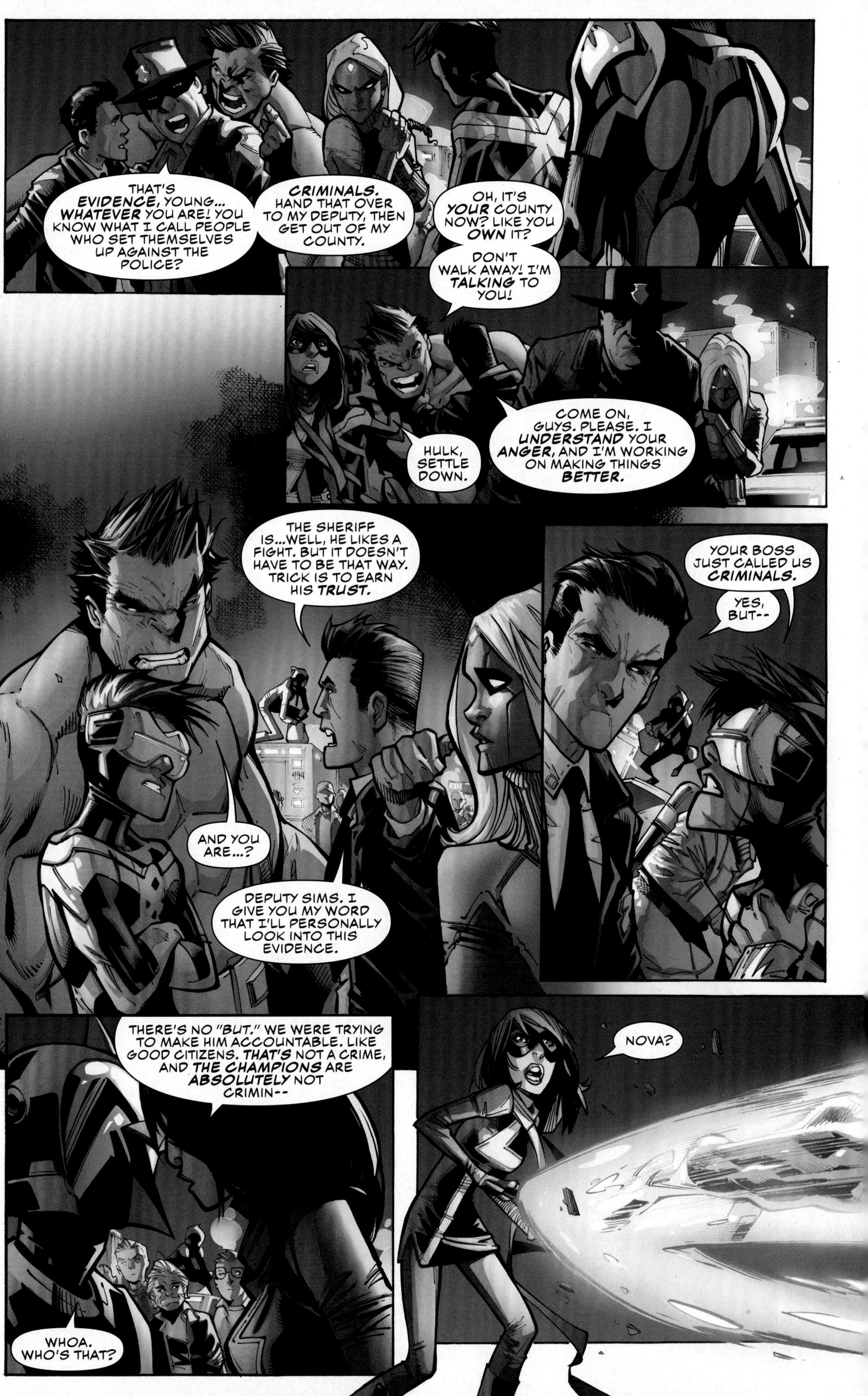
THAT'S EVIDENCE, YOUNG... WHATEVER YOU ARE! YOU KNOW WHAT I CALL PEOPLE WHO SET THEMSELVES UP AGAINST THE POLICE?
CRIMINALS. HAND THAT OVER TO MY DEPUTY, THEN GET OUT OF MY COUNTY.
OH, IT'S YOUR COUNTY NOW? LIKE YOU OWN IT?
DON'T WALK AWAY! I'M TALKING TO YOU!
HULK, SETTLE DOWN.
COME ON, GUYS. PLEASE. I UNDERSTAND YOUR ANGER, AND I'M WORKING ON MAKING THINGS BETTER.
THE SHERIFF IS...WELL, HE LIKES A FIGHT. BUT IT DOESN'T HAVE TO BE THAT WAY. TRICK IS TO EARN HIS TRUST.
AND YOU ARE...?
DEPUTY SIMS. I GIVE YOU MY WORD THAT I'LL PERSONALLY LOOK INTO THIS EVIDENCE.
YOUR BOSS JUST CALLED US CRIMINALS.
YES, BUT--
THERE'S NO "BUT." WE WERE TRYING TO MAKE HIM ACCOUNTABLE. LIKE GOOD CITIZENS. THAT'S NOT A CRIME, AND THE CHAMPIONS ARE ABSOLUTELY NOT CRIMIN--
WHOA. WHO'S THAT?
NOVA?

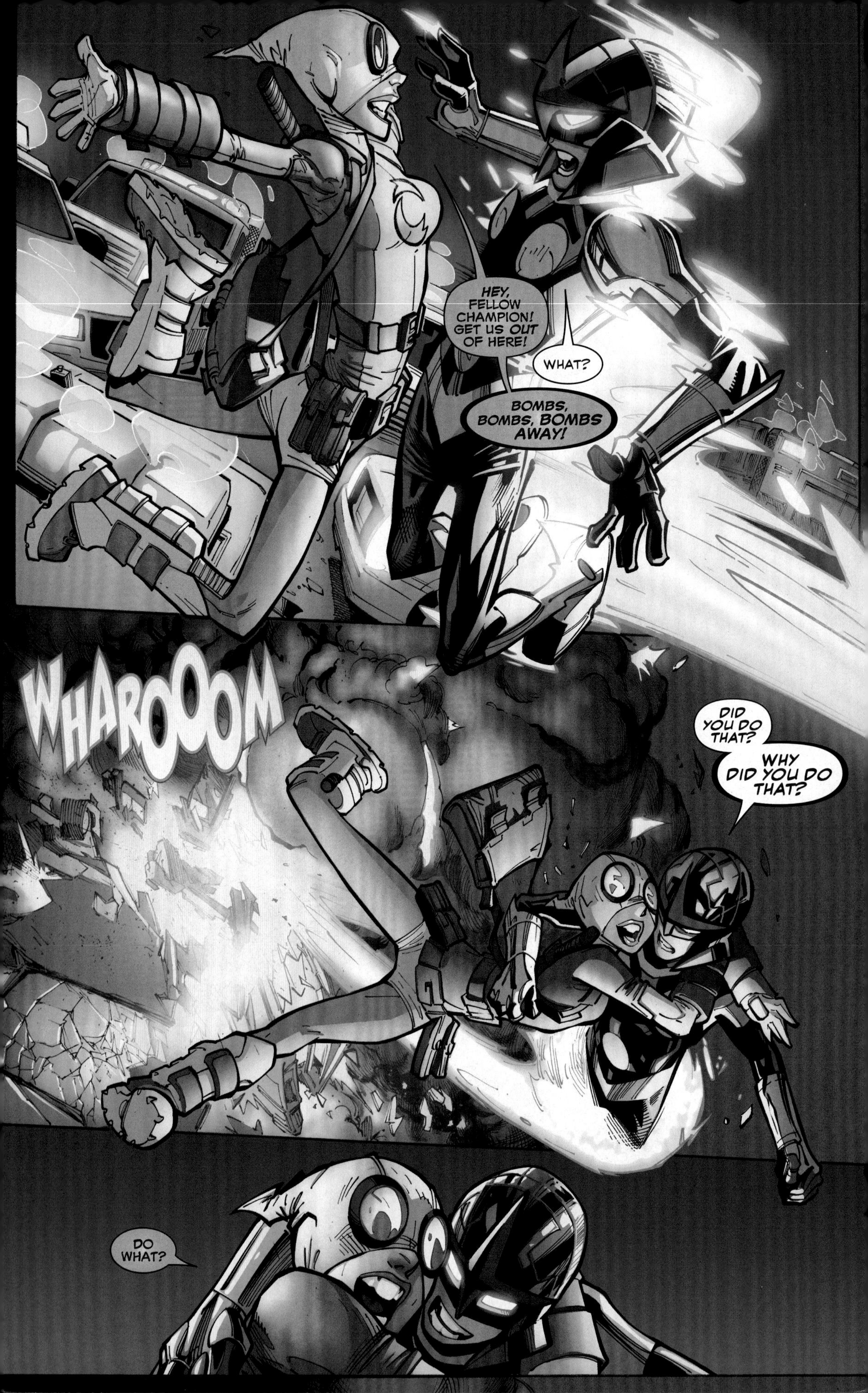
HEY, FELLOW CHAMPION! GET US OUT OF HERE!
WHAT?
BOMBS, BOMBS, BOMBS AWAY!
WHAROOOM
DID YOU DO THAT?
WHY DID YOU DO THAT?
DO WHAT?

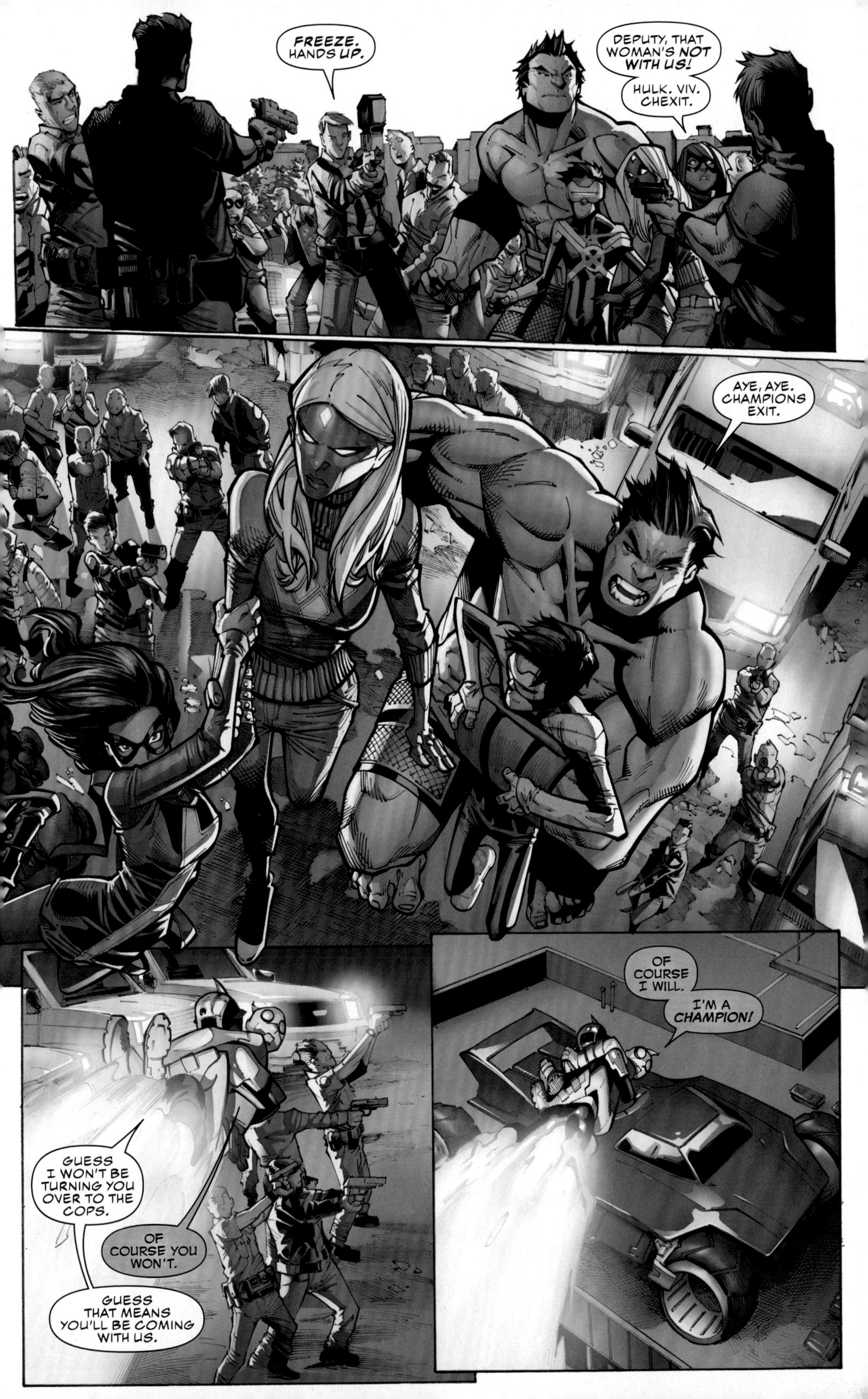
FREEZE. HANDS UP.
DEPUTY, THAT WOMAN'S NOT WITH US!
HULK. VIV. CHEXIT.
AYE, AYE. CHAMPIONS EXIT.
GUESS I WON'T BE TURNING YOU OVER TO THE COPS.
OF COURSE YOU WON'T.
GUESS THAT MEANS YOU'LL BE COMING WITH US.
OF COURSE I WILL.
I'M A CHAMPION!

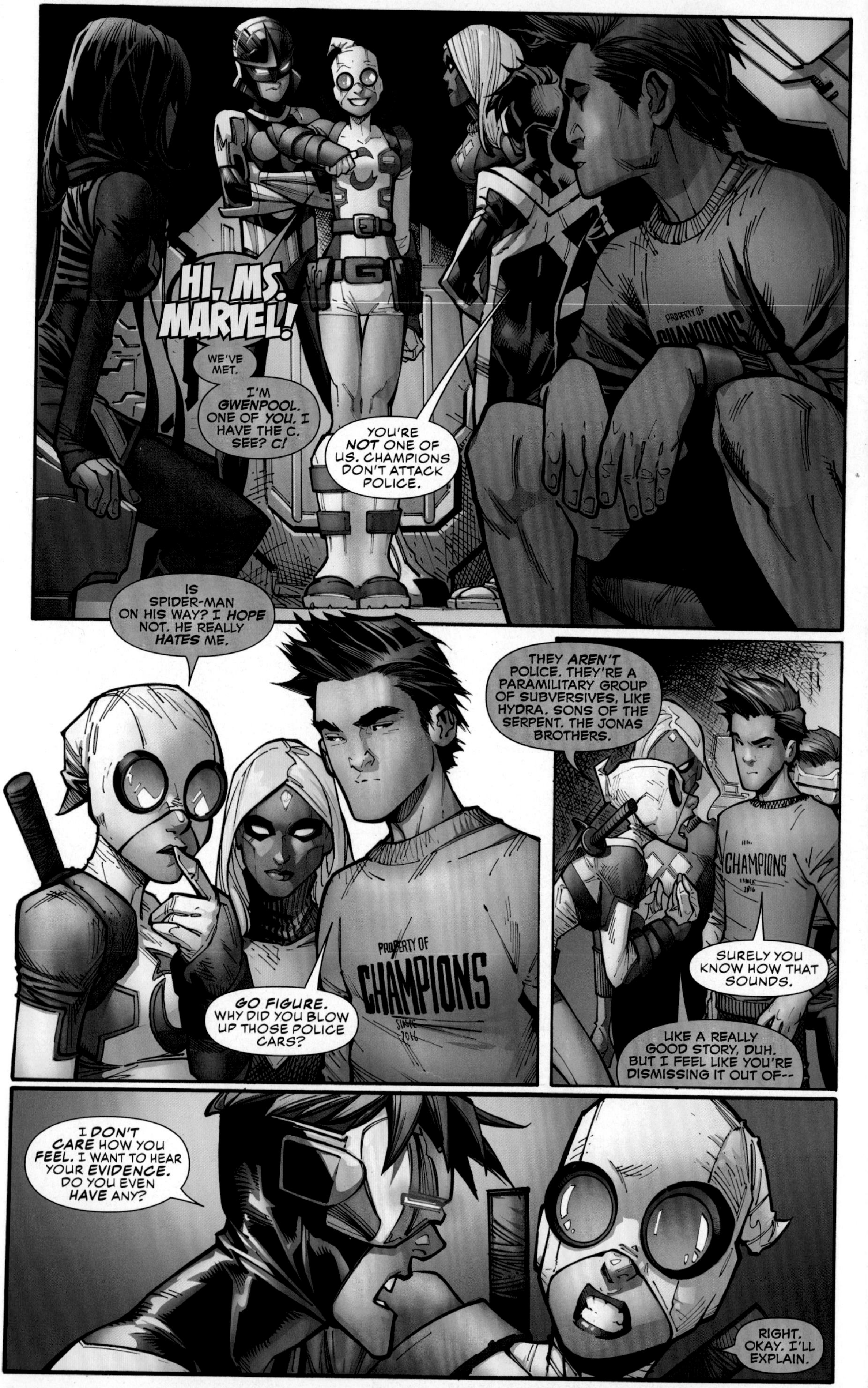
HI, MS. MARVEL!
WE'VE MET.
I'M GWENPOOL. ONE OF YOU. I HAVE THE C. SEE? C!
YOU'RE NOT ONE OF US. CHAMPIONS DON'T ATTACK POLICE.
PROPERTY OF CHAMPIONS
IS SPIDER-MAN ON HIS WAY? I HOPE NOT. HE REALLY HATES ME.
GO FIGURE. WHY DID YOU BLOW UP THOSE POLICE CARS?
PROPERTY OF CHAMPIONS
THEY AREN'T POLICE. THEY'RE A PARAMILITARY GROUP OF SUBVERSIVES, LIKE HYDRA. SONS OF THE SERPENT. THE JONAS BROTHERS.
SURELY YOU KNOW HOW THAT SOUNDS.
LIKE A REALLY GOOD STORY, DUH. BUT I FEEL LIKE YOU'RE DISMISSING IT OUT OF--
CHAMPIONS
I DON'T CARE HOW YOU FEEL. I WANT TO HEAR YOUR EVIDENCE. DO YOU EVEN HAVE ANY?
RIGHT. OKAY. I'LL EXPLAIN.

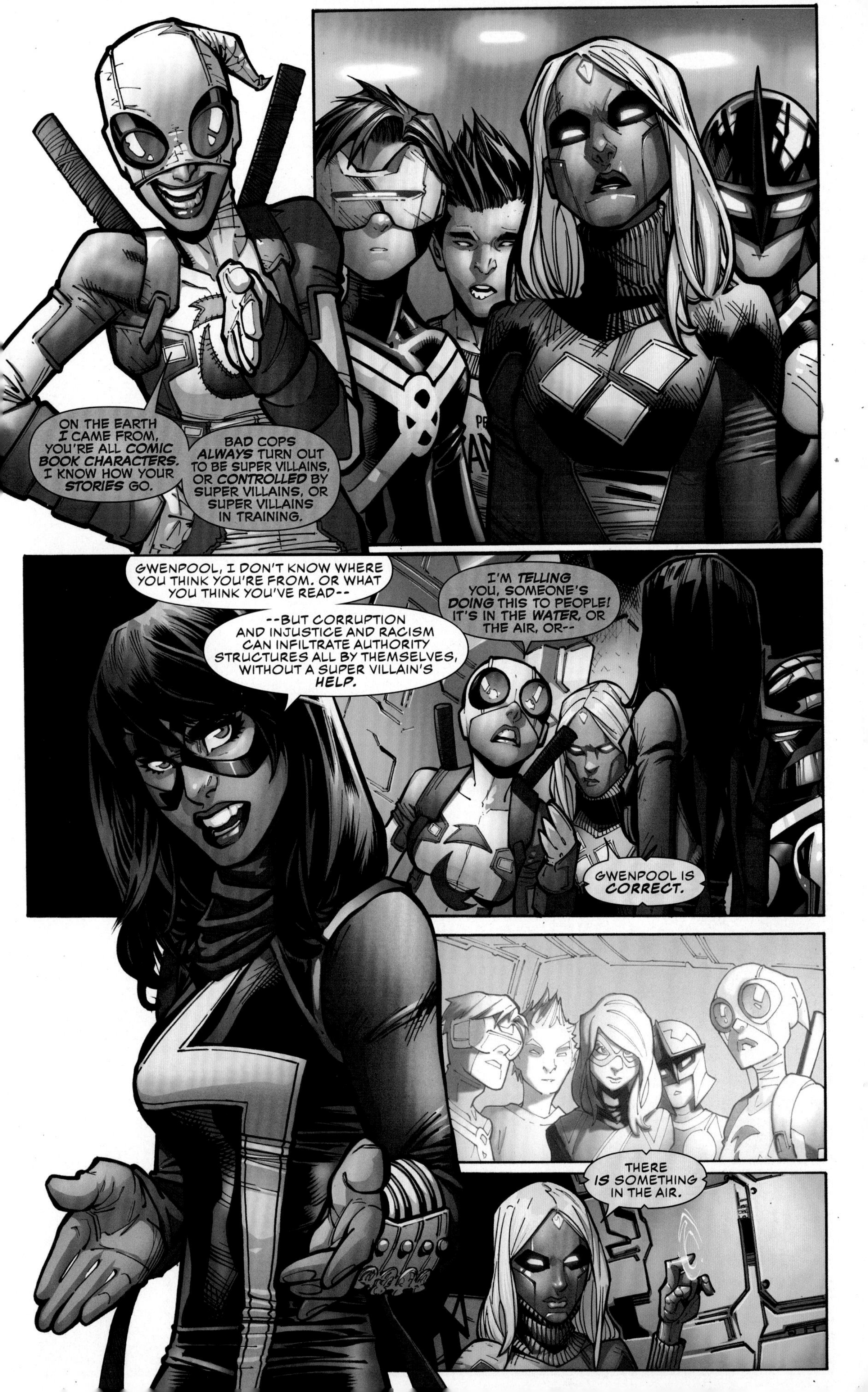
ON THE EARTH I CAME FROM, YOU'RE ALL COMIC BOOK CHARACTERS. I KNOW HOW YOUR STORIES GO.
BAD COPS ALWAYS TURN OUT TO BE SUPER VILLAINS, OR CONTROLLED BY SUPER VILLAINS, OR SUPER VILLAINS IN TRAINING.
GWENPOOL, I DON'T KNOW WHERE YOU THINK YOU'RE FROM. OR WHAT YOU THINK YOU'VE READ--
--BUT CORRUPTION AND INJUSTICE AND RACISM CAN INFILTRATE AUTHORITY STRUCTURES ALL BY THEMSELVES, WITHOUT A SUPER VILLAIN'S HELP.
I'M TELLING YOU, SOMEONE'S DOING THIS TO PEOPLE! IT'S IN THE WATER, OR THE AIR, OR--
GWENPOOL IS CORRECT.
THERE IS SOMETHING IN THE AIR.

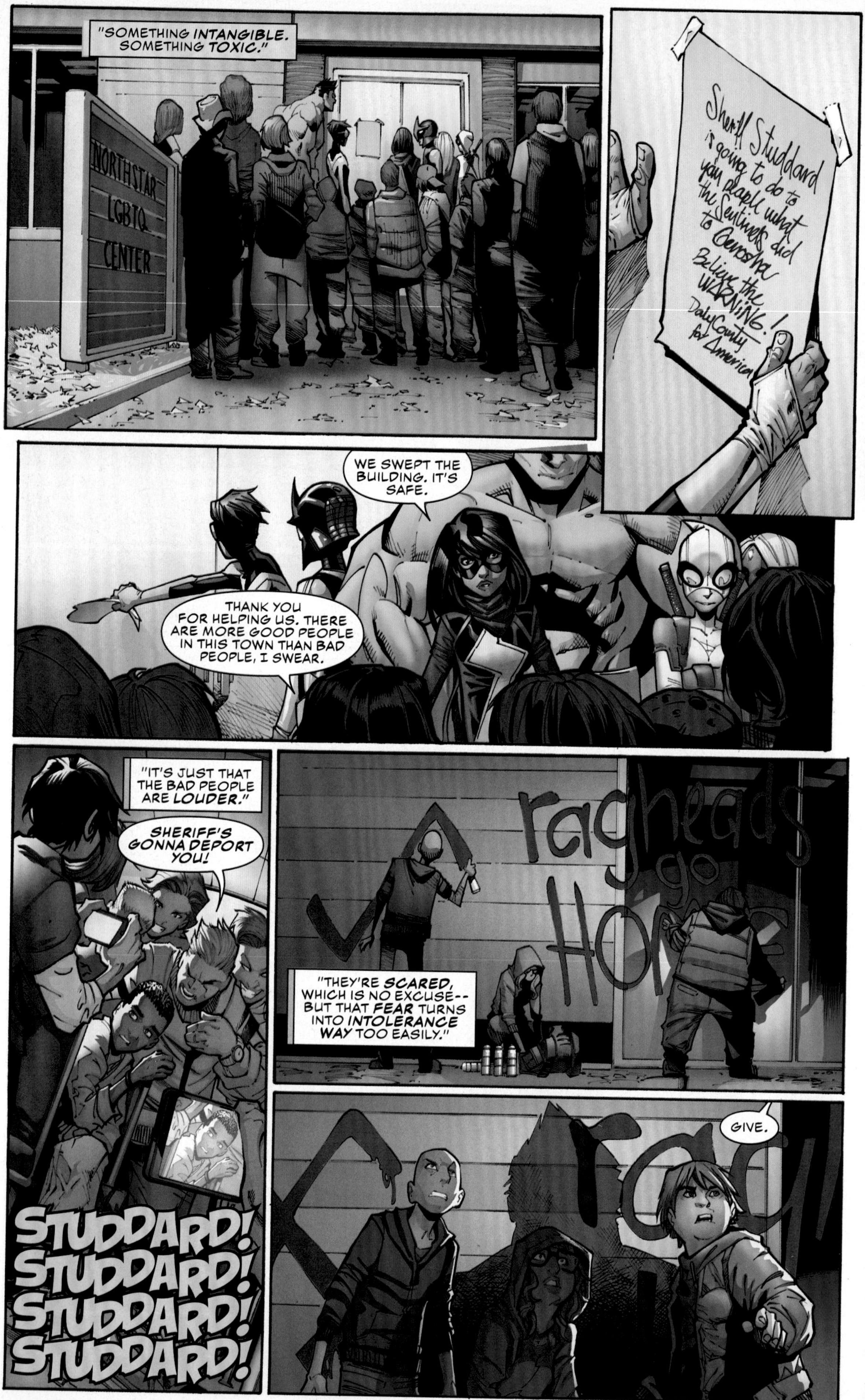
"SOMETHING INTANGIBLE. SOMETHING TOXIC."
NORTHSTAR LGBTQ CENTER
Sheriff Studdard is going to do to you people what the Sentinels did to Genosha
Believe the WARNING!
Daly County for America
WE SWEPT THE BUILDING. IT'S SAFE.
THANK YOU FOR HELPING US. THERE ARE MORE GOOD PEOPLE IN THIS TOWN THAN BAD PEOPLE, I SWEAR.
"IT'S JUST THAT THE BAD PEOPLE ARE LOUDER."
SHERIFF'S GONNA DEPORT YOU!
STUDDARD! STUDDARD! STUDDARD! STUDDARD!
ragheads go
"THEY'RE SCARED, WHICH IS NO EXCUSE-- BUT THAT FEAR TURNS INTO INTOLERANCE WAY TOO EASILY."
GIVE.

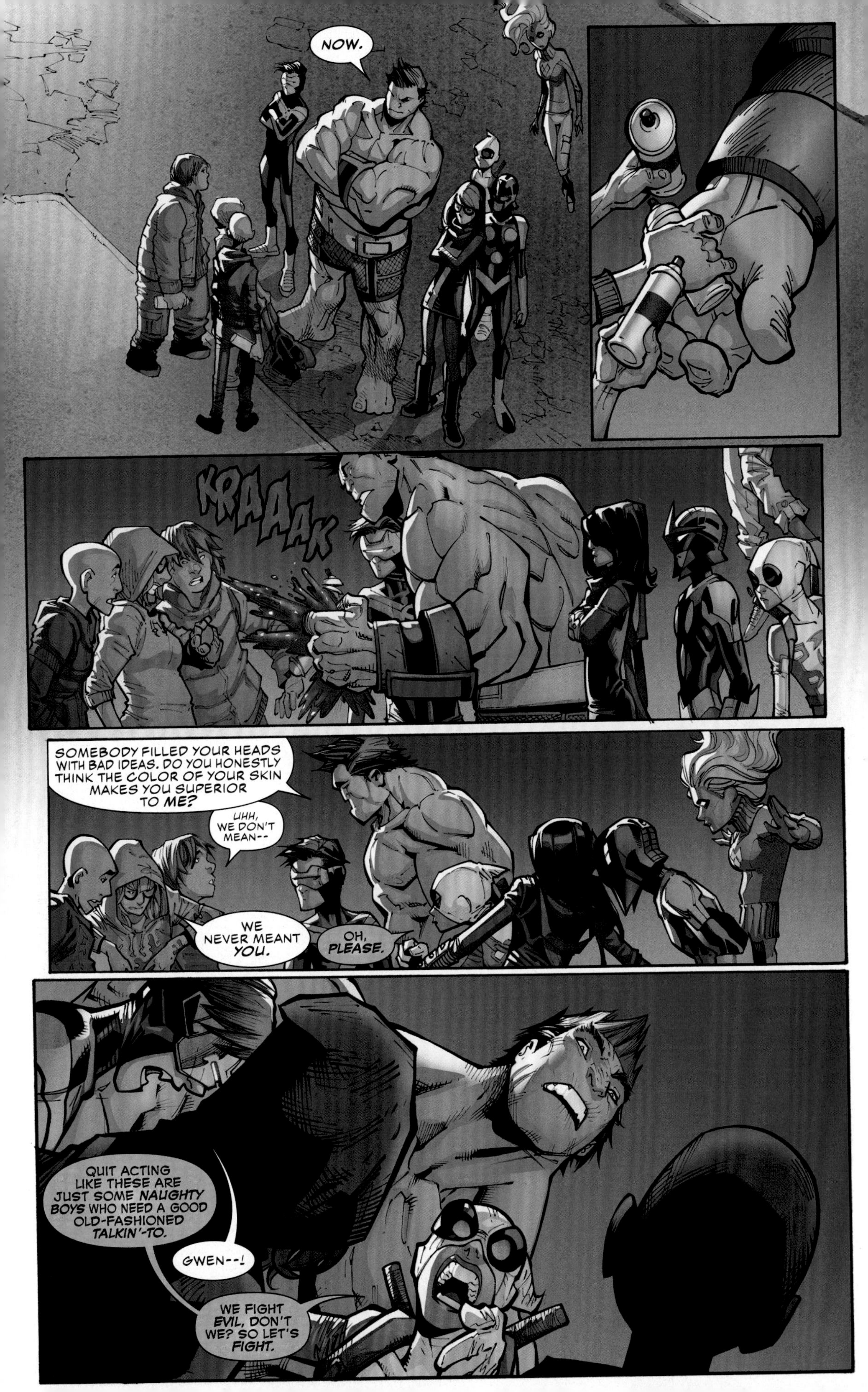
NOW.
KRAAAAK
SOMEBODY FILLED YOUR HEADS WITH BAD IDEAS. DO YOU HONESTLY THINK THE COLOR OF YOUR SKIN MAKES YOU SUPERIOR TO ME?
UHH, WE DON'T MEAN--
WE NEVER MEANT YOU.
OH, PLEASE.
QUIT ACTING LIKE THESE ARE JUST SOME NAUGHTY BOYS WHO NEED A GOOD OLD-FASHIONED TALKIN'-TO.
GWEN--!
WE FIGHT EVIL, DON'T WE? SO LET'S FIGHT.

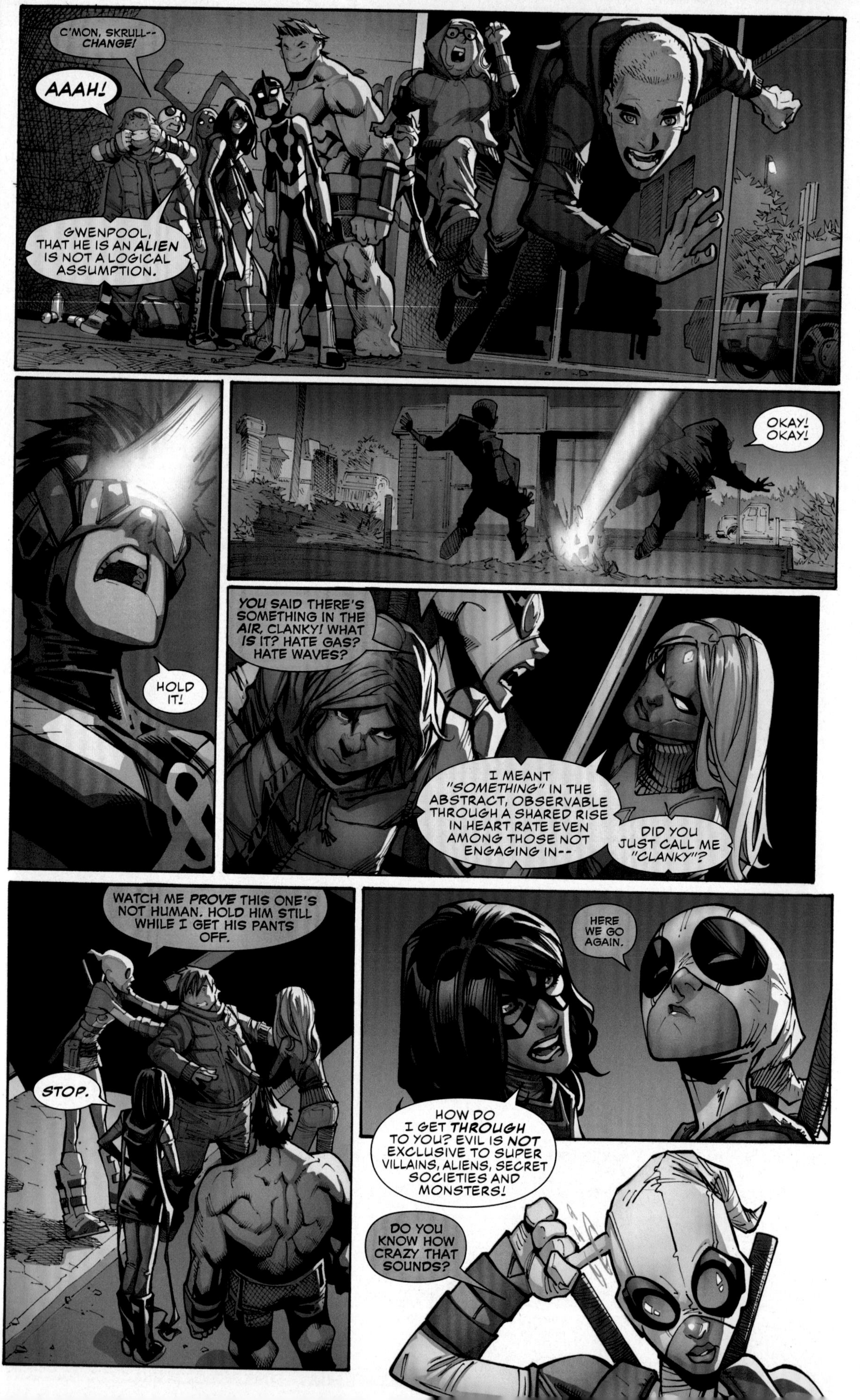
C'MON, SKRULL-- CHANGE!
AAAH!
GWENPOOL, THAT HE IS AN ALIEN IS NOT A LOGICAL ASSUMPTION.
HOLD IT!
OKAY! OKAY!
YOU SAID THERE'S SOMETHING IN THE AIR, CLANKY! WHAT IS IT? HATE GAS? HATE WAVES?
I MEANT "SOMETHING" IN THE ABSTRACT, OBSERVABLE THROUGH A SHARED RISE IN HEART RATE EVEN AMONG THOSE NOT ENGAGING IN--
DID YOU JUST CALL ME "CLANKY"?
WATCH ME PROVE THIS ONE'S NOT HUMAN. HOLD HIM STILL WHILE I GET HIS PANTS OFF.
STOP.
HERE WE GO AGAIN.
HOW DO I GET THROUGH TO YOU? EVIL IS NOT EXCLUSIVE TO SUPER VILLAINS, ALIENS, SECRET SOCIETIES AND MONSTERS!
DO YOU KNOW HOW CRAZY THAT SOUNDS?

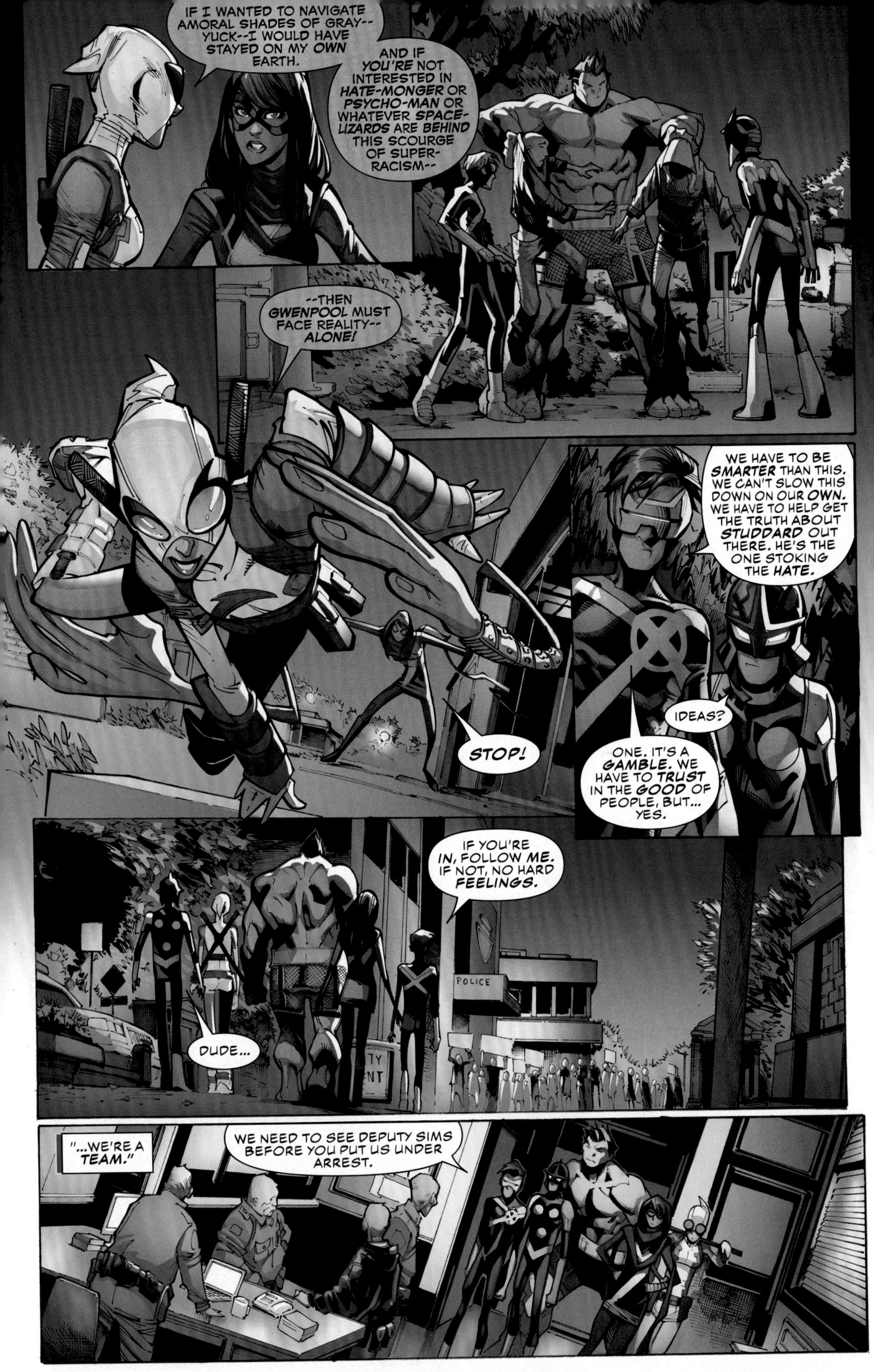

IF I WANTED TO NAVIGATE AMORAL SHADES OF GRAY--YUCK--I WOULD HAVE STAYED ON MY OWN EARTH.
AND IF YOU'RE NOT INTERESTED IN HATE-MONGER OR PSYCHO-MAN OR WHATEVER SPACE-LIZARDS ARE BEHIND THIS SCOURGE OF SUPER-RACISM--
--THEN GWENPOOL MUST FACE REALITY--ALONE!
STOP!
WE HAVE TO BE SMARTER THAN THIS. WE CAN'T SLOW THIS DOWN ON OUR OWN. WE HAVE TO HELP GET THE TRUTH ABOUT STUDDARD OUT THERE. HE'S THE ONE STOKING THE HATE.
IDEAS?
ONE. IT'S A GAMBLE. WE HAVE TO TRUST IN THE GOOD OF PEOPLE, BUT... YES.
IF YOU'RE IN, FOLLOW ME. IF NOT, NO HARD FEELINGS.
DUDE...
POLICE
"...WE'RE A TEAM."
WE NEED TO SEE DEPUTY SIMS BEFORE YOU PUT US UNDER ARREST.

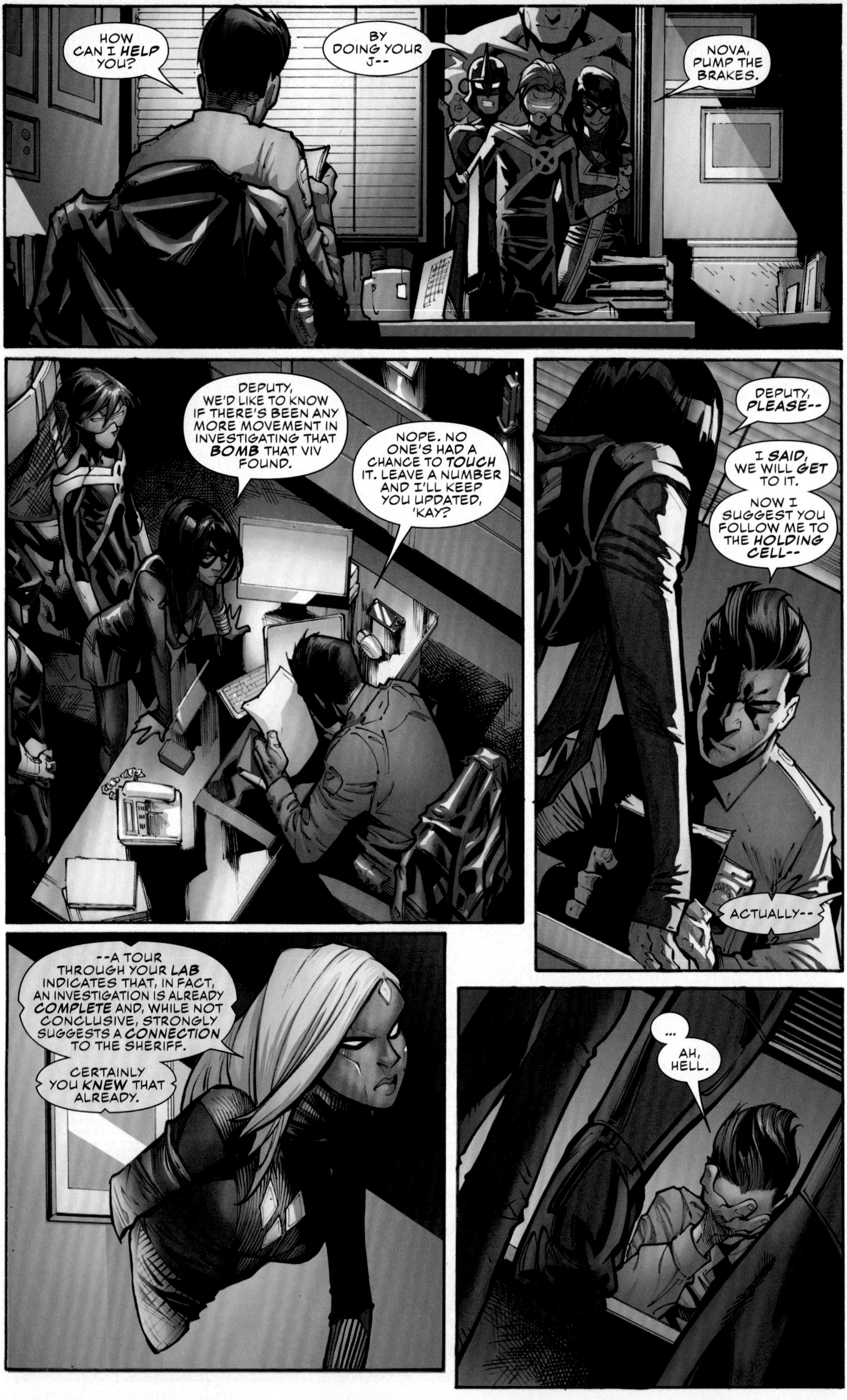
HOW CAN I HELP YOU?
BY DOING YOUR J--
NOVA, PUMP THE BRAKES.
DEPUTY, WE'D LIKE TO KNOW IF THERE'S BEEN ANY MORE MOVEMENT IN INVESTIGATING THAT BOMB THAT VIV FOUND.
NOPE. NO ONE'S HAD A CHANCE TO TOUCH IT. LEAVE A NUMBER AND I'LL KEEP YOU UPDATED, 'KAY?
DEPUTY, PLEASE--
I SAID, WE WILL GET TO IT.
NOW I SUGGEST YOU FOLLOW ME TO THE HOLDING CELL--
ACTUALLY--
--A TOUR THROUGH YOUR LAB INDICATES THAT, IN FACT, AN INVESTIGATION IS ALREADY COMPLETE AND, WHILE NOT CONCLUSIVE, STRONGLY SUGGESTS A CONNECTION TO THE SHERIFF.
CERTAINLY YOU KNEW THAT ALREADY.
...
AH, HELL.

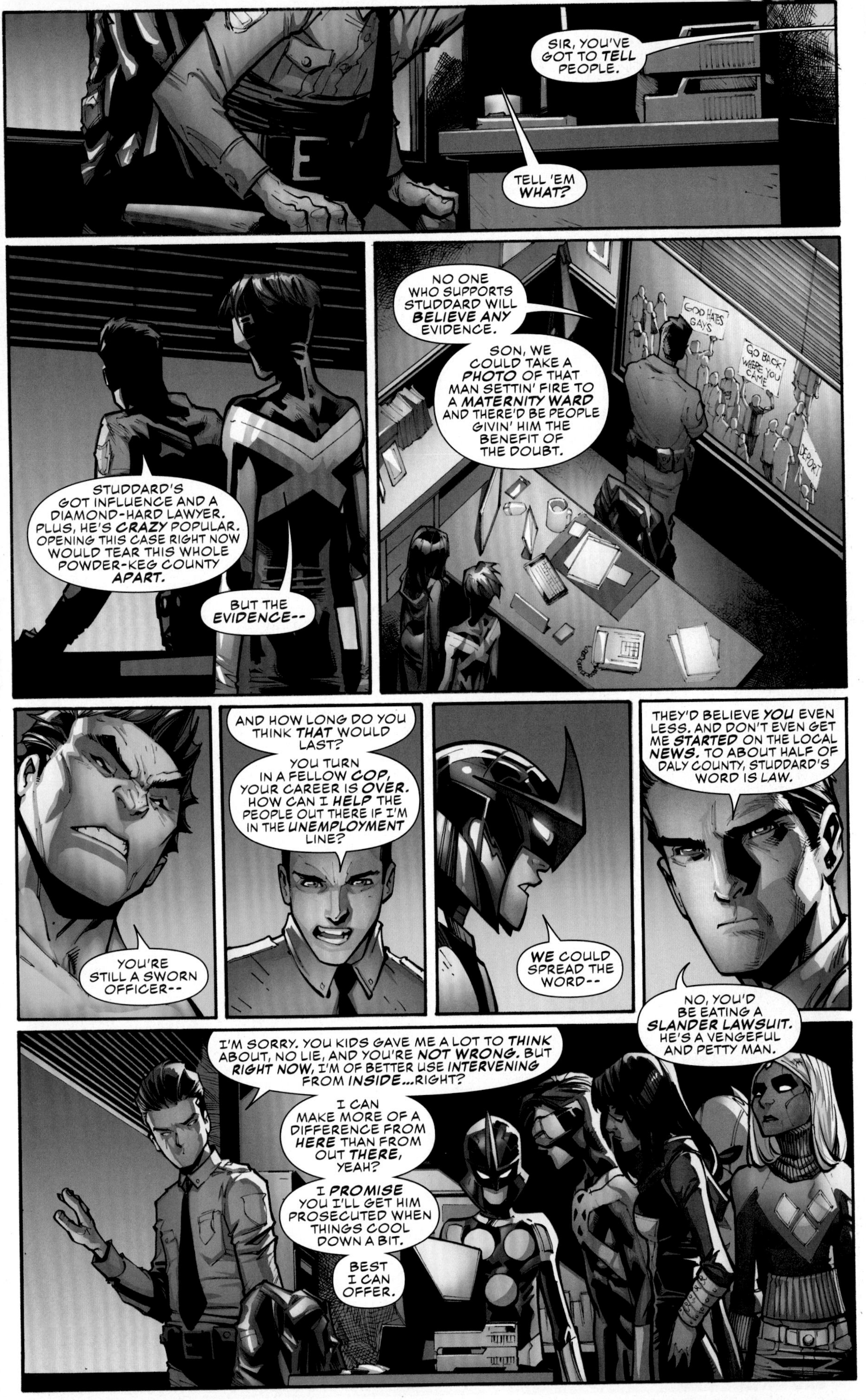
SIR, YOU'VE GOT TO TELL PEOPLE.
TELL 'EM WHAT?
STUDDARD'S GOT INFLUENCE AND A DIAMOND-HARD LAWYER. PLUS, HE'S CRAZY POPULAR. OPENING THIS CASE RIGHT NOW WOULD TEAR THIS WHOLE POWDER-KEG COUNTY APART.
BUT THE EVIDENCE--
NO ONE WHO SUPPORTS STUDDARD WILL BELIEVE ANY EVIDENCE.
SON, WE COULD TAKE A PHOTO OF THAT MAN SETTIN' FIRE TO A MATERNITY WARD AND THERE'D BE PEOPLE GIVIN' HIM THE BENEFIT OF THE DOUBT.
GOD HATES GAYS
GO BACK WHERE YOU CAME
DEPORT
YOU'RE STILL A SWORN OFFICER--
AND HOW LONG DO YOU THINK THAT WOULD LAST?
YOU TURN IN A FELLOW COP, YOUR CAREER IS OVER. HOW CAN I HELP THE PEOPLE OUT THERE IF I'M IN THE UNEMPLOYMENT LINE?
WE COULD SPREAD THE WORD--
THEY'D BELIEVE YOU EVEN LESS. AND DON'T EVEN GET ME STARTED ON THE LOCAL NEWS. TO ABOUT HALF OF DALY COUNTY, STUDDARD'S WORD IS LAW.
NO, YOU'D BE EATING A SLANDER LAWSUIT. HE'S A VENGEFUL AND PETTY MAN.
I'M SORRY. YOU KIDS GAVE ME A LOT TO THINK ABOUT, NO LIE, AND YOU'RE NOT WRONG. BUT RIGHT NOW, I'M OF BETTER USE INTERVENING FROM INSIDE...RIGHT?
I CAN MAKE MORE OF A DIFFERENCE FROM HERE THAN FROM OUT THERE, YEAH?
I PROMISE YOU I'LL GET HIM PROSECUTED WHEN THINGS COOL DOWN A BIT.
BEST I CAN OFFER.

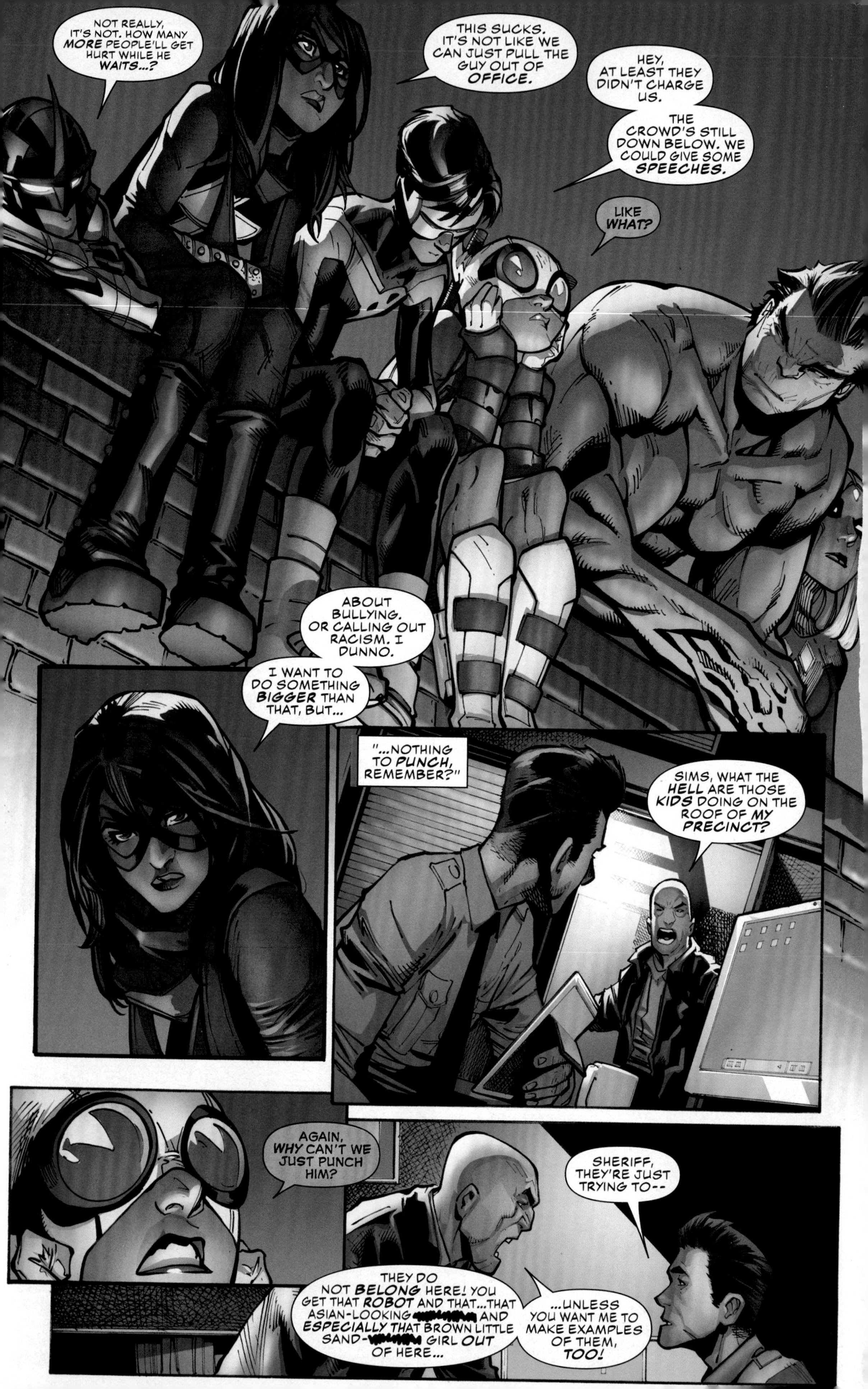

NOT REALLY, IT'S NOT. HOW MANY MORE PEOPLE'LL GET HURT WHILE HE WAITS...?
THIS SUCKS. IT'S NOT LIKE WE CAN JUST PULL THE GUY OUT OF OFFICE.
HEY, AT LEAST THEY DIDN'T CHARGE US.
THE CROWD'S STILL DOWN BELOW. WE COULD GIVE SOME SPEECHES.
LIKE WHAT?
ABOUT BULLYING. OR CALLING OUT RACISM. I DUNNO.
I WANT TO DO SOMETHING BIGGER THAN THAT, BUT...
"...NOTHING TO PUNCH, REMEMBER?"
SIMS, WHAT THE HELL ARE THOSE KIDS DOING ON THE ROOF OF MY PRECINCT?
AGAIN, WHY CAN'T WE JUST PUNCH HIM?
SHERIFF, THEY'RE JUST TRYING TO--
THEY DO NOT BELONG HERE! YOU GET THAT ROBOT AND THAT...THAT ASIAN-LOOKING [redacted] AND ESPECIALLY THAT BROWN LITTLE SAND-[redacted] GIRL OUT OF HERE...
...UNLESS YOU WANT ME TO MAKE EXAMPLES OF THEM, TOO!

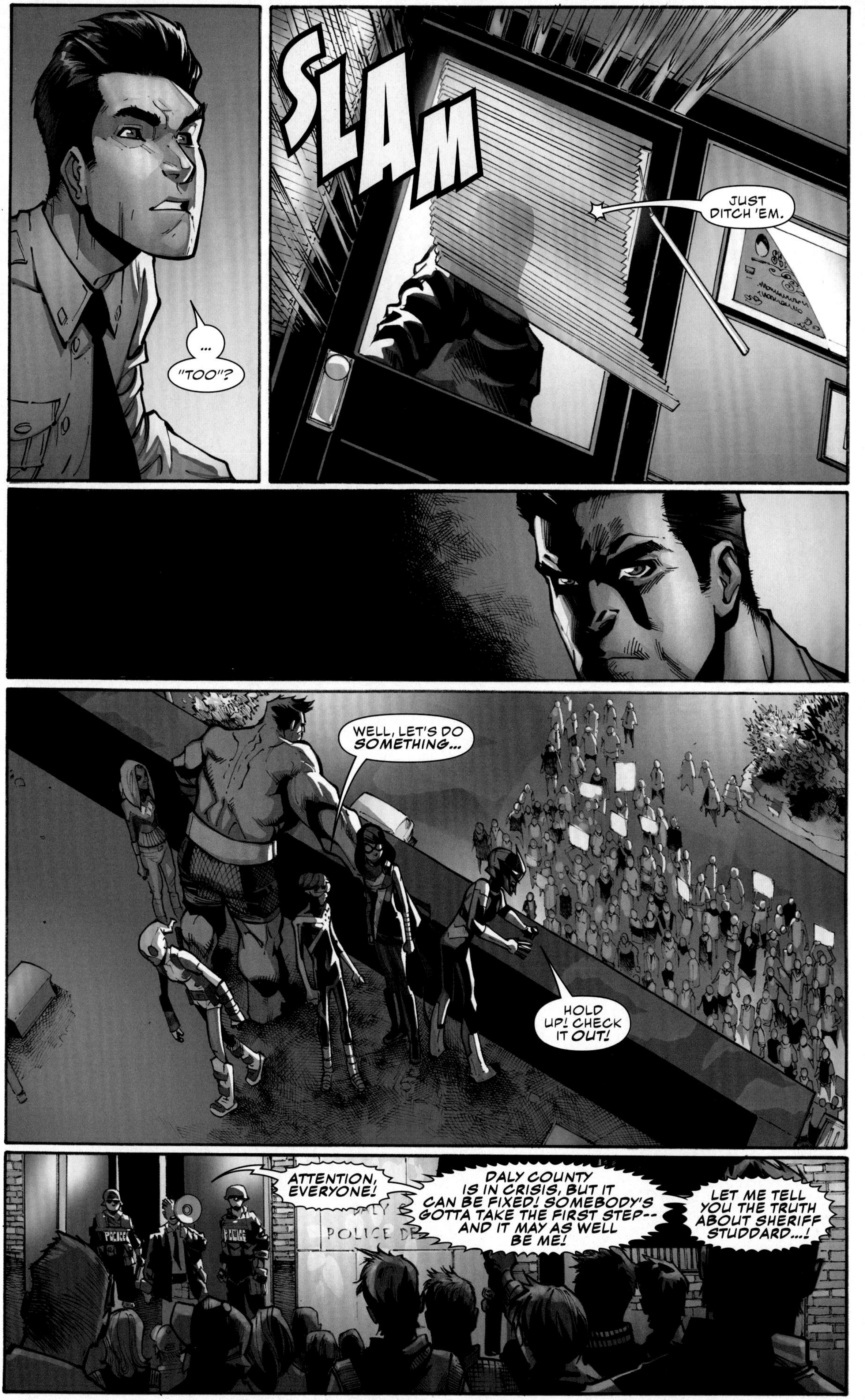
...
"TOO"?
SLAM
JUST DITCH 'EM.
WELL, LET'S DO SOMETHING...
HOLD UP! CHECK IT OUT!
ATTENTION, EVERYONE!
DALY COUNTY IS IN CRISIS, BUT IT CAN BE FIXED! SOMEBODY'S GOTTA TAKE THE FIRST STEP-- AND IT MAY AS WELL BE ME!
LET ME TELL YOU THE TRUTH ABOUT SHERIFF STUDDARD...!

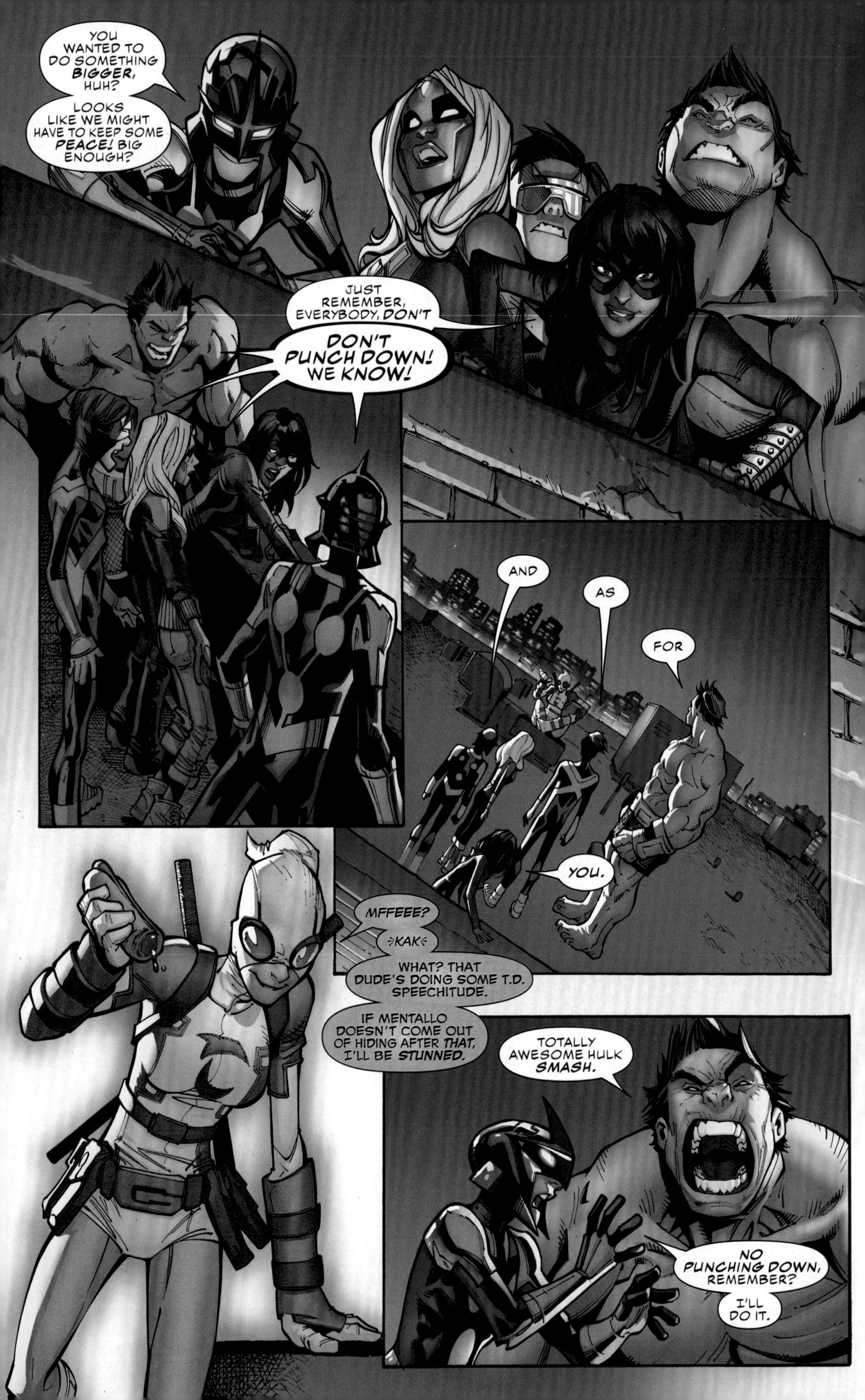

YOU WANTED TO DO SOMETHING BIGGER, HUH?
LOOKS LIKE WE MIGHT HAVE TO KEEP SOME PEACE! BIG ENOUGH?
JUST REMEMBER, EVERYBODY, DON'T
DON'T PUNCH DOWN! WE KNOW!
AND
AS
FOR
YOU.
MFFEEE?
KAK
WHAT? THAT DUDE'S DOING SOME T.D. SPEECHITUDE.
IF MENTALLO DOESN'T COME OUT OF HIDING AFTER THAT, I'LL BE STUNNED.
TOTALLY AWESOME HULK SMASH.
NO PUNCHING DOWN, REMEMBER?
I'LL DO IT.

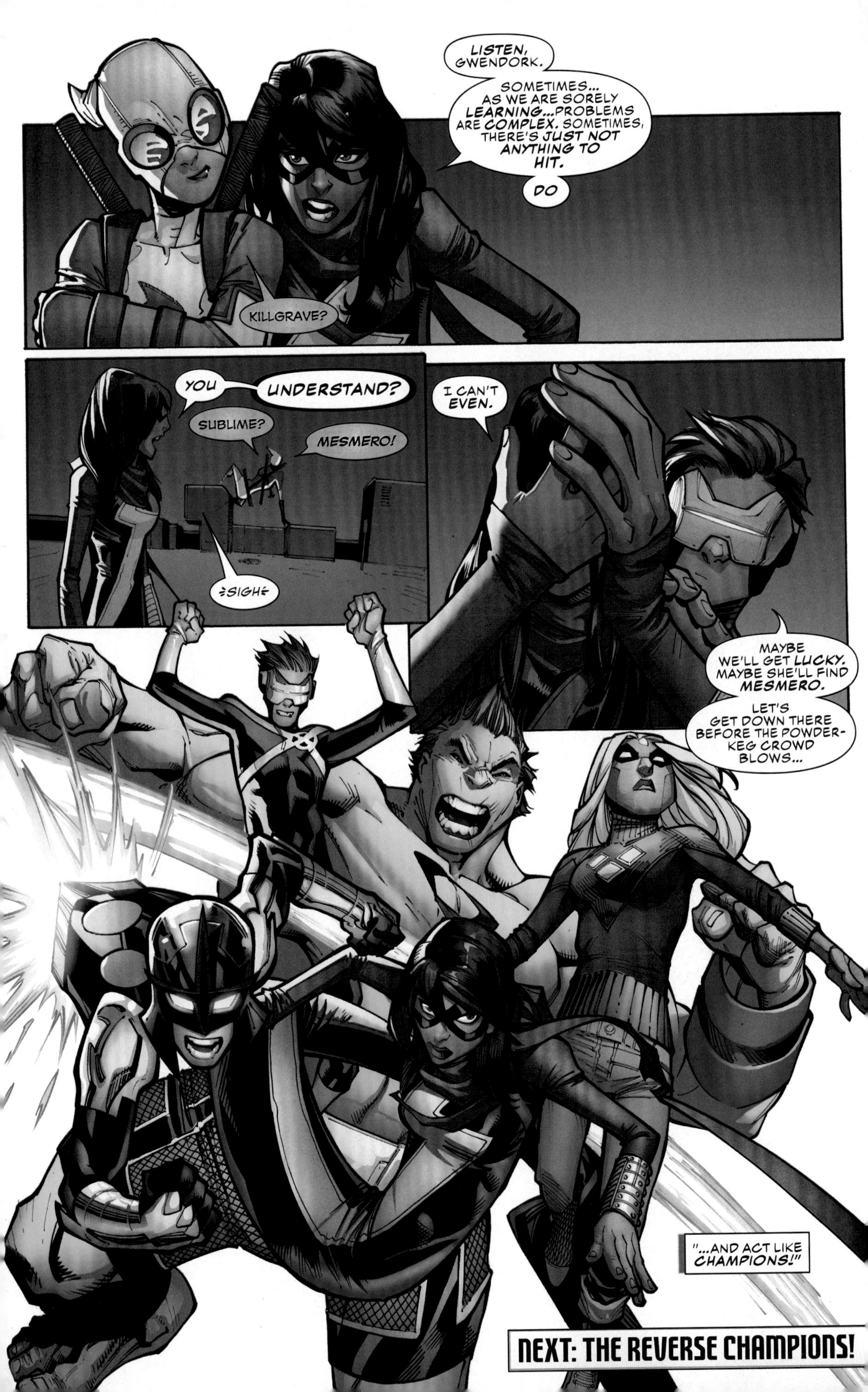
LISTEN, GWENDORK.
SOMETIMES... AS WE ARE SORELY LEARNING...PROBLEMS ARE COMPLEX. SOMETIMES, THERE'S JUST NOT ANYTHING TO HIT.
DO
KILLGRAVE?
YOU
UNDERSTAND?
SUBLIME?
MESMERO!
⋛SIGH⋚
I CAN'T EVEN.
MAYBE WE'LL GET LUCKY. MAYBE SHE'LL FIND MESMERO.
LET'S GET DOWN THERE BEFORE THE POWDER-KEG CROWD BLOWS...
"...AND ACT LIKE CHAMPIONS!"
NEXT: THE REVERSE CHAMPIONS!

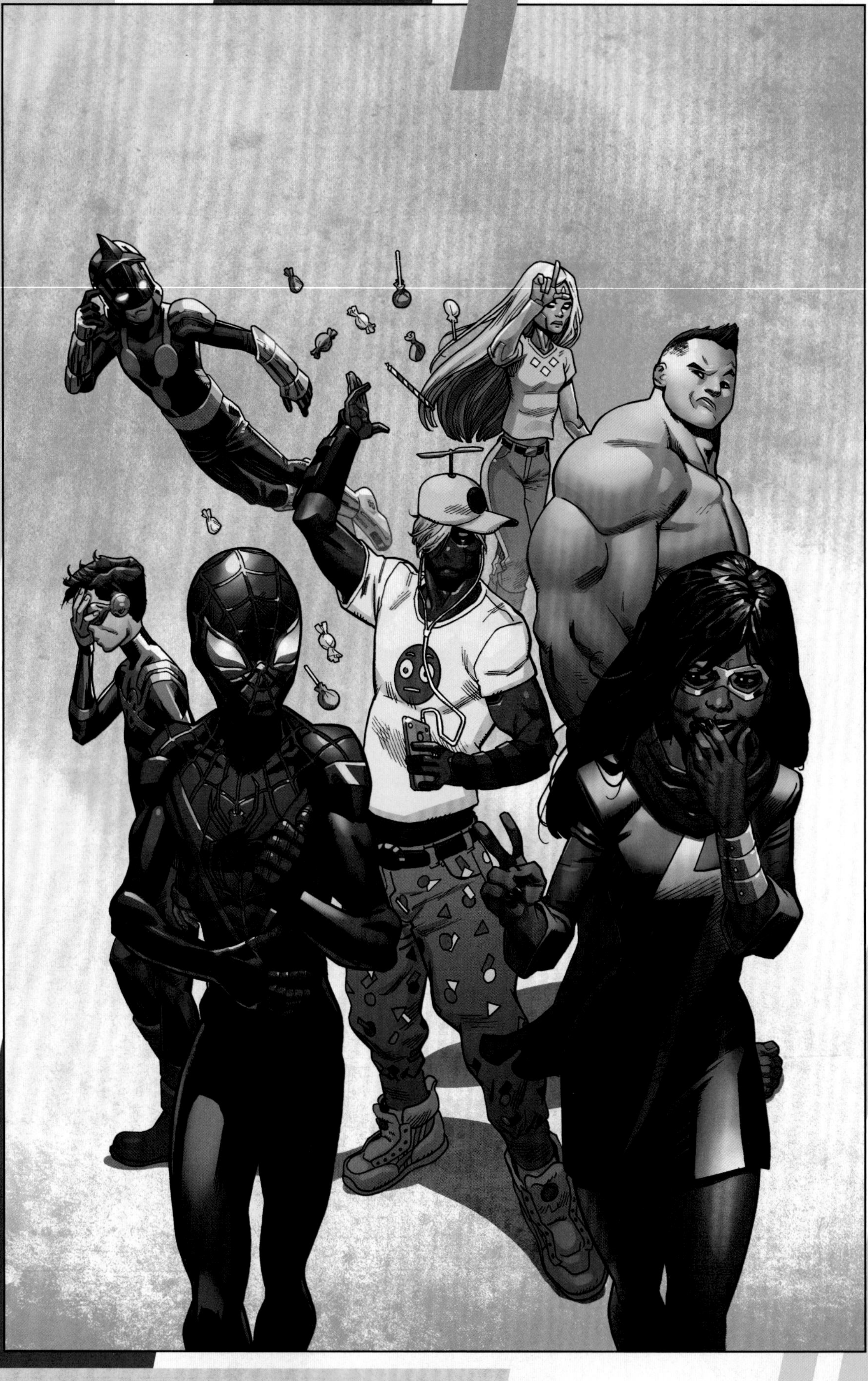

#1 VARIANT BY **MIKE HAWTHORNE & MATT MILLA**

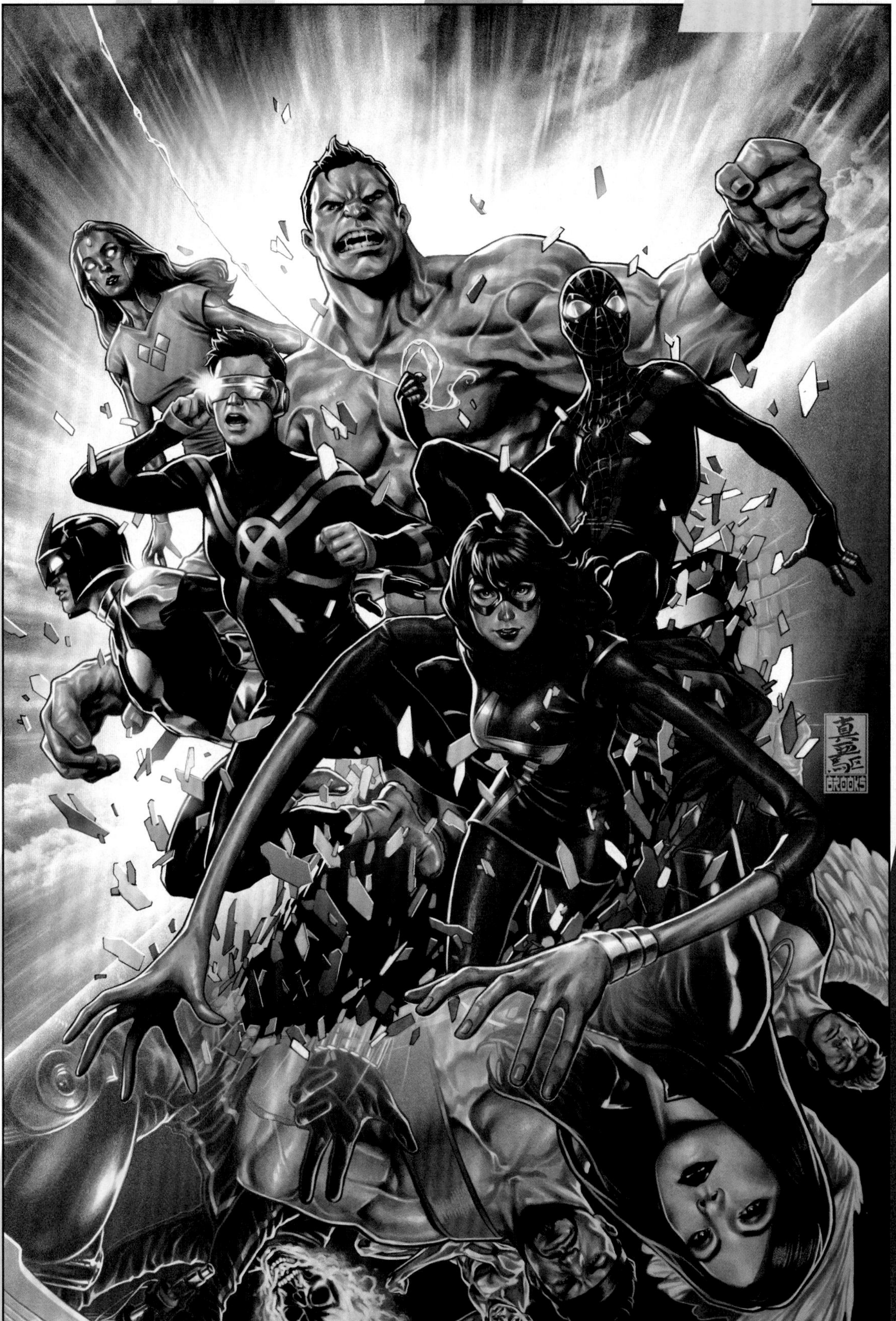
BROOKS

#X VARIANT BY **MARK BROOKS**

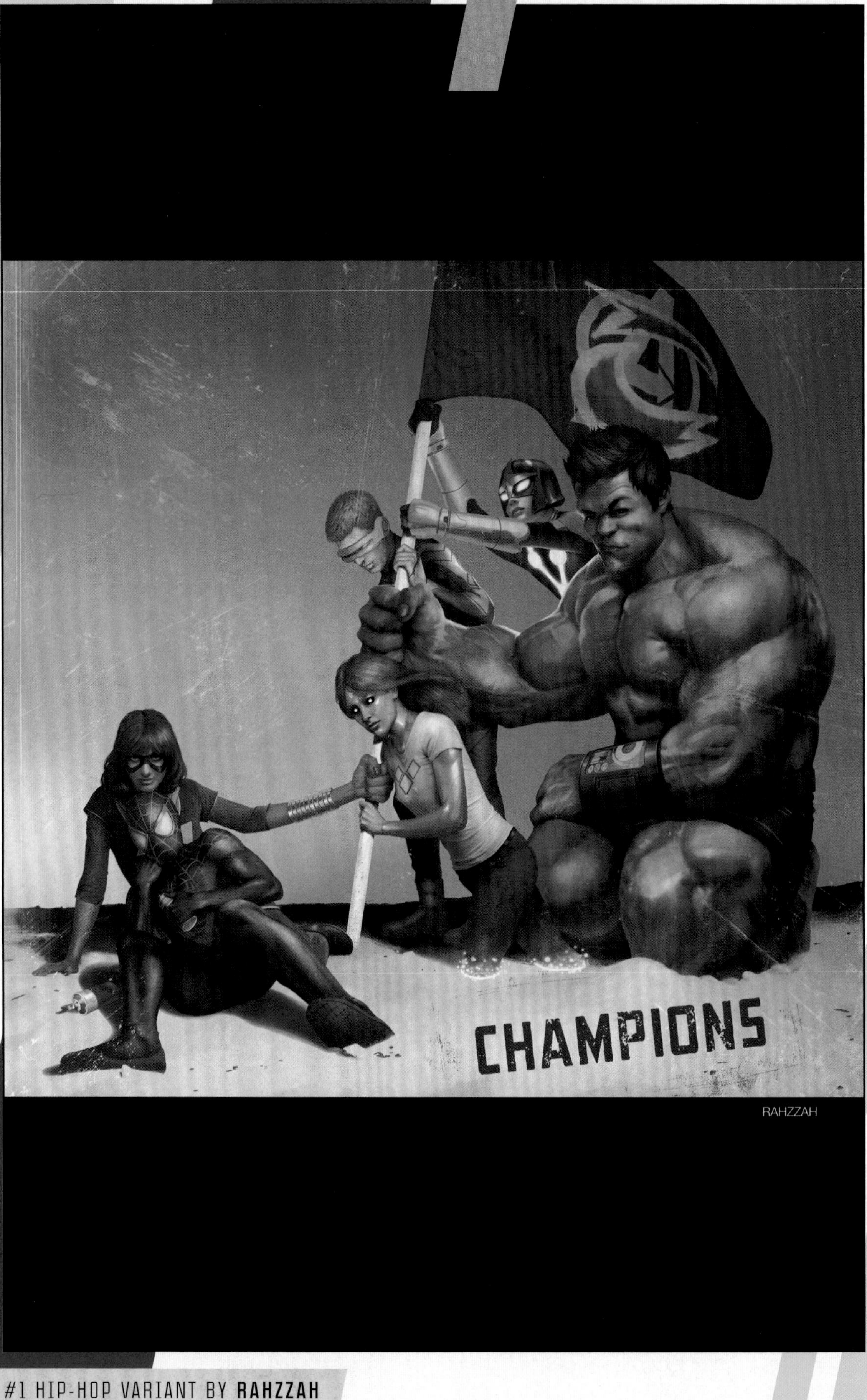
CHAMPIONS
RAHZZAH

#1 HIP-HOP VARIANT BY **RAHZZAH**

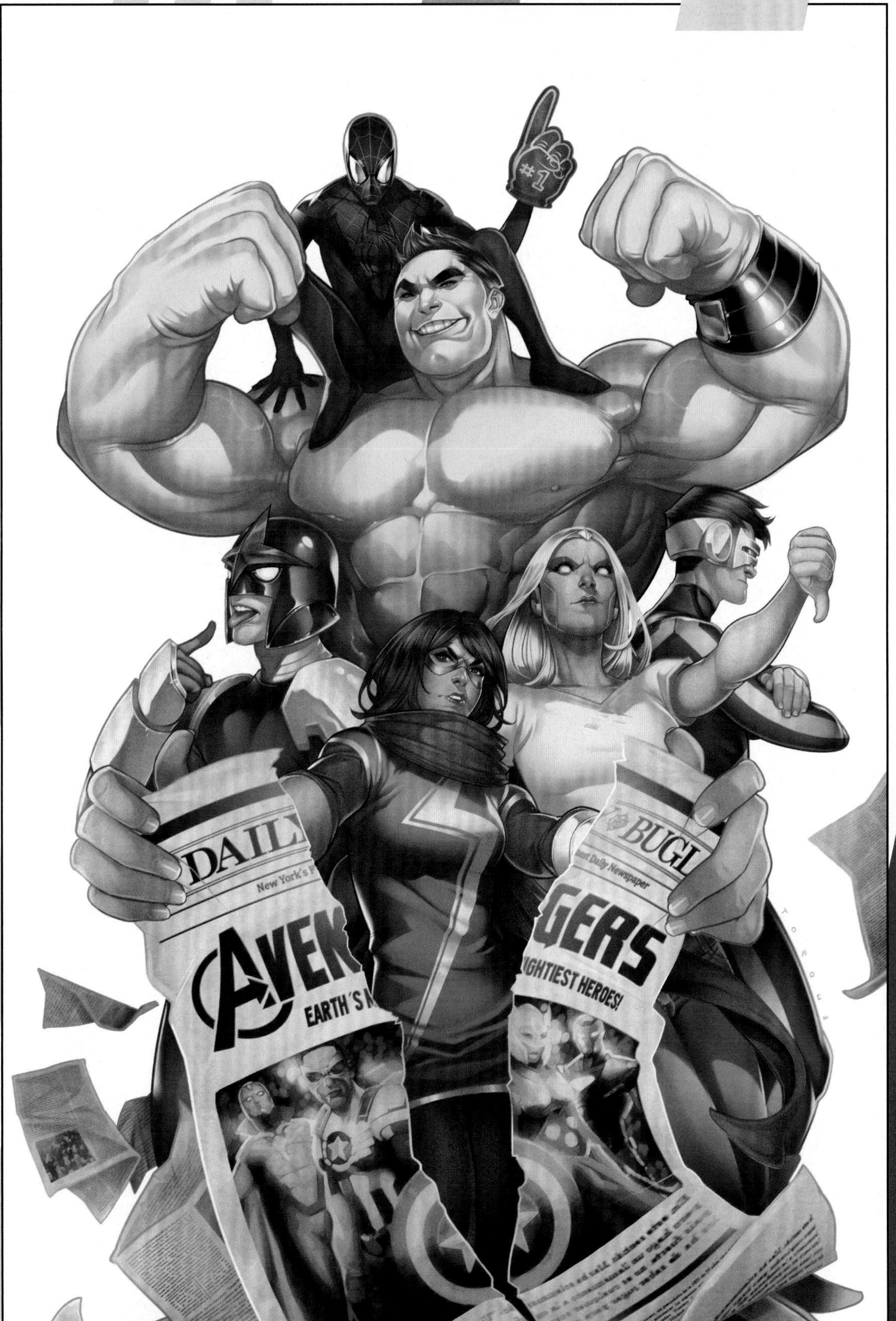
#1
DAIL
New York's F
BUGL
ent Daily Newspaper
AVEN
GERS
EARTH'S M
IGHTIEST HEROES!
TORQUE

#1 VARIANT BY **ELIZABETH TORQUE**

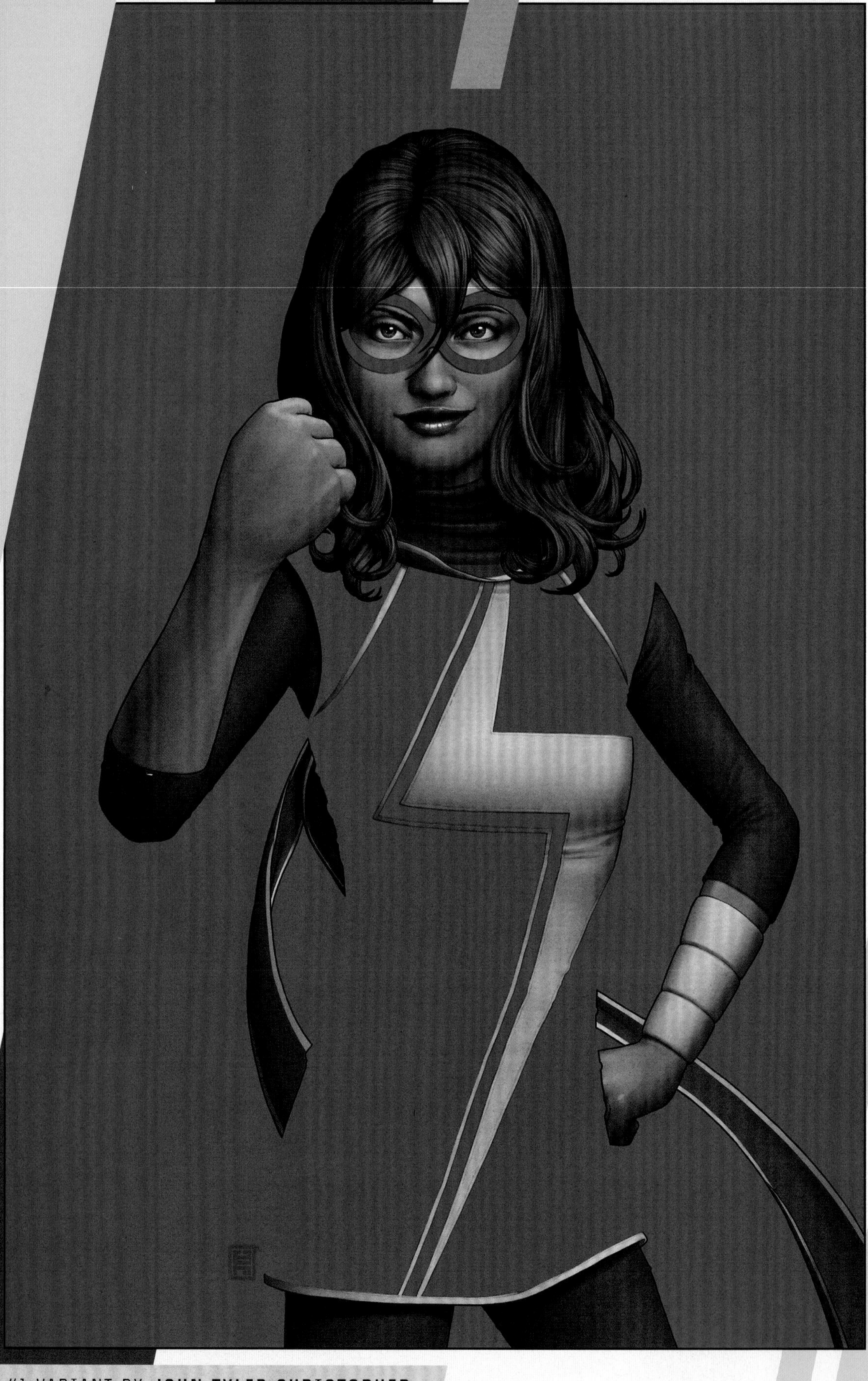

#1 VARIANT BY **JOHN TYLER CHRISTOPHER**

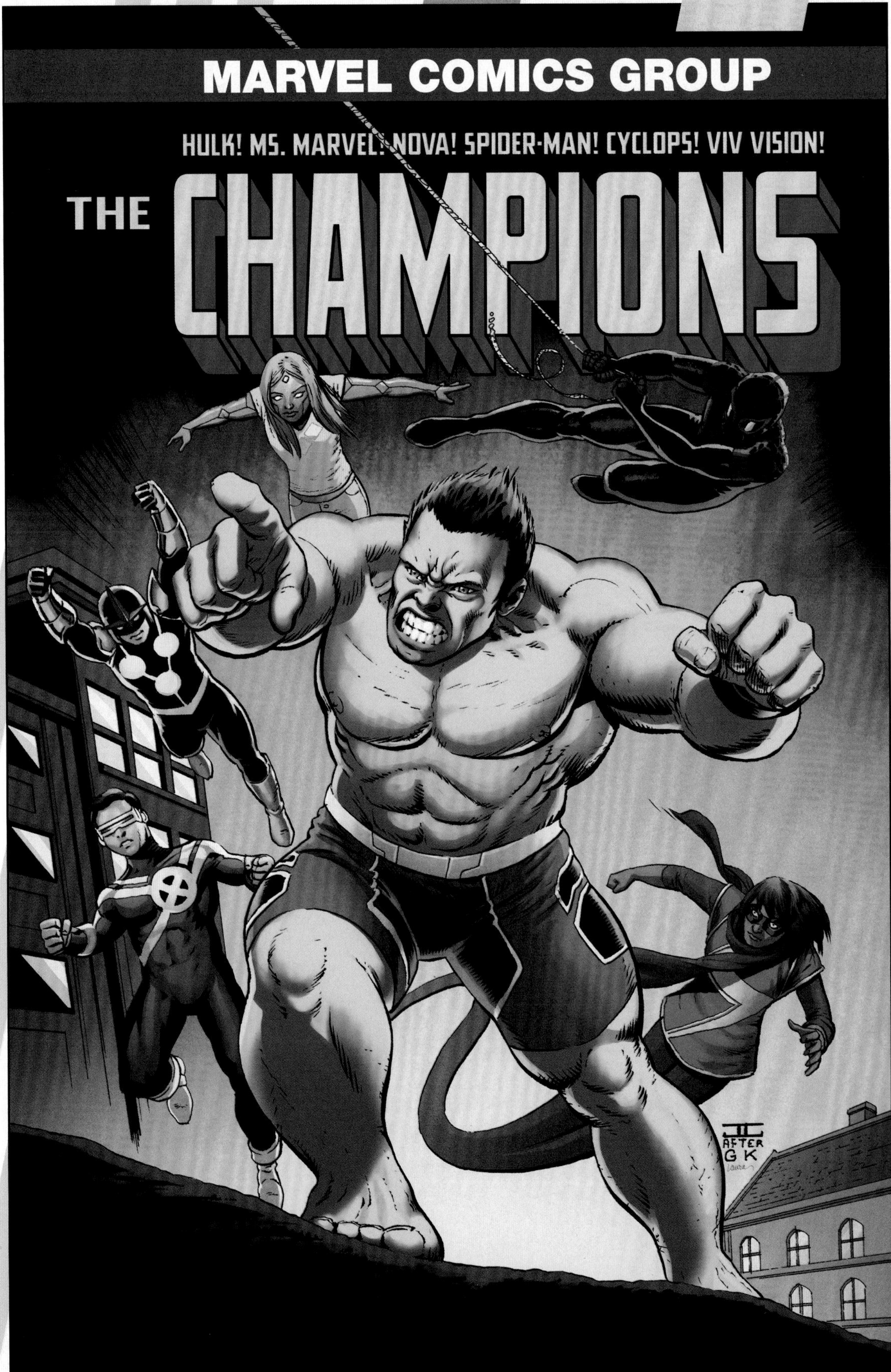
MARVEL COMICS GROUP
HULK! MS. MARVEL! NOVA! SPIDER-MAN! CYCLOPS! VIV VISION!
THE CHAMPIONS

#1 VARIANT BY **JOHN CASSADAY & LAURA MARTIN**

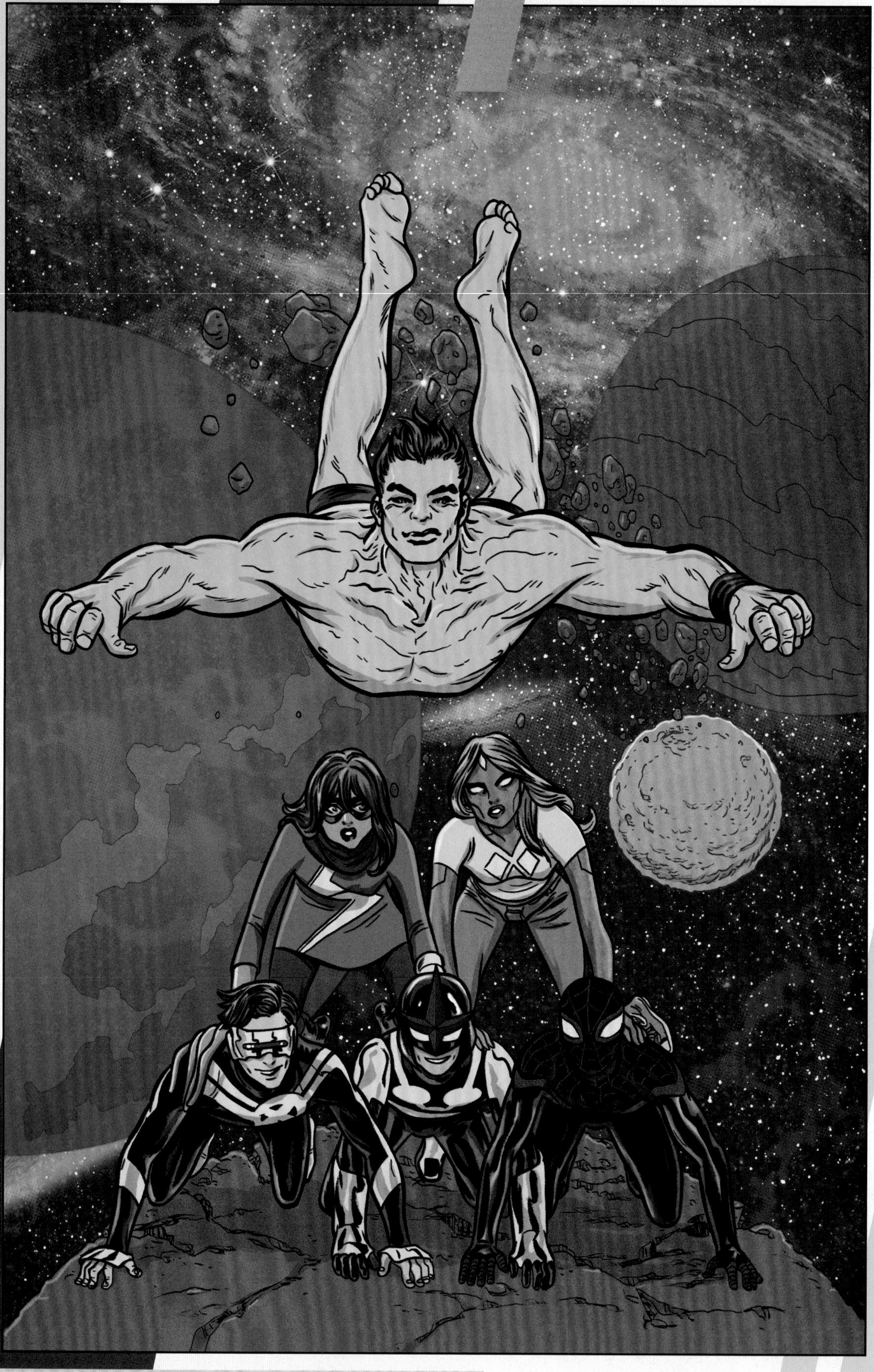

#1 VARIANT BY **MIKE ALLRED & LAURA ALLRED**

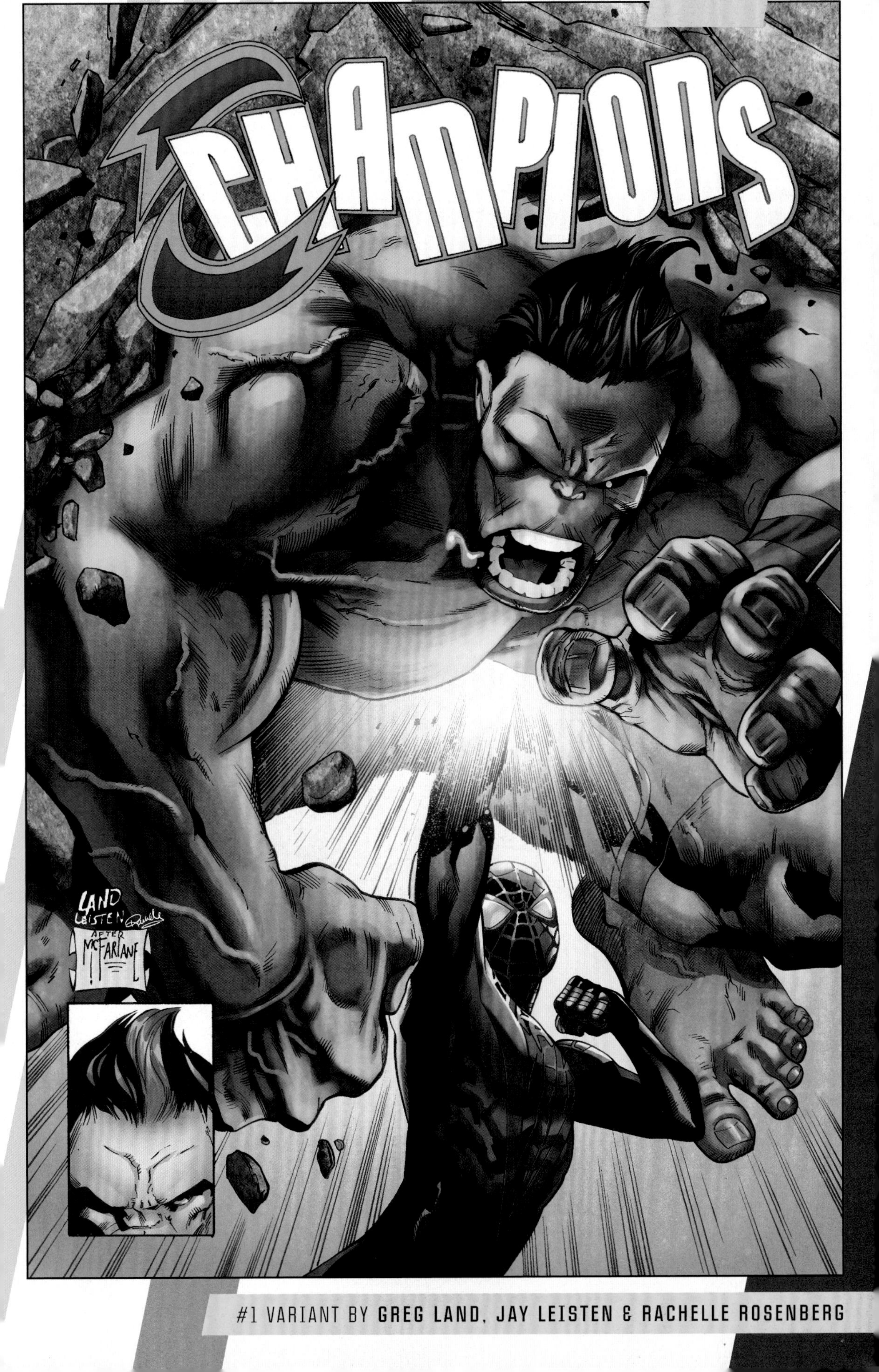
CHAMPIONS
LAND
LEISTEN
AFTER
McFARLANE

#1 VARIANT BY **GREG LAND, JAY LEISTEN & RACHELLE ROSENBERG**

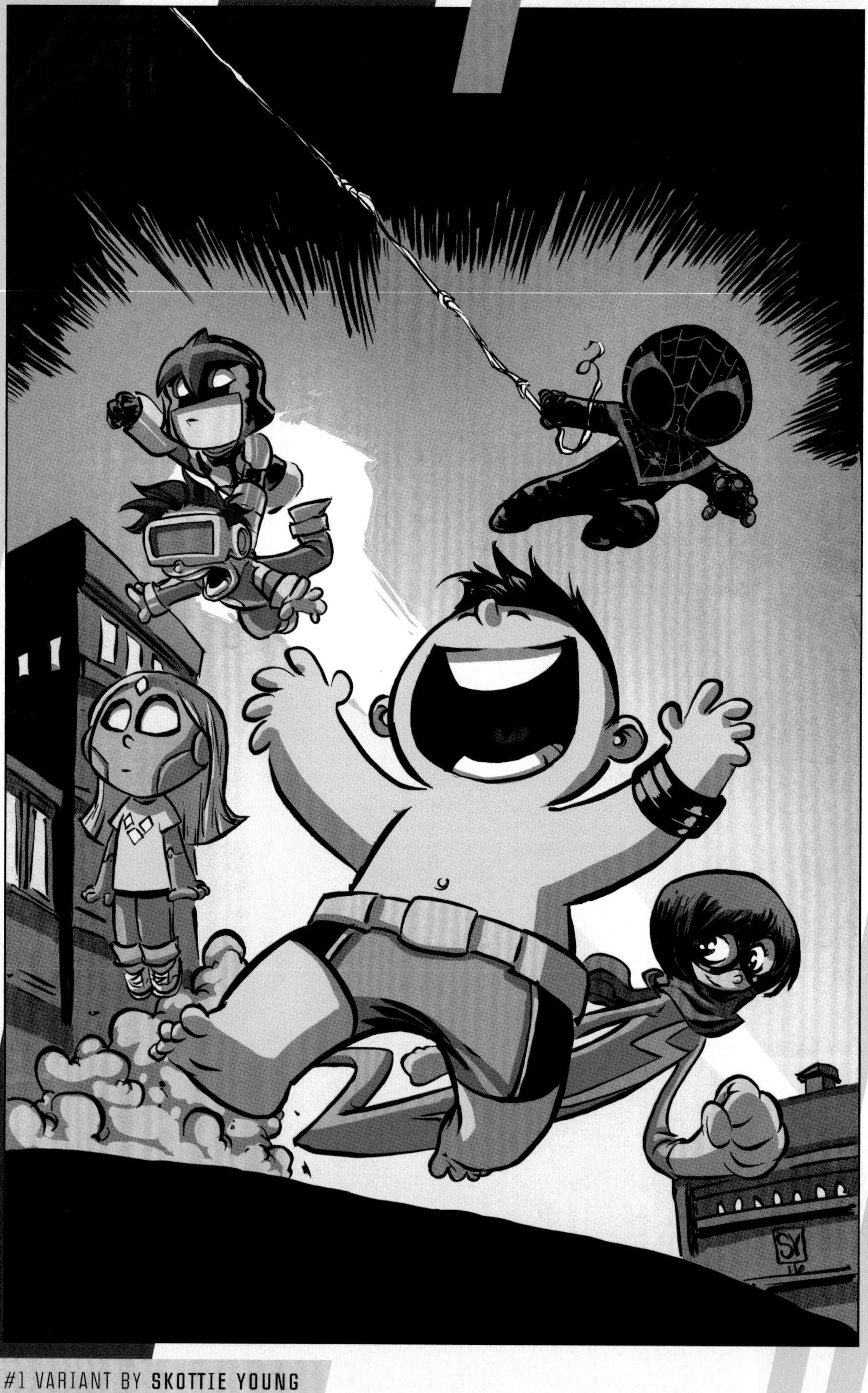

#1 VARIANT BY **SKOTTIE YOUNG**

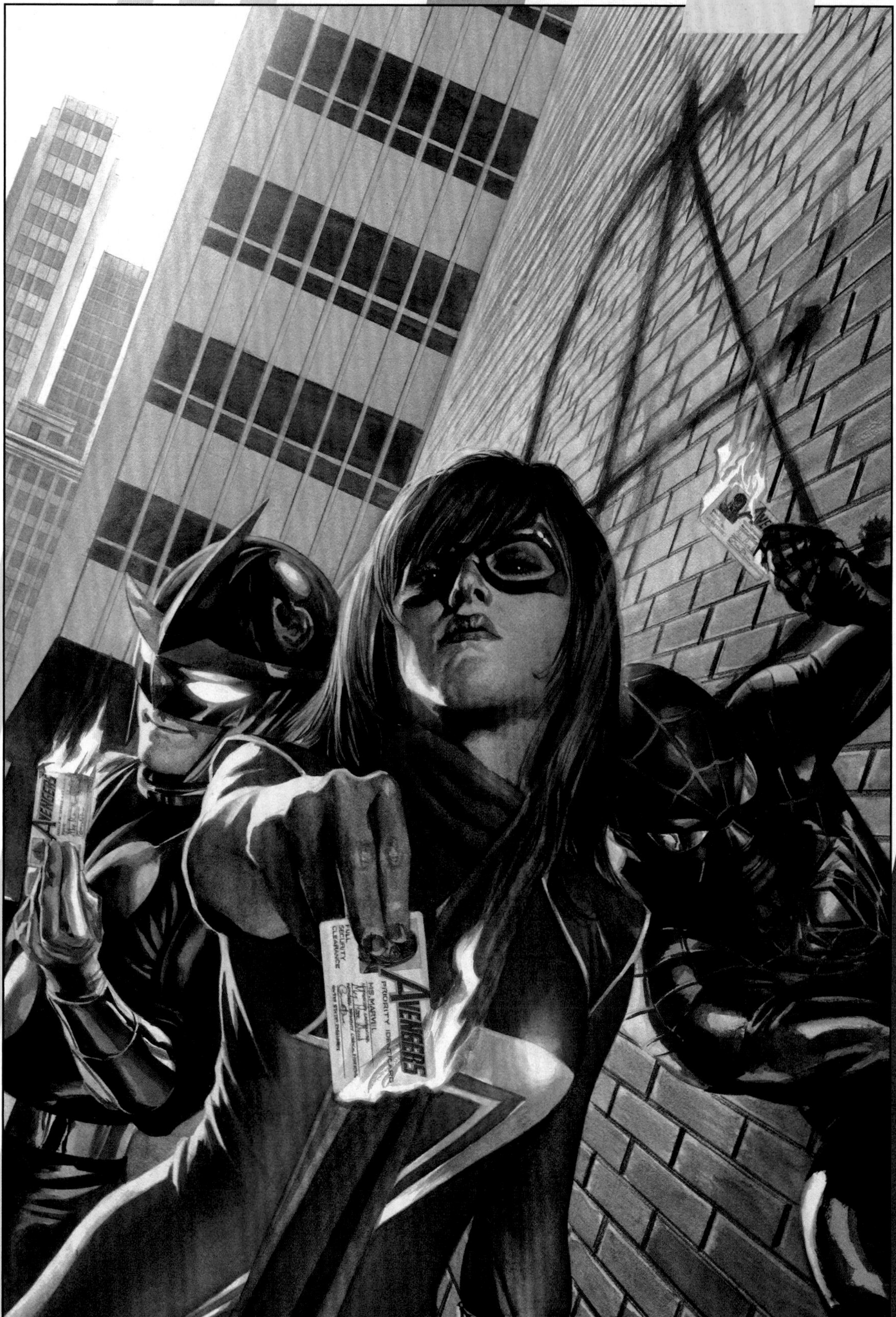
FULL
SECURITY
CLEARANCE
AVENGERS
PRIORITY
MS.MARVEL

#1 VARIANT BY **ALEX ROSS**

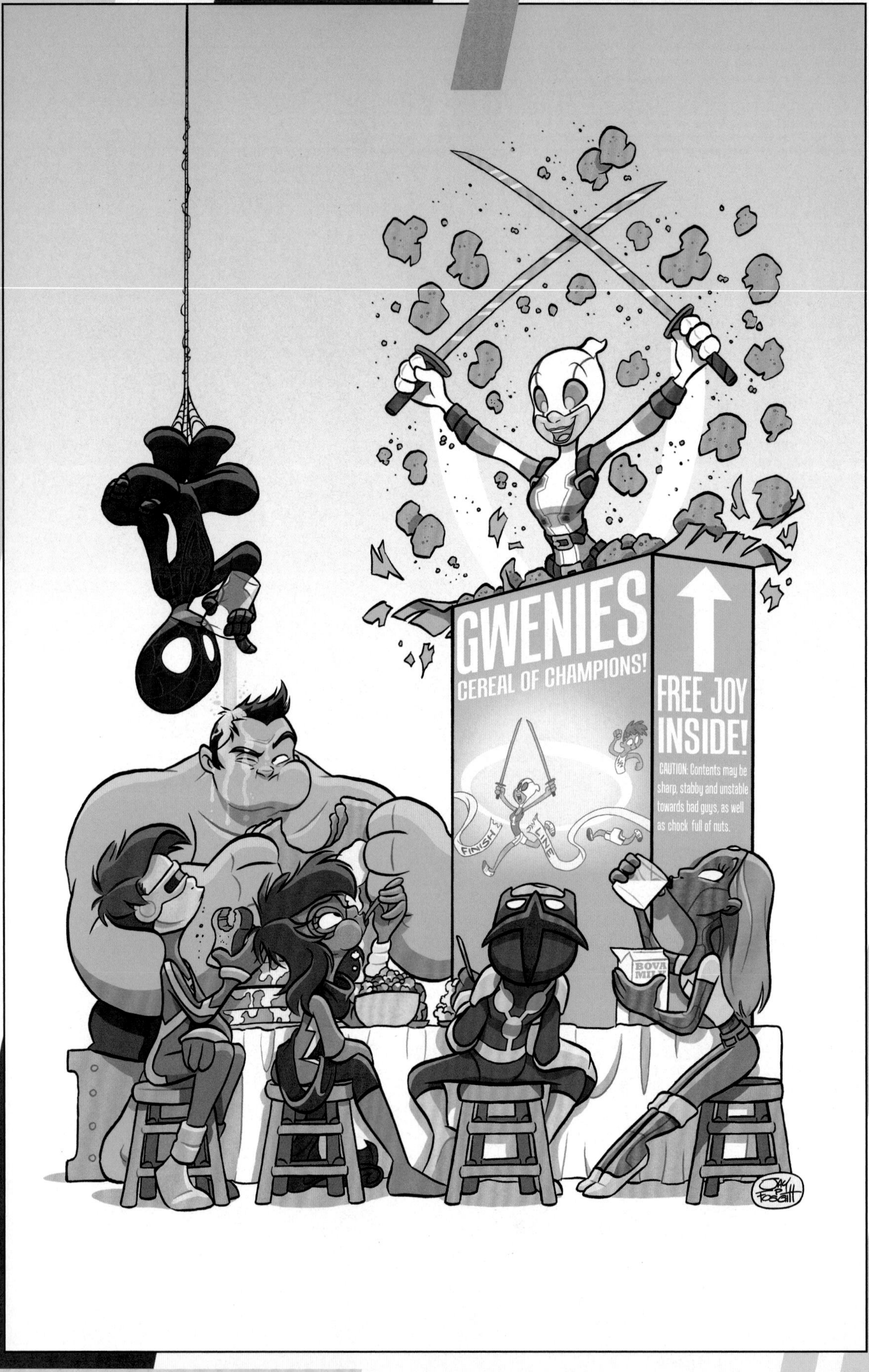
GWENIES
CEREAL OF CHAMPIONS!
FREE JOY INSIDE!
CAUTION: Contents may be sharp, stabby and unstable towards bad guys, as well as chock full of nuts.
FINISH
LINE
BOVA MILK

#1 PARTY VARIANT BY **JAY FOSGITT**

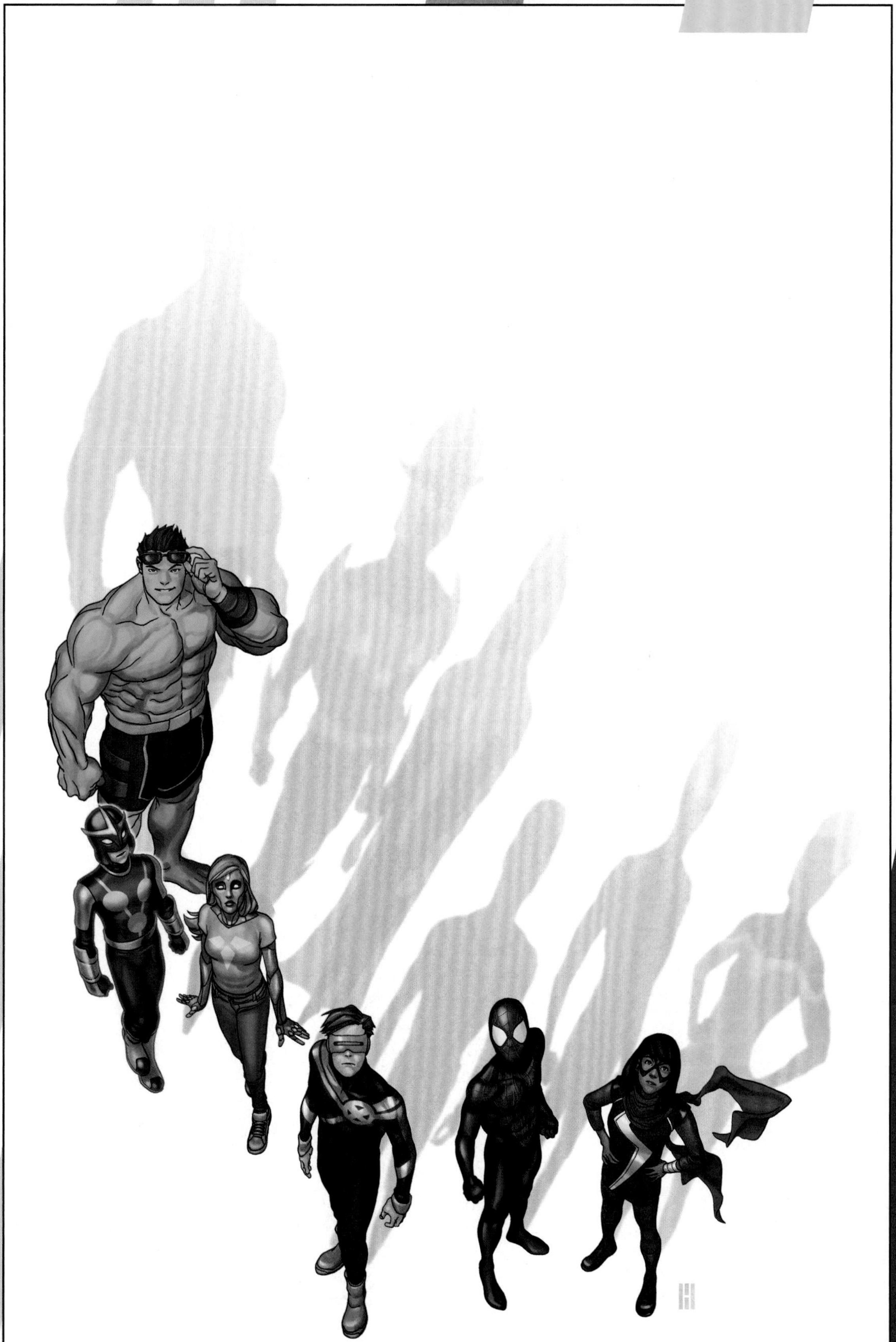

#2 VARIANT BY **MIKE CHOI**

#2 DIVIDED WE STAND VARIANT BY
MIKE MCKONE & ANDY TROY

#2 VARIANT BY **PASCAL CAMPION**

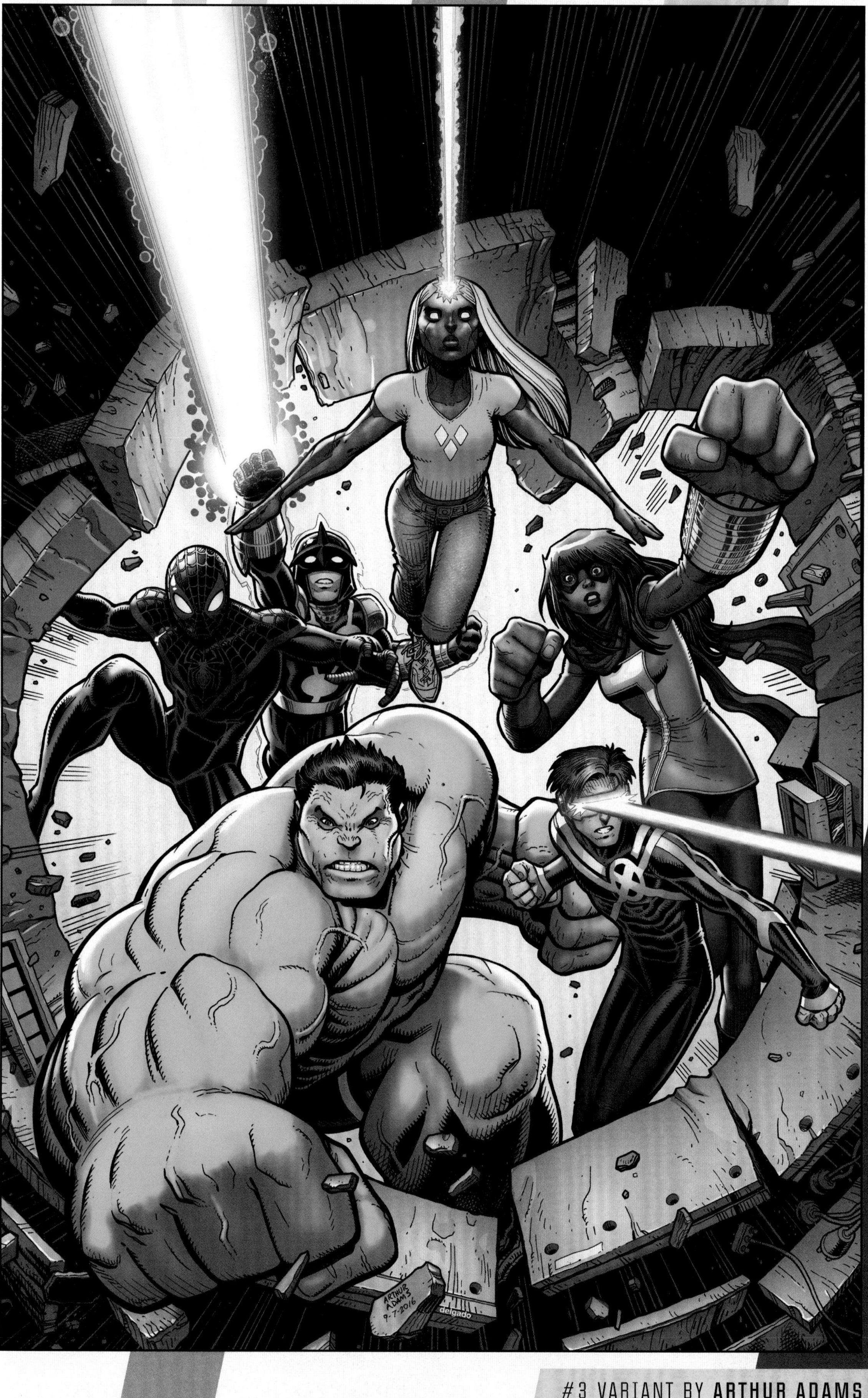
ARTHUR ADAMS 9-7-2016
delgado

#3 VARIANT BY **ARTHUR ADAMS**

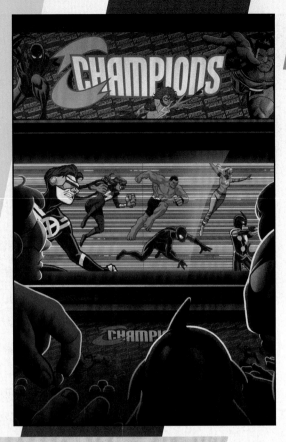

#5 VARIANT BY **JOE QUINONES**

#5 CORNER BOX VARIANT BY **JOE JUSKO**

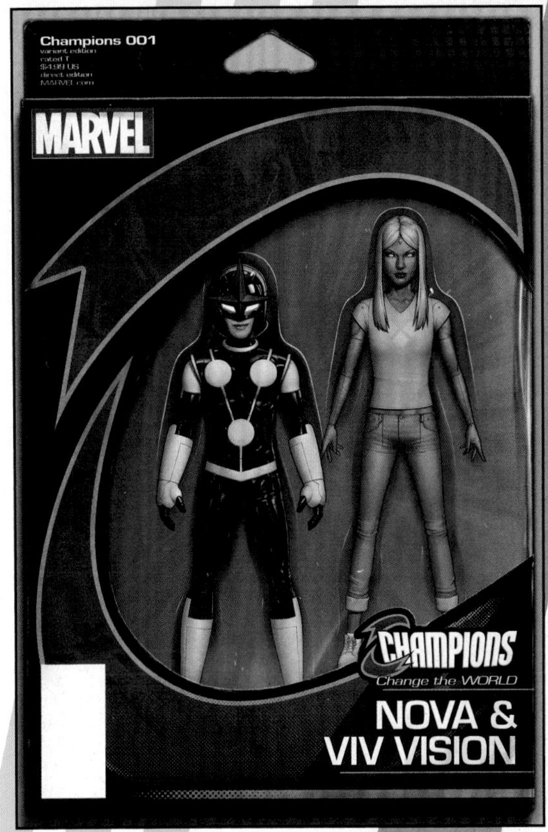
Champions 001
MARVEL
CHAMPIONS
Change the WORLD
NOVA &
VIV VISION

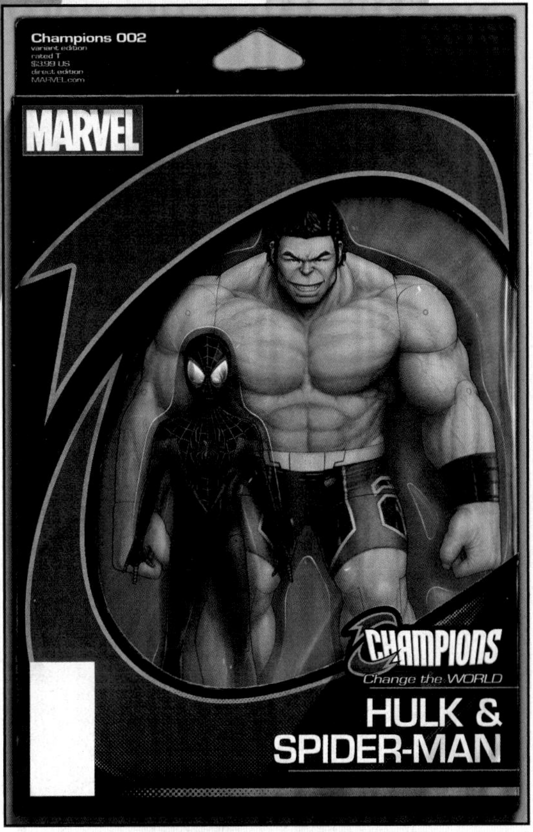
Champions 002
MARVEL
CHAMPIONS
Change the WORLD
HULK &
SPIDER-MAN

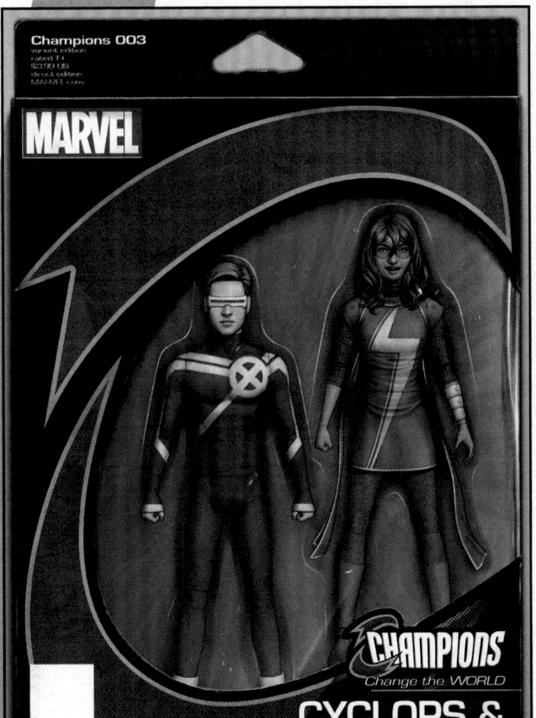
Champions 003
MARVEL
CHAMPIONS
Change the WORLD
CYCLOPS &
MS. MARVEL

#1-3 ACTION FIGURE VARIANTS BY **JOHN TYLER CHRISTOPHER**

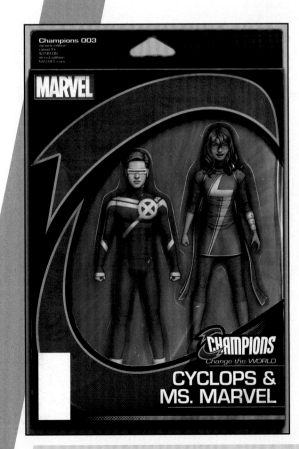

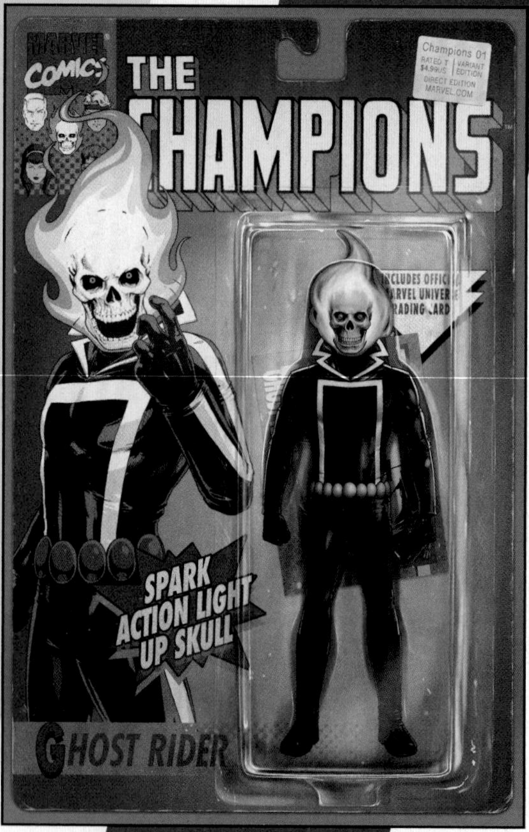
MARVEL COMICS
THE CHAMPIONS
Champions 01 RATED T $4.99US VARIANT EDITION DIRECT EDITION MARVEL.COM
SPARK ACTION LIGHT UP SKULL
GHOST RIDER

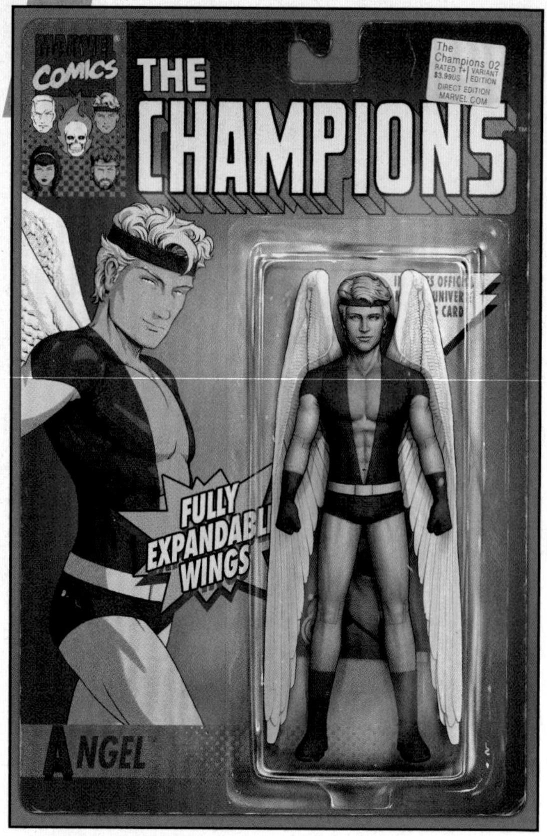
MARVEL COMICS
THE CHAMPIONS
The Champions 02 RATED T+ $3.99US VARIANT EDITION DIRECT EDITION MARVEL.COM
FULLY EXPANDABL WINGS
ANGEL

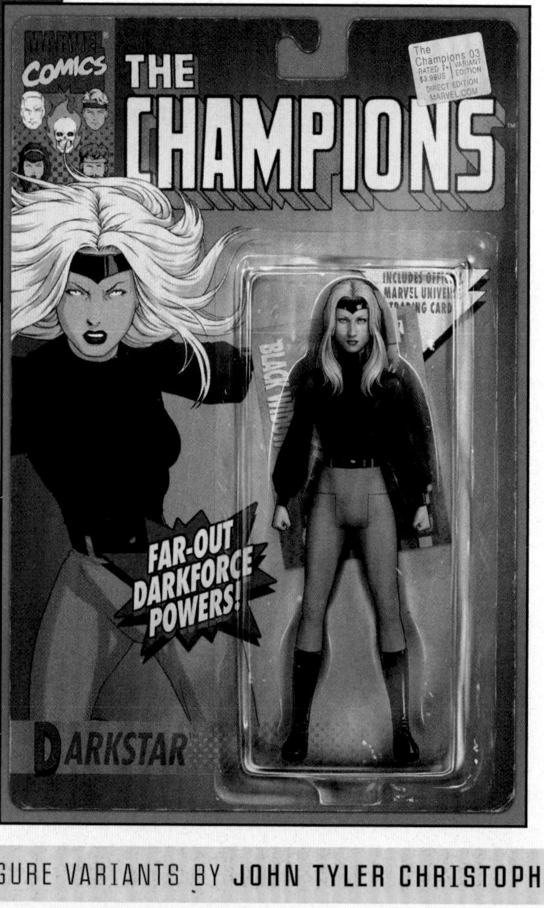
MARVEL COMICS
THE CHAMPIONS
The Champions 03 RATED T+ $3.99US VARIANT EDITION DIRECT EDITION MARVEL.COM
FAR-OUT DARKFORCE POWERS!
DARKSTAR

#1-3 CLASSIC ACTION FIGURE VARIANTS BY **JOHN TYLER CHRISTOPHER**